D0845170

*Recent
Homiletical
Thought*

Recent Homiletical Thought

An Annotated Bibliography

Volume 2, 1966–1979

Edited by

A. Duane Litfin
and Haddon W. Robinson

Baker Book House

Grand Rapids, Michigan

Contents

Preface

"Almost everyone has an opinion about preaching." That's the opening line editors William Toohey and William Thompson used to introduce their bibliography, *Recent Homiletical Thought*, in 1967.[1] In the last decade and a half, opinions about preaching have, if anything, increased. The words of the ancient preacher in Ecclesiastes could have been written about the study of homiletics: "Of making many books there is no end." In the pages that follow we have attempted to catalogue for preachers, scholars, and students the discussions about preaching that have taken place from 1965 until 1979.

In several ways we have followed the excellent lead of Toohey and Thompson. Our bibliography, like theirs, consists of topically arranged references to (1) books, (2) periodical articles, and (3) theses and dissertations. We have annotated the books and articles, and these annotations describe rather than evaluate. Each entry appears only once, and we have added an index of authors. In addition we have retained the format and topical categories used in the first volume and have excluded from the bibliography sermon anthologies and books of preaching helps.

On the other hand we have done a few things differently. For example, we have broadened the list of periodicals covered from 36 to over 100. For that reason, even though we cover only half as many years, we include more articles than does the first volume. While this bibliography may be less selective, it is more exhaustive.

Second, we have not identified articles as Catholic or Protestant. Where the identification seemed obvious, it served no purpose. Where the identification was less obvious, we felt the determination not worth the effort. While such labeling might on occasion serve some purpose, in the last analysis the worth of an author's contribution must be determined from the writing itself, not from a denominational label.

Third, much of the research behind this bibliography was conducted by students enrolled in the Master of Theology program at Dallas Theological Seminary. The use of students—rather than professionals—contains downside risks. In some ways, perhaps, attention to details so important in bibliographic work may suffer (though

---

1. *Recent Homiletical Thought: A Bibliography, 1935–1965* (Nashville: Abingdon, 1967). Abbreviated in annotations below as RHT[1].

such carefulness is by no means characteristic of all professionals either). We have attempted to minimize this risk through increased supervision. The advantage in using student labor lies in the sheer amount of work that can be accomplished.

The students drew upon the combined libraries of Dallas Theological Seminary, Perkins School of Theology, University of Dallas, and Southwestern Baptist Theological Seminary for virtually all their materials. We're grateful to these schools and their librarians for their assistance.

It is impossible to edit an extensive bibliography without forming some impressions about recent homiletical literature. We share these observations with anyone who reads them for whatever they may be worth. First, some topics appear to have suffered from overkill: the need to preach the Bible, the need to preach the Bible relevantly, humor and preaching, the need to understand and address contemporary culture, the purpose and procedure for getting congregational feedback, and black preaching.

Second, we were also a bit surprised by subjects that were seldom discussed: Jewish preaching, television preachers, women preachers, the preacher's personal life and preparation. We also found a scarcity of comprehensible titles for theses and dissertations.

Third, we came up with five random observations about recent homiletical literature in general: (1) This body of literature brings forward a new generation of writers who did not appear at all in the previous volume. By the same token some of the standard writers of the past did not make it in, except perhaps in reprints. (2) A large quantity of applied "research" comes from the ubiquitous Doctor of Ministry programs. We wondered what, if anything, it ever can or will amount to. (3) We think we have spotted the rise and fall of so-called "dialogue" preaching. While all effective preaching is dialogic, the fad of two people carrying on a conversation in the pulpit apparently has not stuck. (4) We were impressed—in fact overwhelmed—by the expectations that writers place on preachers. No mere human could possibly fulfill the conglomeration of demands set forth in this literature. To say the least, the expectations are unrealistic. And (5) we suffered a touch of depression from sifting through the avalanche of literature. Much of it sounds like keen insight into the obvious. We urge our students to preach less but preach better: in writing about preaching, too, less could be better (perhaps some cynic will suggest that we follow our own advice).

We also agree with Toohey's and Thompson's counsel that a bibliography of this scope is no task for perfectionists. Errors and a certain unevenness are unavoidable. Despite the best efforts of contributors, editors, and publisher, mistakes and omissions inevitably occur. Readers who have spotted such lapses are invited to bring their lists to the attention of the editors (but gently, please!).

As Toohey and Thompson also noted in their preface to the first volume, "The compilation of this bibliography has been a labor of love by a great many persons," not least in our case Allan Fisher of Baker Book House. As professionals in the field of homiletics, the editors commend Baker Book House for its willingness to take on a publishing project such as this one. Since bibliographies have all the excitement of a telephone directory, such ventures seldom contribute much to the profit side of the ledger. This volume stands as additional evidence of Baker's strong commitment to the field of preaching.

To quote Toohey and Thompson one last time, we "commend this book to the world of scholarship with the prayer that the living God may use it to facilitate the preaching of his Word."

A. DUANE LITFIN
HADDON W. ROBINSON

Contributors

Timothy L. Bartlett
Craig Baynham
Marshall L. Brantmeier
R. David Bruce
Edward G. Caplinger
W. Gordon Dunaway
L. Andrews Hamilton
Jimmy S. Irvin
G. William Knepper, Jr.
Lawrence G. McConnell
Murry W. McMurry
Gerald S. Mathisen
David J. Mitchell
Raymond E. Mummert
Alan J. Pineault
Tony Simpson
Michael W. Walker
Lonnie V. Williford

Books

Abbey, Merrill R.
Communication in Pulpit and Parish. Philadelphia: Westminster, 1973. 1
237 pp. Applies modern communication research to all aspects of pastoral communication.

Adams, Douglas G.
Humor in the American Pulpit: From George Whitefield Through Henry 2
Ward Beecher. North Aurora, Ill.: Sharing, 1975. 273 pp. A historical and theological analysis of the significance of humor in American preaching.

Adams, Jay E.
Pulpit Speech: A Textbook for Use in the Classroom or Study. Nutley, N.J.: 3
Presbyterian and Reformed, 1971. 169 pp. A text for both ministers and students, relating preaching to such topics as the use of narrative, the role of persuasion, style, and effective delivery. A list of suggested projects concludes each chapter.

Alexander, James W.
Thoughts on Preaching: Being Contributions to Homiletics. Edinburgh: 4
Banner of Truth, 1975. 318 pp. A reprint (New York: Scribner, 1861). A posthumous collection of the author's thoughts on preaching as written in his journal, in periodical articles, or in letters to young ministers.

Armstrong, James
Telling Truth: The Foolishness of Preaching in a Real World. Waco, Tex.: 5
Word, 1977. 114 pp. An exhortation to return to preaching that is intellectually rigorous, personally challenging, and socially relevant.

Baird, John E.
Preparing for Platform and Pulpit. Grand Rapids: Baker, 1976. 222 pp. A 6

reprint (Nashville: Abingdon, 1968). Originally designed for the classroom, this volume gives an orderly presentation of the basic principles of public speaking, beginning with an introduction of speech theory and moving to sermon delivery.

Baumann, J. Daniel
An Introduction to Contemporary Preaching. Grand Rapids: Baker, 1972. 7
302 pp. An introduction to preaching that builds upon the three basic elements of the author's definition of preaching: communication, biblical truth, and behavior change.

Baxter, Batsell Barrett
The Heart of the Yale Lectures. Grand Rapids: Baker, 1975. 345 pp. A 8
reprint (New York: Macmillan, 1947). See RHT[1], entry 11.

Speaking for the Master: A Study of Public Speaking for Christian Men. 9
Grand Rapids: Baker, 1972. 134 pp. A reprint (New York: Macmillan, 1954).
See RHT[1], entry 12.

Beale, Lawrence L.
Toward a Black Homiletic. New York: Vantage, 1978. 10

Beecher, Henry Ward
Yale Lectures on Preaching. Saint Clair Shores, Mich.: Scholarly, 1976. 3 11
vols. in 1. A reprint (New York: Fords, Howard, Hulbert, 1887). Lyman Beecher Lectures, 1872-1874. Deals with the personal elements of preaching, auxiliary forces and external implements of the preacher, and the use of Christian doctrine in relation to the community.

Best, Ernest
From Text to Sermon: Responsible Use of the New Testament in Preaching. 12
Atlanta: John Knox, 1978. 117 pp. An analysis of the process of applying the historical message of the Bible to contemporary times.

Black, James M.
The Mystery of Preaching. Grand Rapids: Zondervan, 1978. 277 pp. A 13
reprint (New York: Revell, 1935). James Sprunt Lectures, 1924, Union Theological Seminary, Richmond. Treats the principles and practice of preaching.

Blackwood, Andrew W.
The Fine Art of Preaching. Grand Rapids: Baker, 1976. 180 pp. A reprint 14
(New York: Macmillan, 1937). See RHT[1], entry 16.

Preaching from the Bible. Grand Rapids: Baker, 1974. 247 pp. A reprint 15
(New York: Abingdon-Cokesbury, 1941). See RHT[1], entry 17.

Boddie, Charles Emerson

God's "Bad Boys." Valley Forge, Pa.: Judson, 1972. 125 pp. A collection of   16
controversial and influential black preachers and scholars.

Boden, Evan H.

Guide for the Lay Preacher: Helps for Sermon Preparation and Delivery.   17
Valley Forge, Pa.: Judson, 1979. 70 pp. A discussion of the process for concep-
tualizing, delivering, and evaluating the sermon.

Bradford, Charles E.

Preaching to the Times: The Preaching Ministry in the Seventh-day   18
Adventist Church. Washington, D.C.: Review and Herald, 1975. 144 pp.

Brooks, Phillips

Lectures on Preaching. Grand Rapids: Baker, 1978. 281 pp. A reprint (New   19
York: Dutton, 1877). Lyman Beecher Lectures, 1877. See RHT[1], entry 26.

Brown, H. C., Jr.

A Christian Layman's Guide to Public Speaking. Nashville: Broadman,   20
1966. 76 pp. A Southern Baptist Theological Seminary professor offers practical help for laymen desiring to speak more effectively. He discusses eight steps
in the process of preparing a speech.

A Quest for Reformation in Preaching. Waco, Tex.: Word, 1968. 251 pp.   21
Provides guidelines for properly understanding the scope, practical procedures, and functional elements of preaching, and the nature of the sermon
and the sermon text. Included are annotated texts of ten sermons by Karl
Barth and others.

Browne, Robert E. C.

The Ministry of the Word. Philadelphia: Fortress, 1976. 128 pp. Discusses   22
the sermon as metaphor and the general area of style.

Buechner, Frederick

Telling the Truth: The Gospel as Tragedy, Comedy and Fairy Tale. San   23
Francisco: Harper & Row, 1977. 97 pp. Helps the preacher make the Gospel
stories relevant by employing a contemporary and imaginative style.

Burke, John

Gospel Power: Toward the Revitalization of Preaching. New York: Alba,   24
1978. 131 pp. A Catholic writer discusses the necessity of renewed emphasis on
preaching within his church.

Buttrick, George A.

Jesus Came Preaching: Christian Preaching in the New Age. Grand   25
Rapids: Baker, 1970. 251 pp. A reprint (New York: Scribner, 1931). Lyman

Beecher Lectures, 1931. Covers the preacher's approach to a new age and the content of his message. It focuses on the centrality of Christ in preaching and on the person of the preacher.

Colquhoun, Frank
Christ's Ambassadors: The Priority of Preaching. Philadelphia: West- **26** minster, 1965. Reprinted—Grand Rapids: Baker, 1979. 93 pp. An Anglican clergyman presents a case for the priority of preaching in light of the authority, message, and responsibility of the minister.

Cooke, Bernard J.
Ministry to Word and Sacraments. Philadelphia: Fortress, 1976. 686 pp. A **27** general study of the Christian ministry, including historical and theological reflections of the ministry.

Cox, James W.
A Guide to Biblical Preaching. Nashville: Abingdon, 1976. 142 pp. A "how **28** to" book covering the aspects of biblical preaching from introduction to conclusion.

Learning to Speak Effectively. London: Hodder & Stoughton, 1966. Re- **29** printed—Grand Rapids: Baker, 1974. 62 pp. A brief work based on ten basic rules for speech-making. It is aimed primarily at the layman and gives only brief attention to the sermon.

Craddock, Fred B.
As One Without Authority: Essays on Inductive Preaching. Enid, Okla.: **30** Phillips University, 1971. Reprinted—Nashville: Abingdon, 1979. 168 pp. A constructive criticism of deductive sermon structure with a suggestion that preachers employ the more open inductive style.

Overhearing the Gospel. Nashville: Abingdon, 1978. 144 pp. Lyman **31** Beecher Lectures, 1978. A new approach to preaching and teaching the gospel to those who no longer want to hear directly.

Crum, Milton, Jr.
Manual on Preaching. Valley Forge, Pa.: Judson, 1977. 189 pp. A manual **32** on sermon preparation, highlighting the blend of information from the text and insight from experience.

Demaray, Donald E.
An Introduction to Homiletics. Grand Rapids: Baker, 1974. 156 pp. An **33** Asbury Theological Seminary professor devotes sections to the preacher, the sermon, and the preaching.

Preacher Aflame! Grand Rapids: Baker, 1972. 87 pp. Brief lectures on the **34** divine molding of the gospel communicator, the crucial place of listening, and the communicative power of the Bible.

Edwards, O. C., Jr.
The Living and Active Word: One Way to Preach from the Bible Today. 35
New York: Seabury, 1975. 178 pp. A step-by-step method for constructing sermons that relate Scripture to the challenge of being a Christian in today's world. The book's second half consists of examples of the type of preaching the author advocates.

Erdahl, Lowell O.
Preaching for the People. Nashville: Abingdon, 1976. 127 pp. Addresses 36
three questions: Why should I preach? What should I preach? How should I preach? The third question, involving sermon preparation and delivery, receives the most attention.

Fant, Clyde E.
Preaching for Today. New York: Harper & Row, 1975. 212 pp. A former 37
homiletics professor at Southwestern Baptist Theological Seminary bridges the gap between the theological and practical aspects of preaching. Unique is the emphasis on "incarnational preaching."

Fasol, Al, ed.
Selected Readings in Preaching: Classic Contributions from Preaching 38
Masters. Grand Rapids: Baker, 1979. 127 pp. Includes readings on the nature of, approaches to, and essential qualities for effective preaching by such men as Phillips Brooks, G. Campbell Morgan, James S. Stewart, Charles Haddon Spurgeon, Halford E. Luccock, and Andrew W. Blackwood.

Ford, D. W. Cleverley
Preaching Today. London: Epworth, 1969. 108 pp. An English scholar 39
attempts to define the role of contemporary preaching. He cites objections to preaching and then answers them by discussing the origins, content, form, place, and future of preaching.

Francis, David
The ABC of Preaching. London: Epworth, 1968. 141 pp. Comprised of 40
articles written for *Preacher's Quarterly* and *Local Preacher's Magazine.*

Gilmore, Alec
Tomorrow's Pulpit. Valley Forge, Pa.: Judson, 1975. 95 pp. Edwin Stephen 41
Griffith Lectures, 1973, Cardiff Baptist College. Relates the author's experimental work in the preaching ministry.

Griffin, Emory A.
The Mind Changers: The Art of Christian Persuasion. Wheaton, Ill.: 42

Tyndale, 1976. 228 pp. An explanation and application of some classical theories and techniques of persuasion.

Griffith, [Arthur] Leonard
   The Need to Preach. London: Hodder & Stoughton, 1971. 126 pp. Finch   **43**
Lectures, 1970, Western North Carolina Conference of the Methodist Church.
Deals with the theory of preaching, and includes four sermons that grow out
of that theory.

Hall, Thor
   The Future Shape of Preaching. Philadelphia: Fortress, 1971. 160 pp. James   **44**
Sprunt Lectures, 1970, Union Theological Seminary, Richmond. Makes a
case for a new kind of homiletic that will be relevant to a rapidly changing
communicative, theological, and ecclesiastical context.

Holmes, George
   Toward an Effective Pulpit Ministry. Springfield, Mo.: Gospel, 1971.   **45**
176 pp. A general work on preaching theory and methodology by a leading
Assemblies of God pastor and teacher.

Horne, Chevis F.
   Crisis in the Pulpit: The Pulpit Faces Future Shock. Grand Rapids: Baker,   **46**
1975. 144 pp. Presents a strong case for the future of the pulpit ministry in
today's world, fully aware of the crisis facing the institutional church and its
preaching.

Jackson, Edgar N.
   A Psychology for Preaching. New York: Hawthorn, 1974. 191 pp. A reprint   **47**
(Great Neck, N.Y.: Channell, 1961). See RHT[1], entry 273.

Johnson, Joseph A., Jr.
   The Soul of the Black Preacher. Philadelphia: Pilgrim, 1971. 173 pp. A   **48**
study of black Christian experience in America, including the quest for black
identity. It analyzes what the Christian faith has to say about the condition of
black Americans.

Keck, Leander E.
   The Bible in the Pulpit: The Renewal of Biblical Preaching. Nashville: **49**
Abingdon, 1978. 172 pp. Assesses the impact and contribution of the his-
torical-critical understanding of the Bible, and contains a new perspective on
what makes preaching "biblical."

Killinger, John
   The Centrality of Preaching in the Total Task of the Ministry. Waco, Tex.:   **50**
Word, 1969. 123 pp. Describes the place of preaching in the minister's life and

its relationship to his other major responsibilities. It contends that in the work of the ministry, preaching is central.

Killinger, John, ed.
Experimental Preaching. Nashville: Abingdon, 1973. 175 pp. Convinced   **51**
that homiletical change is necessary, a professor at Vanderbilt Divinity School uses some sample sermons to exhibit the imaginative, creative forms he hopes will replace traditional ones.

Lewis, Ralph L.
Speech for Persuasive Preaching. Wilmore, Ky.: Asbury Theological Semi-   **52**
nary, 1968. 286 pp. A speech professor describes the relationship of the five canons of speech to the "five persuasive pressures" inherent in preaching situations.

Lloyd-Jones, D. Martyn
Preaching and Preachers. Grand Rapids: Zondervan, 1971. 325 pp. Based on   **53**
lectures at Westminster Theological Seminary, this thorough work presents a philosophy of preaching representative of traditional preaching and of the conservative British church.

Lockyer, Herbert
The Art and Craft of Preaching. Grand Rapids: Baker, 1975. 118 pp. A basic   **54**
introduction to preaching and the preacher.

Macartney, Clarence Edward
Preaching Without Notes. Grand Rapids: Baker, 1976. 186 pp. A reprint   **55**
(New York: Abingdon-Cokesbury, 1946). Discusses the role of gospel preaching, illustration, sermon preparation, biographical preaching, and the minister's occupation.

McLaughlin, Raymond W.
Communication for the Church. Grand Rapids: Zondervan, 1968. 228 pp.   **56**
A professor at Denver Conservative Baptist Seminary relates basic principles of communication to the work of the church and to the communication of the gospel. The book focuses on both preaching and interpersonal communication.

The Ethics of Persuasive Preaching. Grand Rapids: Baker, 1979. 215 pp. A   **57**
detailed presentation and explanation of how sermonic persuasion can be ethically responsible.

McWilliam, Stuart W.
Called to Preach. Edinburgh: Saint Andrew, 1969. 97 pp. Warrack Lectures,   **58**
1969. On the task, world, technique, and personality of the preacher, and on the mass media's influence on preaching.

Malcomson, William L.
The Preaching Event. Philadelphia: Westminster, 1968. 144 pp. A series of **59**
brief, often unrelated essays on three aspects of the preaching event—the
congregation, the preacher, and the message—from a variety of viewpoints.
The author is a Baptist pastor and teacher.

Marcel, Pierre Charles
The Relevance of Preaching. Translated by Rob Roy McGregor. Grand **60**
Rapids: Baker, 1977. 110 pp. A reprint (1963). See RHT[1], entry 91.

Massey, James Earl
The Responsible Pulpit. Anderson, Ind.: Warner, 1974. 115 pp. A Church **61**
of God pastor stresses the imperative to preach with responsible faith, commitment, hermeneutics, and homiletics. He conveys insights on sermon
content from the preaching of Jesus and on sermon delivery from the preaching of blacks.

Mast, Russell L.
Preach the Word. Newton, Kans.: Faith and Life, 1968. 90 pp. Addresses, **62**
essays, and lectures on preaching.

Meyer, F. B.
Expository Preaching: Plans and Methods. Grand Rapids: Baker, 1974. 127 **63**
pp. A reprint (New York: Doran, 1912). Pleads for the expository method of
preaching.

Mitchell, Henry H.
Black Preaching. Philadelphia: Lippincott, 1970. 248 pp. Critically ana- **64**
lyzes the history, theory, practice, and theology of black preaching.

The Recovery of Preaching. New York: Harper & Row, 1977. 175 pp. **65**
Examines black preaching from a cultural and psychological viewpoint.

Morris, Colin M.
The Word and the Words. Nashville: Abingdon, 1975. 174 pp. Defends **66**
preaching as central to the modern church, suggests avenues for sermons to
follow, and guides the preacher in preparing and delivering sermons.

Morrow, Thomas M.
Worship and Preaching. Rev. ed. Edited by Raymond J. Billington and **67**
James B. Bates. London: Epworth, 1967. 175 pp. See RHT[1], entry 96.

O'Neal, Glenn F.
Make the Bible Live: A Basic Guide for Preachers and Teachers. Winona **68**
Lake, Ind.: B.M.H., 1972. 136 pp. Rev. ed. 1979. 142 pp.

Oxnam, G. Bromley
Preaching in a Revolutionary Age. Freeport, N.Y.: Books for Libraries, **69**
1971. 207 pp. A reprint (New York: Abingdon-Cokesbury, 1944). Lyman
Beecher Lectures, 1944. See RHT[1], entry 101.

Pack, Frank, and Meador, Prentice, Jr.
Preaching to Modern Man. Abilene, Tex.: Biblical Research, 1969. 180 pp. **70**
Two Church of Christ preachers discuss the nature of contemporary preaching
from the standpoint of the audience, speaker, and message.

Pennington, Chester A.
God Has a Communication Problem. New York: Hawthorn, 1976. 144 pp. **71**
An argument for creativity in the preparation of sermons is followed by
suggestions for preparing creative messages.

Perry, Lloyd M.
Biblical Preaching for Today's World. Chicago: Moody, 1973. 208 pp. **72**
Lyman Stewart Lectures, 1972, Talbot Theological Seminary. A homiletician
at Trinity Evangelical Divinity School deals with subjects that have been
neglected by present-day homileticians.

Porteous, Alvin C.
Preaching to Suburban Captives. Valley Forge, Pa.: Judson, 1979. 125 pp. **73**

Rad, Gerhard von
Biblical Interpretations in Preaching. Translated by John E. Steely. Nash- **74**
ville: Abingdon, 1977. 125 pp. Lectures on several biblical passages are prefixed
with a discussion of the relationship of exegesis and preaching.

Rahner, Karl, ed.
The Renewal of Preaching: Theory and Practice. New York: Paulist, 1968. **75**
204 pp. A series of articles on preaching and a bibliographical survey,
produced by the Roman Catholic Concilium to help in understanding the
present difficulties in preaching and the Church's mission to proclaim.

Randolph, David James
The Renewal of Preaching. Philadelphia: Fortress, 1969. 148 pp. A call for **76**
renewal in preaching. It emphasizes an interpretation of the biblical text
based on a new hermeneutic and related to life's concrete situation.

Read, David H. C.
Sent from God: The Enduring Power and Mystery of Preaching. Nashville: **77**
Abingdon, 1974. 112 pp. Lyman Beecher Lectures, 1973. The pastor of Madison
Avenue Presbyterian Church, New York, makes a statement about preaching.
He discusses theological background, listening, evangelism in an electronic
age, and sermon preparation.

Reese, James M.
Preaching God's Burning Word. Collegeville, Minn.: Liturgical, 1975. **78**
135 pp. Insists that the preacher enter into the experience of God in preaching.

Reid, Clyde H.
The Empty Pulpit: A Study in Preaching as Communication. New York: **79**
Harper & Row, 1967. 122 pp. Counteracts the lack of meaning and relevance
in contemporary preaching with a discussion of communication and its relationship to the pulpit.

Reu, Johann Michael
Homiletics: A Manual of the Theory and Practice of Preaching. Translated **80**
by Albert Steinhaeuser. Grand Rapids: Baker, 1967. 639 pp. A reprint (Chicago:
Wartburg, 1922). A Lutheran scholar helps to fill a void in the homiletical
literature produced by Lutherans in America.

Rohrbach, Peter Thomas
The Art of Dynamic Preaching: A Practical Guide to Better Preaching. **81**
Garden City, N.Y.: Doubleday, 1965. 190 pp. A Catholic view of the preacher's
task in this "age of renewal" in preaching. Considered are the arts of public
speaking, persuasion, and preaching. Practical exercises conclude each
section.

Sangster, William Edwin
The Approach to Preaching. Grand Rapids: Baker, 1974. 112 pp. A reprint **82**
(Philadelphia: Westminster, 1952). See RHT[1], entry 113.

Power in Preaching. Grand Rapids: Baker, 1976. 110 pp. A reprint (New **83**
York: Abingdon, 1958). Fondren Lectures, Southern Methodist University. See
RHT[1], entry 114.

Scherer, Paul
The Word God Sent. Grand Rapids: Baker, 1977. 285 pp. A reprint (New **84**
York: Harper & Row, 1965). See RHT[1], entry 117.

Schmaus, Michael
Preaching as a Saving Encounter. Translated by J. Holland Smith. Staten **85**
Island, N.Y.: Alba, 1966. 151 pp. The translation of a German work focusing
on the function of doctrinal preaching, those who are to do that preaching,
and its relevancy to those who hear it.

Schneider, Stanley D.
As One Who Speaks for God: The Why and How of Preaching. Min- **86**
neapolis: Augsburg, 1965. 120 pp. A Lutheran professor explains the purpose
and procedure of traditional preaching.

Sittler, Joseph
 The Anguish of Preaching. Philadelphia: Fortress, 1966. 77 pp. Zimmer-   **87**
man Lectures, 1966, Lutheran Theological Seminary, Gettysburg. Addresses
the relationship of preaching to several immediate problems confronting the
church.

Skinner, Craig
 The Teaching Ministry of the Pulpit: Its History, Theology, Psychology,   **88**
and Practice for Today. Grand Rapids: Baker, 1973. 255 pp. A conservative
Australian pastor and educator stresses the importance of biblical teaching
from the pulpit, examining the subject from historical, theological, psychological, and practical viewpoints.

Smith, Arthur L., ed.
 Language, Communication, and Rhetoric in Black America. New York: **89**
Harper & Row, 1972. 399 pp. An informative work on black communication.

Spurgeon, Charles Haddon
 Encounter with Spurgeon. Edited by Helmut Thielicke. Translated by   **90**
John W. Doberstein. Grand Rapids: Baker, 1975. 283 pp. A reprint (Philadel-
phia: Fortress, 1963). See RHT[1], entry 129.

Stanfield, Vernon L., et al.
 Homiletics. Grand Rapids: Baker, 1972. 156 pp. Ten contemporary pastors   **91**
and teachers write on various aspects of homiletics, combining to give an
overview of the subject.

Steimle, Edmund A.; Niedenthal, Morris J.; and Rice, Charles L.: eds.
 Preaching the Story. Philadelphia: Fortress, 1980. 208 pp.   **92**

Stevenson, Dwight E.
 In the Biblical Preacher's Workshop. Nashville: Abingdon, 1967. 223 pp.   **93**
Bridges the gap between biblical exegesis and homiletics, and gives guidance
in dealing with passages of medium length. The author, a professor at Lexington Theological Seminary, provides both principles and illustrations.

Sweazy, George E.
 Preaching the Good News. Englewood Cliffs, N.J.: Prentice-Hall, 1976.   **94**
347 pp. A basic text for students and preachers by a professor at Princeton
Theological Seminary.

Taylor, William M.
 The Ministry of the Word. Grand Rapids: Baker, 1975. 318 pp. A reprint   **95**
(New York: Randolph, 1876). Lyman Beecher Lectures, 1876. Designed for the
young minister, this work discusses the importance of various aspects of the
ministry.

Turnbull, Ralph G.
The Preacher's Heritage, Task, and Resources. Grand Rapids: Baker, 1968. **96**
178 pp. Includes the substance of lectures and messages the author, a retired
pastor, delivered at various seminaries and pastors' conferences.

Warren, Max A. C.
The Day of the Preacher. London: Mowbray, 1967. 53 pp. Deals with the **97**
content, not the technique, of preaching. The author takes account not only
of the gospel but also of the world in which it is proclaimed.

Wedel, Alton F.
The Mighty Word: Power and Purpose of Preaching. St. Louis: Concordia, **98**
1977. 39 pp. An apologetic, based on biblical data, for the centrality of preaching in the life of the church.

Welsh, Clement
Preaching in a New Key: Studies in the Psychology of Thinking and **99**
Listening. Philadelphia: United Church, 1974. 128 pp. Lester Bradner Lectures, 1971, Episcopal Theological School. Focuses on the listener by exploring
the psychology of thinking and listening. The author relies heavily on recent
communication theory.

West, Emerson Roy
How to Speak in Church. Salt Lake City: Deseret, 1976. 168 pp. **100**

White, Douglas M.
The Excellence of Exposition. Neptune, N.J.: Loizeaux, 1977. 191 pp. An **101**
evangelical argument for expository preaching, emphasizing the use of an
"extended passage" and based on Bible-study methods and homiletical
craftsmanship.

White, R. E. O.
A Guide to Preaching: A Practical Primer of Homiletics. Grand Rapids: **102**
Eerdmans, 1973. 251 pp. A basic text for aspiring and beginning preachers,
covering the aim, technique, and continuing disciplines of preaching.

Wiersbe, Warren W.
Walking with the Giants: A Minister's Guide to Good Reading and Great **103**
Preaching. Grand Rapids: Baker, 1976. 289 pp. A compilation of articles
written for *Moody Monthly*, studying a preacher or a book of the past.

Wiseman, Neil B., ed.
Biblical Preaching for Contemporary Man. Kansas City: Beacon Hill, 1976. **104**
160 pp. Articles on various dimensions of biblical preaching, written by the
outstanding preachers and teachers of the Church of the Nazarene.

Yohn, David Waite
The Contemporary Preacher and His Task. Grand Rapids: Eerdmans, **105**
1969. 159 pp. The minister of the Church of Christ at Dartmouth College
discusses the task and purpose of today's preacher by examining his relationship to historical antecedents, the nature of the preaching ministry, and the
Bible's unity, authority, and exposition.

Preaching and Theology

Abbey, Merrill R.
The Word Interprets Us. New York: Abingdon, 1967. 208 pp. Emphasizes **106**
the importance of biblical interpretation and preaching and includes an
analysis of the use of the Bible in the pulpit.

Church, Aloysius
The Theology of the Word of God. Notre Dame, Ind.: Fides, 1970. 96 pp. **107**
Based on the documents of the Second Vatican Council and modern writings,
this work studies Christ's presence in the spoken word, the stages of preaching,
and the place of the laity, bishop, and priest in preaching.

Harrop, G. Gerald
Elijah Speaks Today: The Long Road into Naboth's Vineyard. Nashville: **108**
Abingdon, 1975. 175 pp. Suggests a way to use the Old Testament prophets in
speaking to the socio-economic system of today. The story of Elijah and
Naboth's vineyard is developed to illustrate this process.

Jahsmann, Allan Hart
Power Beyond Words: Communication Systems of the Spirit and Ways of **109**
Teaching Religion. St. Louis: Concordia, 1969. 180 pp. Concerned with the
appropriation of the power of God and the ministry of the Holy Spirit in the
communicative and educational programs of the church.

Jones, J. Ithel
The Holy Spirit and Christian Preaching. London: Epworth, 1967. 78 pp. **110**
Gay Lectures, 1965, Southern Baptist Seminary. Develops the place of the
Holy Spirit in the activity of Christian proclamation.

Kaiser, Walter C., Jr.
The Old Testament in Contemporary Preaching. Grand Rapids: Baker, **111**
1973. 135 pp. An evangelical Old Testament scholar attempts to restore the
church's confidence in the Old Testament by arguing for its importance and
encouraging an increase in its use in preaching.

Kraus, Hans Joachim
The Threat and the Power. Translated by Keith Crim. Richmond: John **112**

Knox, 1971. 107 pp. Pleads for a return to the concept of the "authority of preaching" as a treatment for "the plight of preaching in the Protestant church."

McCurley, Foster R., Jr.
Proclaiming the Promise: Christian Preaching from the Old Testament. 113
Philadelphia: Fortress, 1974. 160 pp. Demonstrates the necessity of using all the tools and results of modern biblical research in order to proclaim the Word of God to twentieth-century Christians. The author places this discussion within the context of the Old Testament.

Miller, Donald G.
Fire in Thy Mouth. Grand Rapids: Baker, 1976. 160 pp. A reprint (Nash- 114
ville: Abingdon, 1954). See RHT¹, entry 180.

Pitt-Watson, Ian
Preaching: A Kind of Folly. Philadelphia: Westminster, 1978. 109 pp. An 115
expansion of the Warrack Lectures, highlighting the necessity of theology in preaching.

Rahner, Hugo
A Theology of Proclamation. Edited by Joseph Halpin. Translated by 116
Richard Dimmler et al. New York: Herder and Herder, 1968. 216 pp. Lectures examining the relationship of kerygma to various aspects of the dogmatic theology of Roman Catholicism.

Stewart, James S.
A Faith to Proclaim. Grand Rapids: Baker, 1972. 160 pp. A reprint (New 117
York: Scribner, 1953). Lyman Beecher Lectures, 1952. See RHT¹, entry 201.

Stuempfle, Herman G., Jr.
Preaching Law and Gospel. Philadelphia: Fortress, 1978. 95 pp. An 118
analysis of the theological foundations of preaching from a Lutheran perspective.

Worley, Robert C.
Preaching and Teaching in the Earliest Church. Philadelphia: Westminster, 119
1967. 199 pp. Sets forth a theory of the nature of teaching and preaching and their relationship in the early church. It is based on an analysis of C. H. Dodd's theory.

Topics of Preaching

Blackwood, Andrew W.
Preaching from Samuel. Grand Rapids: Baker, 1975. 256 pp. A reprint 120

(New York: Abingdon-Cokesbury, 1946). Consists of expositional helps for the preacher. Most chapters in I and II Samuel are dealt with to uncover preaching material.

Cosser, William
   Preaching the Old Testament. London: Epworth, 1967. 79 pp. Shows the   121
preacher that he can use the Old Testament as an effective vehicle in his
preaching. It explains the relevance of the Old Testament to the New and
solves some problems encountered when preaching from the Old Testament.

Daane, James
   The Freedom of God: A Study of Election and Pulpit. Grand Rapids: 122
Eerdmans, 1973. 208 pp. A Reformed theologian presents a doctrinal study of
God's elective decree and then explains how that doctrine can be effectively
preached. This study in the relationship between theology and homiletics is
unique.

Greidanus, Sidney
   Sola Scriptura: Problems and Principles in Preaching Historical Texts.   123
Toronto: Wedge, 1970. 259 pp. An examination of the hermeneutical-
homiletical controversy prominent in Holland in the 1930s and 1940s. The
author offers guidelines for interpreting and preaching historical passages.

Jackson, Edgar N.
   How to Preach to People's Needs. Grand Rapids: Baker, 1970. 191 pp. A   124
reprint (New York: Abingdon, 1956). See RHT[1], entry 274.

Kemp, Charles F.
   The Preaching Pastor. St. Louis: Bethany, 1966. 251 pp. Building upon a   125
belief in the close relationship between preaching and pastoral care, this work
introduces the role of preaching in meeting needs and fostering growth.
Sermons by men such as Horace Bushnell, Harry Emerson Fosdick, and
Phillips Brooks illustrate preaching's ability to meet human needs.

Luecke, Richard Henry
   Violent Sleep: Notes Toward the Development of Sermons for the Modern   126
City. Philadelphia: Fortress, 1969. 154 pp. Studies ways to develop sermons for
contemporary urban America, emphasizing the relationship of scriptural
exegesis to present-day problems.

Stuempfle, Herman G., Jr., ed.
   Preaching in the Witnessing Community. Philadelphia: Fortress, 1973.   127
118 pp. Displays the relationship of evangelism to preaching and of the gospel
to daily life and important social issues.

Taylor, Richard S.
Preaching Holiness Today. Kansas City: Beacon Hill, 1968. 216 pp. This   **128**
doctrinal study of holiness from a Nazarene viewpoint includes principles
for preaching this doctrine. It is illustrated by homiletical outlines and
suggestions.

The Preacher

Adams, Jay E.
Shepherding God's Flock. Vol. 1, *The Pastoral Life.* Nutley, N.J.: Presby-   **129**
terian and Reformed, 1975. 164 pp. Deals with the preacher's personal life, his
call to the ministry, and his care of the congregation. An exercise follows each
major section.

Shepherding God's Flock: A Preacher's Handbook on Pastoral Ministry,   **130**
Counseling, and Leadership. 3 vols. in 1. Grand Rapids: Baker, 1979. See
entry 129 above.

Blackwood, Andrew W.
The Growing Minister: His Opportunities and Obstacles. Grand Rapids: **131**
Baker, 1977. 192 pp. A reprint (New York: Abingdon, 1960). Discusses areas of
growth for the minister as well as obstacles to his growth.

Echlin, Edward P.
The Priest as Preacher, Past and Future. Notre Dame, Ind.: Fides, 1973.   **132**
91 pp. Demonstrates the centrality of preaching in the ministry of the priest
through a historical study. The work's purpose is to help meet the laity's
demands for better preaching.

Huxtable, [William] John F.
"The Preacher's Integrity" and Other Lectures. London: Epworth, 1966.   **133**
189 pp. Lectures on the preacher's integrity in his treatment of the Bible and
in other areas of the ministry and the church.

McCabe, Joseph E.
How to Find Time for Better Preaching and Better Pastoring. Philadelphia: **134**
Westminster, 1973. 112 pp. Citing pressures that reduce a minister's ability to
both pastor and preach, the author suggests ways to improve the minister's
management of time and increase his effectiveness.

Morgan, G. Campbell.
The Ministry of the Word. Grand Rapids: Baker, 1970. 252 pp. A reprint   **135**
(London: Hodder & Stoughton, 1919). Looks at the Christian ministry solely
from the viewpoint of New Testament ideals.

Stalker, James
  The Preacher and His Models. Grand Rapids: Baker, 1967. 284 pp. A   136
reprint (New York: Hodder & Stoughton, 1891). Lyman Beecher Lectures, 1891.
Views preaching in its relationship to the pastor's other roles.

Stewart, James S.
  Heralds of God. Grand Rapids: Baker, 1972. 222 pp. A reprint (London: 137
Hodder & Stoughton, 1946). Warrack Lectures, 1943. See RHT[1], entry 266.

Stott, John R. W.
  The Preacher's Portrait: Some New Testament Word Studies. Grand Rapids: 138
Eerdmans, 1961. 124 pp. Sermons delivered in 1961 at Fuller Theological
Seminary on the subject of God's revealed ideal for the preacher.

Turnbull, Ralph G.
  A Minister's Obstacles. Rev. ed. Grand Rapids: Baker, 1972. 192 pp. A   139
reprint (New York: Revell, 1964). Helps the minister overcome obstacles
peculiar to his calling, such as professionalism, sloth, criticism, pride, and
jealousy.

The Congregation

Deffner, Donald L.
  The Real Word for the Real World: Applying the Word to the Needs of   140
People. St. Louis: Concordia, 1977. 40 pp. Argues for the importance of
need-centered preaching. The author discusses the importance of understanding a congregation's needs, basic human needs in American culture, and the
relationship of these needs to preaching.

Dirks, Marvin J.
  Laymen Look at Preaching: Lay Expectation Factors in Relation to the   141
Preaching of Helmut Thielicke. North Quincy, Mass.: Christopher, 1972.
326 pp. A case study seeking to determine the expectations of those who listen
to preaching.

Fisher, Wallace E.
  Preaching and Parish Renewal. Nashville: Abingdon, 1966. 208 pp. Con-   142
vinced that renewal and biblical preaching are inseparable, a Lutheran pastor
makes a case for the relevance of preaching and of the gospel to human nature
and the world today. He concludes with sermons demonstrating how to
address the gospel to pluralistic gatherings.

Jefferson, Charles E.
  The Building of the Church. Grand Rapids: Baker, 1969. 305 pp. A reprint   143

(New York: Macmillan, 1910). Lyman Beecher Lectures, 1910. Relates the preacher and his preaching to his congregation.

Teikmanis, Arthur L.
Preaching and Pastoral Care. Philadelphia: Fortress, 1968. 144 pp. A reprint   144
(Englewood Cliffs, N.J.: Prentice-Hall, 1964). See RHT[1], entry 279.

Thompson, William D.
A Listener's Guide to Preaching. Nashville: Abingdon, 1966. 110 pp. A   145
book to aid the layman in finding in sermons a renewed means of Christian growth. The author shows him how to share with his minister the responsibility for good preaching and how to be a better listener.

The Setting—Liturgical

Babin, David E.
Week In, Week Out: A New Look at Liturgical Preaching. New York: 146
Seabury, 1976. 140 pp. Explains the role and function of liturgical preaching, and then suggests ways to prepare and present liturgical sermons.

Bass, George M.
The Renewal of Liturgical Preaching. Minneapolis: Augsburg, 1967.   147
166 pp. A Lutheran homiletician relates the liturgical renewal to the sermon. He emphasizes the correspondence of biblical preaching to the Christian year.

Bosch, Paul
The Sermon as Part of the Liturgy. St. Louis: Concordia, 1977. 48 pp.   148
Argues for the use of the liturgical year, stressing the nonverbal message of ritual.

Burke, John, ed.
The Sunday Homily: Scriptural and Liturgical Renewal. Washington,   149
D.C.: Thomist, 1966. 145 pp. Papers delivered at the 1965 Workshop on the Renewal in Scriptural and Liturgical Preaching. The aim is to help the parish priest deliver his Sunday messages in the spirit of renewal envisioned by the Second Vatican Council.

The Setting—Special Occasions

Baillargeon, Anatole, ed.
New Media, New Forms: Contemporary Forms of Preaching. Chicago: 150
Franciscan Herald, 1968. 237 pp. The second of two volumes on various forms of contemporary preaching (for the first, *Handbook for Special Preaching,* see RHT[1], entry 288). These essays focus on the traditional homily, retreats (and

experimental variations of them), media preaching, the Area Mission, and the Week of Reparation.

The Sermon

Asquith, Glenn H.
Preaching According to Plan. Valley Forge, Pa.: Judson, 1968. 79 pp. A   151
Baptist pastor stresses the importance of planning at every stage of sermon
preparation.

Blackwood, Andrew W.
Doctrinal Preaching for Today: Case Studies of Bible Teachings. Grand   152
Rapids: Baker, 1975. 224 pp. A reprint (New York: Abingdon, 1956). See
RHT[1], entry 215.

Expository Preaching for Today: Case Studies of Bible Passages. Grand   153
Rapids: Baker, 1975. 224 pp. A reprint (Nashville: Abingdon-Cokesbury, 1953).
See RHT[1], entry 216.

Planning a Year's Pulpit Work. Grand Rapids: Baker, 1975. 240 pp. A   154
reprint (New York: Abingdon, 1942). See RHT[1], entry 316.

Braga, James
How to Prepare Bible Messages: A Manual on Homiletics for Bible   155
Students. Portland: Multnomah, 1971. 231 pp. A professor at Multnomah
School of the Bible presents a manual on homiletics in the conservative
tradition. Exercises end each chapter.

Brown, H. C., Jr.
Sermon Analysis for Pulpit Power. Nashville: Broadman, 1971. 61 pp.   156
Assists the preacher in objectively analyzing a sermon, before preaching it,
according to the sermon's foundations, construction, and final factors.

Browne, Benjamin P.
Illustrations for Preaching. Nashville: Broadman, 1977. 191 pp. A chapter   157
on how to find illustrative material supplements this topically arranged collection of illustrations.

Cooke, J. B. Deaver
The Carpenter's Way to Build Dynamic Sermons. Drexel Hill, Pa.: Sea-   158
board, 1971. 152 pp.

Dabney, Robert L.
Sacred Rhetoric: A Course of Lectures on Preaching. Saint Clair Shores,   159
Mich.: Scholarly, 1977. 361 pp. A reprint (Richmond: Presbyterian Committee
of Publication, 1870). In these lectures given at Union Theological Seminary

in Richmond, the basic outline of classical rhetoric is used to teach the preparation and presentation of sermons.

Erdahl, Lowell O.
Better Preaching: Evaluating the Sermon. St. Louis: Concordia, 1977. **160**
47 pp. Written especially for veteran preachers who need to reevaluate their preaching.

Fish, Roy J.
Giving a Good Invitation. Nashville: Broadman, 1974. 55 pp. A guide to **161**
giving evangelistic invitations.

Ford, D. W. Cleverley
Preaching at the Parish Communion. Vol. 1, *On the Gospels.* London: **162**
Mowbray, 1967. 125 pp. An introductory chapter on outlining and preparing sermons precedes a series of sermon outlines.

Garrison, Webb B.
Taking the Drudgery out of Sermon Preparation. Grand Rapids: Baker, **163**
1975. 175 pp. A reprint (*Creative Imagination in Preaching.* Nashville: Abingdon, 1960). See RHT[1], entry 325.

Howe, Reuel L.
Partners in Preaching: Clergy and Laity in Dialogue. New York: Seabury, **164**
1967. 127 pp. Describes dialogical preaching involving both clergy and laymen as a means of overcoming the weaknesses of conventional preaching.

Knoche, H. Gerard
The Creative Task: Writing the Sermon. St. Louis: Concordia, 1977. 46 pp. **165**
Insists on the need for creativity in sermons, and suggests ways to cultivate it.

Lehman, Louis Paul
Put a Door on It!: The "How" and "Why" of Sermon Illustration. Grand **166**
Rapids: Kregel, 1975. 102 pp. Discusses the importance of illustrating, how to acquire illustrative material, and how to use it.

Lenski, R. C. H.
The Sermon: Its Homiletical Construction. Grand Rapids: Baker, 1968. **167**
314 pp. A reprint (Columbus: Lutheran Book Concern, 1927). Each section is liberally supported by biblical illustrations reflecting the author's emphasis on biblical exegesis.

Linn, Edmund Holt
Preaching as Counseling: The Unique Method of Harry Emerson Fosdick. **168**
Valley Forge, Pa.: Judson, 1966. 159 pp. This study, based in part on personal interviews, describes the preaching philosophy and methodology of Fosdick.

It is meant to be a memorial to Fosdick and his counseling method of preaching.

Luccock, Halford E.
In the Minister's Workshop. Grand Rapids: Baker, 1977. 254 pp. A reprint **169** (New York: Abingdon-Cokesbury, 1944). See RHT[1], entry 331.

Macpherson, Ian
The Art of Illustrating Sermons. Grand Rapids: Baker, 1976. 219 pp. A **170** reprint (Nashville: Abingdon, 1966). See RHT[1], entry 335.

Mannebach, Wayne C., and Mazza, Joseph M.
Speaking from the Pulpit. Valley Forge, Pa.: Judson, 1969. 127 pp. In this **171** general text two speech professors at secular colleges apply selected areas of speech theory to preaching. They write as laymen interested in increasing the effectiveness of pulpit discourse.

Massey, James Earl
The Sermon in Perspective: A Study of Communication and Charisma. **172** Grand Rapids: Baker, 1976. 116 pp. A work viewing the sermon as communication, commentary, counsel, creation, and charisma.

Milner, Paulinus, ed.
The Ministry of the Word. London: Burns & Oates, 1967. 128 pp. A fruit of **173** the Conference of Practical Liturgy.

Morgan, G. Campbell
Preaching. Grand Rapids: Baker, 1974. 90 pp. A reprint (New York: Revell, **174** 1937). See RHT[1], entry 339.

Pearce, J. Winston
Planning Your Preaching. Nashville: Broadman, 1967. 204 pp. A Baptist **175** pastor argues for the necessity of long-range planning of a preaching program, then supplies eight helpful plans that stress variety and order.

Perry, Lloyd M.
Biblical Sermon Guide: A Step-by-Step Procedure for the Preparation and **176** *Presentation.* Grand Rapids: Baker, 1970. 131 pp. A traditional approach to preparing and presenting the biblical sermon. It suggests many methods to provide variety in outlines.

Rice, Charles L.
Interpretation and Imagination: The Preacher and Contemporary Litera- **177** *ture.* Philadelphia: Fortress, 1970. 172 pp. Urges the enrichment of preaching through the use of various types of contemporary literature. The author sees

this as one way to present the gospel to those who are impervious to biblical and theological terminology.

Sangster, William Edwin
    The Craft of Sermon Construction. Grand Rapids: Baker, 1972. 208 pp. A **178**
reprint (Philadelphia: Westminster, 1951). See RHT[1], entry 347.

Thompson, William D., and Bennett, Gordon C.
    Dialogue Preaching: The Shared Sermon. Valley Forge, Pa.: Judson, 1969. **179**
158 pp. An examination of the history, roles, and values of dialogue preaching in public worship is followed by an anthology of dialogue sermons.

Unger, Merrill F.
    Principles of Expository Preaching. Grand Rapids: Zondervan, 1973. **180**
267 pp. A reprint (1955). See RHT[1], entry 352.

Weisheit, Eldon
    A Sermon Is More than Words. St. Louis: Concordia, 1977. 46 pp. Discusses **181**
the importance, impact, and use of audio-visual material in the sermon.

West, Emerson Roy
    When You Speak in Church: Purpose, Preparation, Presentation. Salt **182**
Lake City: Deseret, 1965. 196 pp. A Mormon author designed this book for anyone desiring to speak more effectively in church. Built upon basic principles of public speaking, it pays special attention to preparing speeches for special occasions.

Wood, John Edwin
    The Preacher's Workshop: Preparation for Expository Preaching. London: **183**
Tyndale, 1965. 64 pp.

Delivery

Abbey, Merrill R.
    Man, Media, and the Message. New York: Friendship, 1970. 159 pp. Written **184**
for the National Council of Churches' Department of Education for Mission, this study discusses the church's need to employ modern media to reach men with its message.

Harms, Paul
    Power from the Pulpit: Delivering the Good News. St. Louis: Concordia, **185**
1977. 55 pp. An explanation of how to deliver a sermon effectively.

Phelps, Arthur Stevens
    Public Speaking for Ministers. Rev. ed. Edited by Lester R. De Koster. **186**

Grand Rapids: Baker, 1964. 167 pp. Discusses factors that contribute to a successful public presentation. Delivery is a major emphasis. The first edition was titled *Speaking in Public.*

Stevenson, Dwight E., and Diehl, Charles F.
Reaching People from the Pulpit: A Guide to Effective Sermon Delivery.   **187**
Grand Rapids: Baker, 1978. 182 pp. A reprint (New York: Harper & Row, 1958). See RHT[1], entry 364.

History—Individual Preachers

Adams, Jay E.
Audience Adaptations in the Sermons and Speeches of Paul. Phillipsburg,   **188**
N.J.: Presbyterian and Reformed, 1976. 107 pp. Analyzes Paul's four recorded sermons and four recorded defenses to determine the extent to which he adapted himself to his audiences. The book's final section suggests ways the preacher today can employ audience adaptation.

The Homiletical Innovations of Andrew W. Blackwood. Phillipsburg,   **189**
N.J.: Presbyterian and Reformed, 1975. 166 pp. Discusses Blackwood's contributions to the field of homiletics and the sources and components of his teaching theory.

Sense Appeal in the Sermons of Charles Haddon Spurgeon. Nutley, N.J.:   **190**
Presbyterian and Reformed, 1975. 70 pp. A study of 425 sermons by Spurgeon to discover his use of sense appeal. Spurgeon's appeal to each of the five senses and the sources of his method are discussed.

Augustine
The Preaching of Augustine: "Our Lord's Sermon on the Mount." Edited   **191**
by Jaroslav Pelikan. Translated by Francine Cardman. Philadelphia: Fortress, 1973. 186 pp. Evaluates this early theologian's exposition and interpretation of the Sermon on the Mount.

Carrithers, Gale H., Jr.
Donne at Sermons: A Christian Existential World. Albany: State University   **192**
of New York, 1972. 329 pp. This study of John Donne's preaching includes discussions of the sermon as it relates to its genre and to Donne's own existential convictions. Texts and analyses of four sermons are included.

Chamberlin, John S.
Increase and Multiply: Arts-of-Discourse Procedure in the Preaching of   **193**
Donne. Chapel Hill: University of North Carolina, 1976. 213 pp. Evaluates John Donne's application of the three arts of rhetoric to preaching. His use of the art of discourse procedure to dilate a sermon is discussed.

Chrysostom, John
The Preaching of Chrysostom: Homilies on the Sermon of the Mount. **194**
Edited by Jaroslav Pelikan. Philadelphia: Fortress, 1967. 239 pp. An introduction to Chrysostom as an exegete, a rhetor, and an expositor of the Sermon on the Mount is followed by his ten homilies on this passage.

Crocker, Lionel, ed.
Harry Emerson Fosdick's Art of Preaching: An Anthology. Springfield: **195**
Thomas, 1971. 295 pp. Fosdick and others analyze his preaching.

Day, Owen T., and Thomas, Nancy C.
The Hallelujah Hole: The Story of a Frontier Preacher. Valley Forge, Pa.: **196**
Judson, 1976. 174 pp. A biography of Frank Day, born in 1862.

Donne, John
Donne's Prebend Sermons. Edited by Janel M. Mueller. Cambridge, Mass.: **197**
Harvard University, 1971. 642 pp. A detailed introduction, five sermons, and notes revealing a great Anglican pastor at the height of his preaching ministry.

Eaton, Arthur W. H.
The Famous Mather Byles, the Noted Boston Tory Preacher, Poet, and Wit, **198**
1707-1788. Boston: Gregg, 1972. 278 pp. A reprint (Boston: Butterfield, 1914).
A biography.

Fant, Clyde E.
Bonhoeffer: Worldly Preaching. Nashville: Nelson, 1975. 191 pp. Based on **199**
Dietrich Bonhoeffer's lectures on preaching at the Confessing Church Seminary in Finkenwalde, this work reveals his intense interest in practical theology. The text of his ten lectures is included.

Gericke, Paul
The Preaching of Robert G. Lee: Adorning the Doctrine of God. Orlando, **200**
Fla.: Christ for the World, 1967. 180 pp. A study of the life and preaching of a great Southern Baptist pastor. The author probes for the reason behind Lee's effectiveness as a preacher.

Gundry, Stanley N.
Love Them In: The Proclamation Theology of D. L. Moody. Chicago: **201**
Moody, 1976. 252 pp. An analysis of Moody's theology and methodology.

Kemmler, Dieter Werner
Faith and Human Reason: A Study of Paul's Method of Preaching as **202**
Illustrated by 1-2 Thessalonians and Acts 17, 2-4. Leiden: Brill, 1975. 225 pp.
A discussion of the role of human reason in Paul's preaching.

Kiessling, Elmer Carl
The Early Sermons of Luther and Their Relation to Pre-Reformation **203**
Sermons. New York: AMS, 1971. 157 pp. A reprint (Grand Rapids: Zondervan, 1935). See RHT[1], entry 379.

Miller, Robert Moats
How Shall They Hear Without a Preacher? The Life of Ernest Fremont **204**
Tittle. Chapel Hill: University of North Carolina, 1971. 524 pp. A biography of the long-time pastor of First Methodist Church, Evanston.

Newman, John Henry
The Preaching of John Henry Newman. Edited by W. D. White. Philadel- **205**
phia: Fortress, 1969. 237 pp. Fifteen sermons by this nineteenth-century churchman and preacher are introduced by a description of his life, his theory of preaching, and the contemporary significance of his preaching.

Roberts, Oral
The Call: An Autobiography. Garden City, N.Y.: Doubleday, 1972. 216 pp. **206**
An autobiography of the well-known evangelist, faith-healer, and university president.

Spykman, Gordon J.
Pioneer Preacher: Albertus Christiaan Van Raalte: A Study of His Sermon **207**
Notes. Grand Rapids: Calvin College and Seminary Library, 1976. 142 pp.

Turner, R. Edward
Proclaiming the Word: The Concept of Preaching in the Thought of **208**
Ellen G. White. Berrien Springs, Mich.: Andrews University, 1980. 182 pp. A study of White's developing concept of preaching and of other factors significant in the early homiletical thought of Adventism.

Weatherhead, A. Kingsley
Leslie Weatherhead: A Personal Portrait. Nashville: Abingdon, 1975. **209**
269 pp. A biography of the British Methodist preacher by his younger son, highlighting his ministry as preacher, writer, and counselor.

History—Groups

Brastow, Lewis O.
Representative Modern Preachers. Freeport, N.Y.: Books for Libraries, 1968. **210**
438 pp. A reprint (New York: Macmillan, 1904). Discusses nine famous preachers: Friedrich Schleiermacher, F. W. Robertson, Henry Ward Beecher, Horace Bushnell, Phillips Brooks, John Henry Newman, Thomas Mozley, Thomas Guthrie, and Charles Haddon Spurgeon.

Demaray, Donald E.
Pulpit Giants: What Made Them Great. Chicago: Moody, 1973. 174 pp.   **211**
Brief portraits of twenty-five leading preachers in the evangelical tradition
from Augustine to Billy Graham. A concluding chapter describes their
common characteristics.

Downey, James
The Eighteenth Century Pulpit: A Study of the Sermons of Butler, Berkeley,   **212**
Secker, Sterne, Whitefield, and Wesley. Oxford: Clarendon, 1969. 263 pp. In
defining the sermon's place in the literary history of eighteenth-century
England, the author analyzes the pulpit oratory of Joseph Butler, George
Berkeley, Thomas Secker, Laurence Sterne, George Whitefield, and John
Wesley.

Fant, Clyde E., and Pinson, William M.
Twenty Centuries of Great Preaching: An Encyclopedia of Preaching. 13   **213**
vols. Waco, Tex.: Word, 1971. This collection of sermons by ninety preachers
(from Christ to the present) includes an introduction to each preacher represented. This covers his life and an analysis of his sermon style.

Jones, Edgar De Witt
American Preachers of To-day: Intimate Appraisals of Thirty-two Leaders.   **214**
Freeport, N.Y.: Books for Libraries, 1971. 317 pp. A reprint (Indianapolis:
Bobbs-Merrill, 1933). An evaluation of leading preachers of the day.

Laymon, Charles M.
They Dared to Speak for God. Nashville: Abingdon, 1974. 176 pp. A dis-   **215**
cussion of representative preaching in the Bible, the men who preached and
the types of preaching.

Newton, Joseph Fort
Some Living Masters of the Pulpit: Studies in Religious Personality.   **216**
Freeport, N.Y.: Books for Libraries, 1971. 261 pp. A reprint (New York: Doran,
1923). Describes the lives and ministries of such leading preachers of the day
as William R. Inge, Charles E. Jefferson, Samuel Parkes Cadman, William A.
Quayle, George W. Truett, and Frank W. Gunsaulus.

Stevenson, Dwight E.
Disciple Preaching in the First Generation: An Ecological Study. Nashville: **217**
Disciples of Christ Historical Society, 1969. 109 pp. Forrest F. Reed Lectures,
1969.

Wagenknecht, Edward
Ambassadors for Christ: Seven American Preachers. New York: Oxford   **218**
University, 1972. 310 pp. An examination of the lives and preaching of Lyman

Beecher, William Ellery Channing, Henry Ward Beecher, Phillips Brooks, D. L. Moody, Washington Gladden, and Lyman Abbott.

History—Periods

Crew, Phyllis Mack
   Calvinist Preaching and Iconoclasm in the Netherlands, 1544-1569. New   **219**
York: Cambridge University, 1978. 221 pp. A scholarly analysis of Dutch
preaching during the Reformation.

Elliott, Emory
   Power and the Pulpit in Puritan New England. Princeton, N.J.: Princeton   **220**
University, 1975. 251 pp. An evaluation of how the Puritan pulpit both
influenced and was influenced by the changing conditions in late-seventeenth-
century Massachusetts.

Gatch, Milton, McC.
   Preaching and Theology in Anglo-Saxon England: Aelfric and Wulfston.   **221**
Toronto: University of Toronto, 1977. 279 pp. Treats Abbott Aelfric and Arch-
bishop Wulfstan II as representatives of preaching and theological method of
the era.

Gotaas, Mary C.
   Bossuet and Vieira: A Study in National, Epochal, and Individual Style.   **222**
New York: AMS, 1970. 155 pp. A reprint (Washington, D.C.: Catholic University of America, 1953). Examines basic principles of preaching style found in
the seventeenth-century Baroque period in France and Portugal, as demon-
strated by two leading representatives.

Herr, Alan Fager
   The Elizabethan Sermon: A Survey and a Bibliography. New York: **223**
Octagon, 1969. 169 pp. A reprint (Philadelphia: University of Pennsylvania,
1940). See RHT[1], entry 424.

Hicks, H. Beecher, Jr.
   Images of the Black Preacher: The Man Nobody Knows. Valley Forge, Pa.:   **224**
Judson, 1977. 158 pp. Surveys images of black preachers from the slavery era to
the present.

Holland, DeWitte, ed.
   Preaching in American History: Selected Issues in the American Pulpit,   **225**
1630-1967. Nashville: Abingdon, 1969. 436 pp. Twenty essays describing and
interpreting some major topics of the American pulpit between 1630 and 1967.
It was prepared under the auspices of the Speech Association of America.

Sermons in American History: Selected Issues in the American Pulpit. **226**
Nashville: Abingdon, 1971. 542 pp. A companion volume to Holland's
Preaching in American History (see entry 225 above). It analyzes the history
of American preaching and presents representative sermons illustrative of the
major issues covered in the first volume. It was prepared under the auspices of
the Speech Communication Association.

Levy, Babette May

Preaching in the First Half Century of New England History. New York: **227**
Russell and Russell, 1967. 222 pp. A reprint (Hartford, Conn.: American
Society of Church History, 1945). See RHT[1], entry 429.

Mann, Jacob, and Sonne, Isaiah

The Bible as Read and Preached in the Old Synagogue: A Study in the **228**
*Cycles of the Readings from Torah and Prophets, as Well as from Psalms, and
in the Structure of the Midrashic Homilies.* New York: Ktav, 1968-1971. 2 vols.
A reprint (Cincinnati: Hebrew Union College, 1940-1966). An outline of the
use of Scripture in the synagogue from the time of the Second Temple to the
thirteenth century. It reveals a process of standardization resulting in uni-
formity throughout Judaism and fathering much that has become common
in Jewish services.

Oliver, Robert T.

History of Public Speaking in America. Boston: Allyn and Bacon, 1965. **229**
583 pp. An historical summary of public speaking in America and the manner
in which it depicts the general flow of history itself.

Pipes, William H.

Say Amen, Brother! Old-Time Negro Preaching: A Study in American **230**
Frustration. Westport, Conn.: Negro Universities, 1970. 211 pp. A reprint
(New York: William-Frederick, 1951). See RHT[1], entry 439.

Seaver, Paul S.

The Puritan Lectureships: The Politics of Religious Dissent, 1560-1662. **231**
Stanford, Calif.: Stanford University, 1970. 411 pp. A study of the nature of the
lectureships, their effectiveness in controlling the pulpit of the established
church, and the church hierarchy's efforts to hinder their success.

Smith, Hilary Dansey

Preaching in the Spanish Golden Age: A Study of Some Preachers of the **232**
Reign of Philip III. New York: Oxford University, 1978. 199 pp.

Turnbull, Ralph G.

A History of Preaching. Vol. 3, *From the Close of the Nineteenth Century* **233**
*to the Middle of the Twentieth Century, and American Preaching During the
Seventeenth, Eighteenth, and Nineteenth Centuries.* Grand Rapids: Baker,

1974. 586 pp. Continues the work done in two previous volumes by Edwin C. Dargan (see RHT[1], entry 421). It discusses American preaching during the last three centuries and European, Canadian, Oriental, and African preaching in the twentieth century.

Vitrano, Steven P.
An Hour of Good News: The Chicago Sunday Evening Club: A Unique   **234**
Preaching Ministry. Chicago: Chicago Sunday Evening Club, 1974. 187 pp. A history of "An Hour of Good News," a unique radio and television program sponsored since 1908 by the Chicago Sunday Evening Club. The program has attracted to its pulpit hundreds of leading preachers and laymen from almost all branches of the church.

Wilson, John F.
Pulpit in Parliament: Puritanism During the English Civil Wars, 1640–   **235**
1648. Princeton, N.J.: Princeton University, 1969. 299 pp. An analysis of what the preaching done in the Long Parliament reveals about the development of Puritanism during that period.

History—Theory

Lessenich, Rolf P.
Elements of Pulpit Oratory in Eighteenth-Century England (1660–1800).   **236**
Köln: Böhlau, 1972. 276 pp. A study of the general theory of the neoclassical sermon and its relationship to latitudinarian doctrine.

Rosenberg, Bruce A.
The Art of the American Folk Preacher. New York: Oxford University,   **237**
1970. 275 pp. An in-depth study of a unique but traditional form of preaching done by blacks in America.

Bibliography

Toohey, William, and Thompson, William D., eds.
Recent Homiletical Thought: A Bibliography, 1935–1965. Nashville: **238**
Abingdon, 1967. 303 pp. A bibliography of homiletical literature published between 1935 and 1965. It includes books, journal articles, and research papers, with the books and articles being annotated.

Articles

Abbey, Merrill R.

"Crisis Preaching for the 70's." *Pulpit Digest* 51 (Feb 1971): 7–12. Argues for **239** a systematized approach to Bible study, which results in messages that better equip people to contend with the daily crises of life.

"Faith Confronts the Secular Mind." *Pulpit Digest* 43 (Apr 1963): 11–18, 66. **240** Suggests ways to make preaching serve a vital role in remaking a world that is increasingly secular. A chapter from *Preaching to the Contemporary Mind* (see RHT[1], entry 268).

Abbott, Glenn C.

"Needed: A Prophetic Breakthrough." *Christianity Today*, 8 July 1966, **241** pp. 14–15. Sees a renewal of the church only in a return both to the Spirit-filled life so obvious in the early church and to the prophetic preaching of the Bible.

Achtemeier, Elizabeth

"The Old Testament in the Church." *Union Seminary Quarterly Review* **242** 12 (Mar 1957): 45–49. Contends that Christians must hear sermons about the God who acted in history in the Old Testament if they are to understand the God who became incarnate in the New.

Adams, James McKee

"The Preacher and His Message." *Review and Expositor* 20 (1923): 3–27. **243** Defends four propositions one must believe in order to remain faithful to the Bible in one's preaching. The discussion centers on biblical inerrancy and authority.

Adams, Jay E.

"Help in Using the Original Languages in Preaching." *Journal of Pastoral* **244** *Practice* 3, 3 (1979): 168–69. Argues for a pragmatic rather than a purist approach to the use of original languages in the preparation of sermons.

Ahern, Barnabas M.
"The Scriptures and Preaching." *Proceedings of the Catholic Homiletic* **245**
Society Charter Convention (1959): 24-29.

Alden, Elder I.
"Another Look at 'Preaching the Word.'" *Baptist Program* (May 1976): 4. **246**

Alexander, E. J.
"Is God Really Gagged?" *TSF News and Reviews* (Spring 1971): 10-13. **247**
Supports the pulpit ministry through an examination of Greek words
meaning "to preach." The author also discusses theological and practical
considerations for the pulpit ministry.

Alexander, James N.
"Evangelism: Preaching and Pastoral." *Expository Times* 60 (1949): 286-89. **248**
Urges Christian preachers to return to their prime task of New Testament
proclamation. Suggestions are made for "recovering our lost evangelism."

"Preaching in Eclipse." *Expository Times* 65 (1953): 8-10. Identifies the **249**
major reasons for the wane in the influence of preaching as its loss of priority
with the preacher and its lack of rich doctrinal content.

Anonymous
"Crisis in the Pulpit." *Christianity Today*, 4 June 1965, pp. 24-25. Probes **250**
the forces that threaten the influence of the Christian pulpit.

"Preaching: The Folly of God." *Christianity Today*, 20 December 1968, **251**
pp. 20-21. Views preaching as the power of God that moves men to action.
Discusses what preaching should be and do.

"Teach us. . . ." *Presbyterian Journal*, 14 June 1972, pp. 9-10. A letter from **252**
a housewife to a new pastor in which she outlines the church's need for solid
Bible preaching and for training in Bible study.

Atwood, Bertram deH.
"Preaching and the New Hermeneutic." *Christian Ministry* 9 (Mar 1978): **253**
15-18. Discusses and illustrates the effects of current biblical criticism and
hermeneutics upon contemporary preaching.

Averill, Lloyd J.
"In Defense of Preaching." *Pulpit Digest* 39 (Aug 1959): 11-14. Contends **254**
that the sermon, when done properly, is not outmoded as a form of
communication.

Aycock, Don M.
"The Relationship Between Preaching and Pastoral Care." *Search* 8 (Fall **255**
1977): 23-26. Discusses preaching as precounseling, the relationship of
preaching to counseling, and the necessary integration of the two.

Ayer, William Ward
"The Art of Effective Preaching." *Bibliotheca Sacra* 124 (1967): 30–41. De- **256**
scribes the elements of effective preaching: a call, intelligent presentation,
logic, polemic, illustration, imagination, and application.

"Preaching to Combat the Present Revolution." *Bibliotheca Sacra* 124 **257**
(1967): 206–17. Describes the type of preaching that can combat the continued
moral, religious, political, and ethical degeneration in society.

"Study Preparation and Pulpit Preaching." *Bibliotheca Sacra* 124 (1967): **258**
106–16. Stresses the necessity of proper study, which does not dampen zeal,
and of more application in preaching.

Babbage, Stuart Barton
"The Preacher's Task *Today*." *Presbyterian Journal*, 2 September 1964, **259**
pp. 7–9. Presents the preacher's task as the proclamation of Christ crucified.
This is identified as the only sure foundation for sound morality, effective
evangelism, and social reform.

Bajema, Henry
"The Wilderness: A Fruitful Field." *Torch and Trumpet* 2 (Aug 1952): 32. **260**
Points out the urgency of preaching and the centrality of the pulpit.

Ball, Charles Ferguson
"The Joy of Preaching." *Christianity Today*, 17 March 1967, pp. 28–29. **261**
Asserts the need to preach with great expectancy, and shows how to plan a
year's sermons and prepare them.

Barr, Browne
"Pop Sermons." *Christian Century*, 17 September 1969, pp. 1190–92. Argues **262**
that the sermon has come upon hard times due to its own decay. The author
traces the blame to both layman and preacher, and he suggests a corrective.

Barth, Markus
"Biblical Preaching Today." *Review and Expositor* 72 (1975): 161–67. **263**
Reprinted in *New Pulpit Digest* 55 (Nov 1975): 17–20. Argues that preaching
must be based on the Bible's authority if it is to have any authority and
credibility of its own. The author sees the exercise of preaching to extend
beyond the formal pulpit.

Baxter, Wendell
"In Defense of Preaching." *Presbyterian Journal*, 11 March 1970, pp. 11, 15. **264**
Appeals to preachers to preach, and insists that the preacher allot adequate
study time and exude a fervent zeal from the Holy Spirit.

Beardslee, William A.
"Teaching and Preaching: The Problem of Place." *Religion in Life* 41 **265**

(1972): 59-68. A philosophical analysis and comparison of preaching and teaching. The author discusses sociological and theological considerations in assessing the present and future of preaching and teaching.

Beauchesne, Richard
    "Preaching, Mystery and Ministry." *Worship* 39 (Aug 1965): 412-17. De-   **266**
velops the thesis that, to communicate the gospel to modern man, preaching
must be personal in content, historical in approach, and testatory in character.

Beckelhymer, Hunter
    "No Posturing in Borrowed Plumes." *Christian Century,* 6 February 1974,   **267**
pp. 138-42. Concludes that plagiarism of another's sermon is dishonest. The
preacher is responsible to wrestle with the text himself; only then will he
preach with spiritual power.

    "Some Current Tensions in Homiletics." *Religion in Life* 42 (1973): 93-102.   **268**
Identifies five tensions in homiletics: (1) craftsmanship vs. spontaneity, (2)
monologue vs. dialogue, (3) proclamation and openness, (4) communication
with sequential logic vs. a barrage of sensations, and (5) the effectiveness of
word and deed in witnessing to Christian faith.

Beenken, Gilbert M.
    "Is Preaching Important?" *Christianity Today,* 12 February 1965, pp. 47-50.   **269**
Supplies reasons why preaching is important, thus deserving the preacher's
utmost in preparation and prayer. This is a sermon on the text II Timothy
4:1-2.

Bell, L. Nelson
    "Babel or Pentecost?" *Christianity Today,* 16 August 1968, pp. 24-25. Sees   **270**
the church in danger of losing its God-given mission—proclaiming the
redemptive message of the gospel.

    "A Call for Realistic Preaching." *Presbyterian Journal,* 23 June 1971, p. 13.   **271**
Defines preaching as the proclamation of the whole counsel of God in the
redemptive work of Christ. It also discusses the centrality of the gospel and
the justification of preaching.

    "He Left the Appendix In." *Presbyterian Journal,* 26 August 1970, p. 13.   **272**
Compares the preacher who deals with doctrinal problems but fails to reach
men's souls to a surgeon who inadvertently leaves in a patient's appendix.

    "Missing—One Knife." *Christianity Today,* 21 August 1970, pp. 34-35. A   **273**
church that does not acknowledge biblical authority or practice biblical
preaching is compared to an ill-prepared surgeon whose patient never heals.

    "Salvation's Alternative." *Christianity Today,* 19 December 1969, pp. 24-25.   **274**
Asserts that the gospel cannot be preached adequately without including the
truth of God's judgment on unredeemed sinners.

"Stones for Bread." *Presbyterian Journal*, 20 January 1971, p. 13. Relates a **275** sermon the author once heard that distorted the gospel message. He stresses the need of presenting the gospel with clarity and to meet needs.

"Urgency." *Christianity Today*, 13 September 1968, pp. 36–37. Argues that **276** the first priority is to preach the Word. This means preaching the cross, which goes beyond treating the symptoms to curing the illness.

"What Has Precedence?" *Christianity Today*, 23 April 1965, p. 25. Amidst **277** the departure of many preachers from the historical gospel, the author affirms the priority of confronting men with sin, redemption, and forgiveness.

Bennetch, John Henry
"The Advantage in Knowing the Biblical Languages." *Bibliotheca Sacra* **278** 100 (1943): 177–87. Defends instruction in the original languages for the preacher in training, based on the contribution of this knowledge to his preaching ministry.

Bennett, T. Miles
"Needed: Prophetic Preaching." *Southwestern Journal of Theology* 3 (Apr **279** 1961): 67–80. Decries the lack of influence that contemporary preaching has on society, and calls for and defines prophetic preaching.

Bennett, Willis
"Play and Its Meaning for Preaching." *Review and Expositor* 47 (1950): **280** 165–72. Shows that play is an attitude, that this attitude can be adapted to preaching, and that constructive play has practical benefits.

Bergland, John
"Ten Tests for Preaching." *Duke Divinity School Review* 41 (1976): 16–20. **281** Lists ten criteria by which to measure the effectiveness of one's preaching.

Berlo, David K.
"Trends in Communication." *Princeton Seminary Bulletin* 61 (Win 1968): **282** 48–56. Discusses communication as a life-long process used in the life-long search for a concept of what is real.

Bird, George L., and Dean, Lillian Harris
"Christians Can Learn from Communications Theorists." *Christianity* **283** *Today*, 20 January 1967, pp. 8–10. Discusses current communication theories and how they inform areas of church life, including the area of preaching.

Bjornard, Reidar B.
"Christian Preaching from the Old Testament." *Review and Expositor* 56 **284** (1959): 8–19. Stresses that the Old Testament too is the Word of God for Christians. The author discusses six major themes in the Old Testament and their

application to Christian truth. These themes are to guide the preacher in his study of the Old Testament.

Blackwell, John A.
"Black Preaching." *Princeton Seminary Bulletin* 65 (July 1972): 37-42.   **285**
Furnishes five basic observations on black preaching and a short summary of its technique.

Blackwood, Andrew W.
"What Is Wrong with Preaching Today?" *Asbury Seminarian* 7 (Win 1953):   **286**
8-18. Uncovers where the pulpit in America needs strengthening.

Blizzard, Samuel W.
"The Training of the Parish Minister." *Union Seminary Quarterly Review*   **287**
11 (Jan 1956): 45-50. A survey reveals that parish ministers feel the need for using the Bible in the parish and making it central in their preaching.

Bloesch, Donald G.
"Can Gospel Preaching Save the Day?" *Eternity* 20 (July 1969): 6-8, 33.   **288**
Affirms that only real gospel preaching can deal with the crises of our time. Preaching must cease to be anthropocentric and should again include the law of God.

Bogle, Paul M.
"The Moral Obligation of Preaching." *Proceedings of the Catholic Homi-*   **289**
letic Society Charter Convention (1960): 23-32.

Boice, James Montgomery
"The Great Need for Great Preaching." *Tenth* (Oct 1974): 2-13. Reprinted   **290**
in *Christianity Today*, 20 December 1974, pp. 7-9. Lists four requirements for effective preaching: (1) commitment to the Bible's authority; (2) an understanding and proclamation of doctrines; (3) an active devotional life; and (4) a love for Christ.

"Manifesto for Effective Preaching." *Eternity* 26 (Oct 1975): 73. Offers six   **291**
guidelines for effective preaching: (1) proclaim the Bible; (2) be clear on inspiration; (3) do not moralize biblical stories; (4) preach great doctrines; (5) have a devotional life; and (6) know the effect of your example on future pastors.

Boland, Edward G.
"A Parish Institute on Preaching." *Pastoral Life* 15 (1967): 13-17. Records   **292**
criticisms of the delivery and structure of sermons preached by pastors who participated in a local institute on preaching.

"The Parish Preachers' Institute." *Pastoral Life* 17 (1969): 32-38. Contains   **293**

criticisms of two sermons preached by participants in the Parish Preachers'
Institute.

Bolton, Robert H.
"The Freest Spot on Earth." *Church Management* 45 (Apr 1969): 9-   **294**
10. Contrasts the preacher's freedom to speak his mind with the limitation
placed upon newspapers, magazines, and television by both advertisers and
consumers.

Bowie, Walter Russell
"Relating Theology to Life." *Pulpit Digest* 34 (Mar 1954): 11-16. Advises   **295**
that every sermon be related to the needs of life and grounded in the faith.

Boyd, James Oscar
"Biblical Theology in the Study and the Pulpit." *Banner of Truth* (Nov   **296**
1975): 1-11. Cites the value of biblical theology in guarding against fads, catch-
words, and trivialities in preaching a text.

Brack, Harold A.
"Hearing the Word." *Religious Communication Today* (Sep 1979): 30-32.   **297**
Furnishes suggestions and methods for improving one's ability to absorb the
Bible's message and thus to communicate it to others better.

Brokhoff, John R.
"An Experiment in Innovative Preaching." *Princeton Seminary Bulletin*   **298**
66 (Oct 1973): 82-97. Describes lessons learned from an experiment with a
Lutheran congregation, testing their reaction to new styles of communication
in the church. The author concludes that the sermon is not dead.

"Hints for Better Preaching." *Pulpit Digest* 58 (Jan 1978): 33. Suggests ten   **299**
practical ways to improve one's preaching.

"Will Tomorrow's Minister Preach?" *Preaching Today* 7 (Jan 1973): 13-15.   **300**
Insists that the sermon is not dead after all.

Brown, H. C., Jr.
"The Primacy of Preaching." *Southwestern Journal of Theology* 5 (Apr   **301**
1963): 85-97. Examines the decadent status of contemporary preaching, and
calls for the primacy of preaching in the minister's work.

Browning, Don
"Should Preaching Be Abolished?" *Encounter* 37 (1976): 1-7. Sees preaching   **302**
as an essential part of Christianity, based on the pattern of Old Testament
prophets and of Jesus Christ. Preaching is to set forth the Christian message
as a mixture of ethics and mystery.

Bruneau, Thomas J.
"Communicative Silences: Forms and Functions." *Journal of Communi-* 303
cation 23 (1973): 17-46. Defines three major forms of silence, then briefly
describes them as they relate to some important human communication
functions.

Brunner, Francis A.
"What Is the Kerygmatic Approach?" *American Ecclesiastical Review* 154 304
(1966): 84-91. Because the kerygmatic approach to preaching is to teach Christ,
the author believes the aim of preaching is conversion and orientation to
Christ Jesus.

Buchli, Virginia, and Pearce, W. Barnett
"Listening Behavior in Coorientational States." *Journal of Communica-* 305
tion 24 (Sum 1974): 62-70. Explores the way in which the prediction of
agreement or disagreement affects the listening of an audience.

Buell, Harold E.
"Pulpit Communication." *Journal of Communication* 4 (1954): 89-93. 306
Suggests ways to improve the sermon's effectiveness as communication.

Burgess, Joseph
"Heresies That Preachers Do." *Dialog* 16 (1977): 114-17. Insists that the 307
preacher exegete first the text, then the congregation. The author also argues
that to proclaim the text is to proclaim law and gospel.

Burke, John
"Faith, Preaching, and Tradition." *American Ecclesiastical Review* 159 308
(1968): 139-54. Explains how effective preaching flows from the preacher's
personal faith, which unites him to the entire believing community and
places him in the historical stream of a living Christian tradition.

"Witness to Faith: The Homily." *American Ecclesiastical Review* 163 (1970): 309
184-95, 270-81, 318-26. Defines the homily as a short sermon integrally related
to a liturgical celebration, discusses the homily's delivery, and offers some
principles of preaching.

Burtner, E. Edwin
"What Preaching Can Do." *Religion in Life* 42 (1973): 235-48. Describes 310
the nature of preaching in the light of both biblical discourse and its affinity
with serious novels or dramas.

Bussis, Dale E.
"Preaching the Sermon." *Princeton Seminary Bulletin* 57 (Mar 1964): 311
41-52. Discusses approaches to preaching, aural and visual codes, and style
and language in preaching.

Bustanoby, Andre

"Getting More Mileage out of Sermons." *Christianity Today*, 29 September 1972, pp. 28–29. Some ideas for spreading the sermon message to the community: e.g., a tape ministry, radio and TV coverage, newspaper ads. **312**

Byrnes, Joseph F.

"Preaching: Present Possibilities and Perennial Value." *Worship* 42 (1968): 14–21. Suggests a method that can help the preacher communicate more effectively in our multimedia world. The author supports his method by examining preachers like Origen, Augustine, and Luther. **313**

Caemmerer, Richard R., Sr.

"Can Preaching Start a Chain Reaction?" *Concordia Theological Monthly* 42 (1971): 173–74. Four surveys related to the sermon and its delivery show that the sermon must start a chain reaction, with the listeners sharing the Word of God with each other during the week. **314**

"Current Contributions to Christian Preaching." *Concordia Theological Monthly* 37 (1966): 38–47. Looks at arguments against using human speech for communicating divine truth, and employs them to challenge the preacher to fulfill his task better. **315**

"The New Hermeneutic and Preaching." *Concordia Theological Monthly* 37 (1966): 99–110. Surveys the hermeneutical approaches to the Bible of such men as Schweitzer, Barth, Bultmann, Robinson, Westermann, Eichrodt, von Rad, and Pannenberg, and shows how their contributions are important to the Christian preacher today. **316**

"The Pendulum of Preaching." *Lutheran Quarterly* 20 (1968): 335–41. Describes the extremes to which preaching swings, and urges the preacher to go beyond the customary in order to change the lives of his hearers. **317**

Campbell, Colin

"Can I Become a More Effective Preacher?" *Homiletic and Pastoral Review* 78 (June 1978): 64–69. Suggests practical ways to improve the quality of one's preaching. **318**

Carlton, John W.

"Using the Arts in Preaching." *Review and Expositor* 61 (1964): 191–205. Sees art as a means to develop the whole man, not just as a homiletical tool. The author discusses how violent, sensual, anti-Christian literature can aid the preacher in understanding society and its view of Christianity. **319**

Cavert, Samuel McCrea

"What Is Biblical Preaching?" *Pulpit Digest* 39 (June 1959): 9–10. Describes biblical preaching as proclamation and communication. **320**

Chafer, Lewis Sperry
"Gospel Preaching." *Bibliotheca Sacra* 95 (1938): 343-64. Calls for plain, 321
simple preaching of the gospel.

Clark, Thomas D.
"An Exploration of Generic Aspects of Contemporary American Christian 322
Sermons." *Quarterly Journal of Speech* 63 (1977): 384-94. Analyzes characteristics peculiar to sermons, derived from a comparison of political, social, and
religious speeches.

Clinard, Gordon
"Changing Emphases in Contemporary Preaching." *Southwestern Journal* 323
of Theology 4 (Apr 1962): 79-91. Analyzes theological and homiletic development in preaching.

Colagreco, Michael
"Wise Words in the Pulpit: Thoughts Prior to the Event." *Dimension* 8 324
(Win 1976): 134-38.

Coleman, Richard J.
"What Aggravates Me About the Preaching I Hear." *Pulpit* 39 (Dec 1968): 325
22-25. Following a lengthy list of sermon criticisms, the author identifies four
areas in which one may evaluate one's preaching. Questions to be used in an
evaluation are included.

Coleman, Robert E.
"An Evangelistic Sermon Checklist." *Christianity Today*, 5 November 1965, 326
pp. 27-28. Offers a series of crucial questions that force the evangelist to think
through his message.

Collins, Patricia
"A Layperson's View of the Homily." *Priest* 34 (Apr 1978): 41-42. A plea for 327
priests to preach the message conveyed by the writers of Scripture. The sermon,
says the author, should be more highly esteemed and include an explanation
of a Scripture text. She supports her argument with documents from the
Second Vatican Council.

Condon, Denis
"Ordained to Preach." *Priest* 34 (Feb 1978): 26-29. Discusses four qualities 328
that should be found in a homily, why priests are ordained, and the awesome
task of producing relevant sermons.

Connors, Joseph M.
"The Perennial Rhetoric as the Framework of Homiletic Theory." *Pro-* 329
ceedings of the Catholic Homiletic Society Charter Convention (1958): 20-40.

Conrad, F. Leslie, Jr.

"Prime Pointers for Preachers." *Christianity Today*, 10 June 1966, pp. 19–   330
20. A compilation of quotations from Andrew W. Blackwood on preaching,
the sermon, and master preachers.

Cook, Charles W.

"Weekly Tidings from the Lord." *Pulpit Digest* 52 (Mar 1972): 7-10, 66.   331
Describes most preaching today as "somewhere between miserable and
wretched," substantiates this with examples, then explains how to spice up
the sermon, its delivery, and its reception.

Copeland, E. Luther

"The Propagation of the Faith." *Review and Expositor* 55 (1958): 300-310.   332
Argues that kerygma, diakonia, and koinonia are the essential marks of the
church. The author defines the kerygma as evangelistic preaching and discusses its nature. Diakonia and koinonia provide the base for kerygma.

Copenhaver, Charles

"The Craft of Preaching." *Minister's Quarterly* 21 (Fall 1965): 1-5. Describes   333
preaching as a craft, requiring the minister to learn sermon construction,
clarity, conviction, change of pace. He must also consider the congregation
an important element in the creation of a sermon.

Corbett, Edward P. J.

"The Sagging Pulpit." *Homiletic and Pastoral Review* 59 (1959): 821-26.   334
An encouragement to preach from the whole Bible, using all the material at
one's disposal. It also recommends reading good literature and listening to
good speakers.

Cowan, Arthur A.

"Suggestions on Preaching the New Testament: Some Difficulties of   335
Exposition and Some Examples of Interpretation." *Expository Times* 66
(1955): 163-67. Discusses biblical topics that are difficult to expound, such as
the demonic, the apocalyptic, and the miraculous, and instructs the preacher
on how to handle them.

Cox, James W.

"Confessional Preaching." *New Pulpit Digest* 55 (Jan 1975): 65.   336

"Evangelistic Preaching." *New Pulpit Digest* 54 (Sep 1974): 51-52.   337

"Humor in the Pulpit." *New Pulpit Digest* 53 (July 1973): 52.   338

"Inspirational Preaching." *New Pulpit Digest* 54 (Sep 1974): 51.   339

"Is Persuasion Allowable in Preaching?" *New Pulpit Digest* 57 (Jan 1977):   340
10-11.

"Plagiarism in the Pulpit." *New Pulpit Digest* 54 (Jan 1974): 60–61. Asks if   341
it is morally right to preach another man's sermon, gives pros and cons, then
concludes with the author's opinion.

"The Preacher's Models." *New Pulpit Digest* 54 (Mar 1974): 46. Shows   342
how famous writers and preachers developed their styles and how one can
adapt these processes to one's own use.

"Preaching with Authority." *New Pulpit Digest* 55 (Jan 1975): 64.   343

"Prophetic Preaching." *New Pulpit Digest* 54 (Nov 1974): 63.   344

"Psychological Preaching." *New Pulpit Digest* 54 (Nov 1974): 63–64.   345

"Teacher-Preaching." *New Pulpit Digest* 55 (Jan 1975): 64–65.   346

"The Uniqueness of Preaching." *Review and Expositor* 64 (1967): 523–33.   347
Argues that the success of preaching cannot be measured by standards applied
to other forms of public speaking. The author considers the uniqueness of
preaching in its three aspects: the speaker, the message, and the audience.

Craddock, Fred B.
"Recent New Testament Interpretation and Preaching." *Princeton Semi-*   348
nary Bulletin 66 (Oct 1973): 76–81. Uses recent trends in New Testament
interpretation to illustrate how biblical studies and preaching lead into and
grow out of each other. The trends have developed from hermeneutics and the
increasingly recognized need for the preacher to overhear—not merely hear—
the text.

Criswell, W. A.
"Why I Preach That the Bible Is Literally True." *Moody Monthly* 69 (Mar   349
1969): 26–27, 36, 64–65, 101. Contends that if the preacher does not accept the
Bible as authoritative, then his message is not authoritative.

Curr, H. S.
"The Foolishness of Preaching." *Evangelical Quarterly* 14 (1942): 139–50.   350
Discusses the nature of preaching and its effectiveness relative to the hearer.

Daane, James
"Sharing Is Not Preaching." *Reformed Journal* 23 (Dec 1973): 6–8. Outlines   351
three reasons why sharing is not preaching: (1) there is a power in preaching
not found in sharing; (2) no one can share Christ, for He can only share
Himself; (3) the word the church proclaims is the life-giving Word.

Danker, Frederick W.
"Laughing with God." *Christianity Today*, 6 January 1967, pp. 16–18.   352
Provides a biblical perspective on humor and laughter, and applies it to the
church and the pulpit.

Darby, James C.
  "Preaching Jesus Christ." *Pulpit Digest* 38 (July 1958): 13–16. Analyzes the   353
primary aim of preaching.

Daves, Michael
  "Is Modern Preaching So Bad?" *Pulpit Digest* 39 (July 1959): 12–14. Refutes   354
the charge that today's preaching is mediocre. The author states that preaching
is not a dead art but is very much alive. This is a response, in part, to entry 498
below.

Davidson, Francis
  "Evangelism for Today." *Evangelical Quarterly* 17 (1945): 241–47. Discusses   355
such aspects of the gospel as its nature and the way to preach it.

Davidson, J. A.
  "A New Concern for Preaching." *Pulpit Digest* 59 (Nov 1979): 30. Bemoans   356
the lack of relevance in preaching today. The author believes good preaching
meets the educational and counseling needs of people.

Dearing, Richard N.
  "Ego-Oriented Preaching." *Journal of Pastoral Care* 26 (1972): 40–49.   357
Analyzes two major preaching styles: ego-oriented and superego-oriented
preaching.

De Jong, Peter Y.
  "How Should We Preach Today?" *Torch and Trumpet* 13 (Feb 1963): 19.   358
Suggests that preachers evaluate their messages in the light of the historical
development of Christian doctrine.

  "The Pillars of Our Church: III, The Place and Purpose of the Pulpit."   359
Torch and Trumpet 6 (Dec 1956): 4–7, 14–21. Deals with the way preaching has
helped to shape the Reformed tradition.

  "Preaching and the Elders." *Torch and Trumpet* 1 (Feb 1952): 8–10. Exhorts   360
elders to listen to the sermon actively and to discuss it with the preacher.

  "What Makes Preaching Truly Great?" *Torch and Trumpet* 16 (Jan 1966):   361
9–11. Analyzes the preaching of P. H. Eldersveld (1911–1965), the radio minister
of the Christian Reformed Church who was responsible for, among other
programs, the "Back to God Hour." The emphasis is on the centrality of
Scripture in the preacher's message.

Demaray, Donald E.
  "The Pastor as Communicator." *Asbury Seminarian* 23 (Jan 1969): 3–6.   362
Advises preachers to (1) limit the subject, (2) involve the people, and (3) speak
from a burning heart of personal experience.

De Rosa, Peter

"Transmitting the Christian Message." *Clergy Review* 50 (1965): 428-32. A   **363**
general overview of the nature of preaching within Roman Catholicism.
Problems are identified and solutions suggested.

de Witt, John Richard

"The Character of Reformed Preaching." *Banner of Truth* (May 1978):   **364**
15-17. Characterizes Reformed preaching as scriptural, practical, simple, and
dynamic.

"Sojourn in the Pew." *Missionary Monthly* 72 (1967): 101-3. Reprinted.   **365**
"From the Pew a Preacher Talks Back to the Pulpit." *Presbyterian Journal*, 19
July 1967, pp. 10-11. And reprinted in *Banner of Truth* (Jan 1968): 33-36.
Speaks out in alarm at the poor quality and false foundations of preaching.
Calls preachers to return to their studies so that they can expound the Word of
God as they preach.

Dial, Howard E.

"The Pulpit Teaching Ministry as Preventive Counseling." *Journal of*   **366**
Pastoral Practice 2 (Win 1978): 157-70. Contends that solid, expository preaching is the best way to prevent emotional problems in a congregation. Suggests
numerous ways in which preaching can offer preventive therapy.

Dirks, Marvin J.

"Credibility in Preaching." *Religious Communication Today* (Sep 1978):   **367**
20-23. Defines credibility, shows the need for it, and identifies hindrances to
it.

Dorff, Francis

"On Preaching God's Word." *Priest* 34 (Nov 1978): 37-38. Lists five factors   **368**
crucial to good sermon preparation, and warns the preacher against five risks.

Edwards, Mark

"Preaching." *Priest* 31 (Sep 1975): 24-29. Offers some answers to three   **369**
questions: (1) To whom do we preach? (2) What are we to preach? (3) Who is
to preach? The focus is on the third, and the answer emphasizes the preacher's
morality and integrity.

Ellis, E. Earle

"What Good Are Hebrew and Greek?" *Christianity Today*, 26 May 1972,   **370**
pp. 8-9. Counteracts the view that the study of biblical languages need no
longer be part of a minister's academic preparation.

Engbers, John

"The Conservative and the Changing Church." *Outlook* 23 (Dec 1973):   **371**
2-9. Contends that one of four essentials for the true conservative is a commitment to preaching.

Engel, James F.
"Fine Tuning for Greater Results." *Spectrum: Christian Communications*   372
2 (Spring 1976): 26–28. Describes four principles of communication strategy
that are rooted in the biblical records and church history.

Erwin, Dan, and Hensley, Wayne
"The Central Activity of the Church." *Princeton Seminary Bulletin* 67   373
(Win 1975): 82–88. The central activity of the church should be preaching,
according to this dialog sermon given in a seminary chapel service.

Evans, J. Ellwood
"Expository Preaching." *Bibliotheca Sacra* 111 (1954): 54–62. Expository   374
preaching is defined and is defended as the superior form of preaching.

Farra, Harry
"The Energizing of Truth." *Christian Ministry* 9 (Sep 1978): 17–19. High-   375
lights the need for fresh, appealing preaching, and suggests ways to make it
so.

"Is Your Preaching Ethical?" *Christian Ministry* 10 (Sep 1979): 17–20.   376
Warns against unethical preaching, furnishing guidelines for ethical practice
in the pulpit and a creed of honesty.

Ferguson, Sinclair B.
"More Thoughts on Preaching." *Banner of Truth* (Mar 1977): 10–16. Points   377
out the need for great preaching, which the author defines as both Reformed
and biblical, both doctrinal and pastoral, both consecutive and expository,
both orthodox and orderly.

Finley, Mitchel B.
"I Want to Hear a Good Sermon." *Priest* 35 (Mar 1979): 10–12. A layman   378
urges priests to preach better homilies, ones that challenge him to change his
life and believe anew in the gospel, and ones that reflect prayerful preparation
and real experience of the everyday world.

Fitch, William
"The Glory of Preaching." *Christianity Today*, 20 January 1967, pp. 22–23.   379
Examines the various aspects of preaching, showing the high privilege that is
the preacher's and the greatness of this form of communicating God's Word.

Ford, Harold W.
"Holding Forth the Word of Life in a Secular Age." *Seminary Review* 17   380
(1971): 83–92. Maintains that the Word preached must change the age, not vice
versa. The author defines secularization and Christianity and describes four
ways the preached word can be secularized.

Francis, David
"With All Thy Mind." *Preacher's Quarterly* 12 (1966): 202-7. Preachers   381
must also be teachers, argues the author, because of the ignorance of Christians. Teachers must be clear, honest, equipped, and gripped.

Francke, A. H.
"The Art of the Preacher." Translated by John D. Manton. *Banner of Truth*   382
(Feb 1970): 35-40. Explains how to teach and preach so as to produce real fruit
in the church.

Freeman, David H.
"Change the Words—Not the Message." *Christianity Today*, 22 July 1966,   383
pp. 14-16. Insists that, while the elements of the message cannot be changed,
our understanding of the message can grow and the words of the message
must be revised to be understood by modern man.

Freeman, Elmer S.
"The Context and Content of Contemporary Preaching." *Theology Today*   384
14 (1957): 335-46. Discusses the secular and religious background of preaching,
the proper content of preaching, and the duty to preach to people's needs.

Frenk, Erdman W.
"A Critique of Contemporary Lutheran Preaching." *Concordia Theologi-*   385
cal Monthly 21 (1950): 721-48.

Fritz, John H. C.
"Essays on Sermonizing." *Concordia Theological Monthly* 20 (1949): 81-99.   386
Discusses the purpose of, choice of text for, and delivery of the sermon.

Fry, Franklin Clark
"Paradoxes of the Ministry Today." *Princeton Seminary Bulletin* 56 (Oct   387
1962): 4-11. Observes four paradoxes of the ministry that affect preaching.

Fueter, Paul D.
"Communicating the Bible." *International Review of Mission* 60 (1971):   388
437-51. Urges the use of "transculturation" in communicating the Bible from
the pulpit and in other settings.

Gaddy, C. Welton
"Preaching That Communicates." *Search* 4 (Win 1974): 12-18. Offers four   389
preaching styles: (1) incarnational, (2) authoritative, (3) confessional, and
(4) dialogical.

Gilmore, J. Herbert, Jr.
"The Preaching Ministry and the Bible." *Review and Expositor* 57 (1960):   390

58-68. Argues that preaching must be based on the Scriptures, explaining them and showing their relevance to the audience.

Glasser, Arthur F.
"The World Needs a Message." *Eternity* 18 (July 1967): 11-13, 34. Defends **391** the continued primacy in evangelism of preaching a message of redemption, and looks at the features of Paul's proclamation of the gospel on Mars Hill.

Gossip, A. J.
"On Preaching the Cross." *Expository Times* 42 (1931): 443-46. Explains **392** why the message of the cross is not being preached today, and shows that the true spirit and dynamic of this message is the key to church renewal.

Graesser, Carl, Jr.
"Preaching from the Old Testament." *Concordia Theological Monthly* 38 **393** (1967): 525-34. Gives five reasons why a pastor should preach from the Old Testament, five difficulties encountered when doing so, and four steps to be followed when preparing a sermon from the Old Testament. The process is illustrated with the text Isaiah 6:1-13.

Grassi, Joseph A.
"The Impact of Scriptural Developments on Preaching." *Homiletic and* **394** *Pastoral Review* 66 (1966): 301-5. Explains how the three stages of tradition through which Jesus' teaching and life came to us can guide the preacher in using the gospel.

Green, Oscar F.
"Humor in Preaching." *Anglican Theological Review* 27 (1945): 116-22. **395** Gives reasons why pulpit humor is not acceptable to many congregations, emphasizes the value of humor, and tells how to handle it properly.

Greenlee, J. Harold
"The Greek New Testament in Preaching." *Asbury Seminarian* 17 (Spring **396** 1963): 17-27. Discusses the effective use of the Greek New Testament in one's pulpit ministry.

Griffith, A[rthur] Leonard
"Ten Marks of an Interesting Sermon." *New Pulpit Digest* 54 (Nov 1974): **397** 14-15.

Gruner, Charles R.
"Effect of Humor on Speaker Ethos and Audience Information Gain." **398** *Journal of Communication* 17 (1967): 228-33. Reports a study that showed "clowning wits" to be popular but without influence. "Sarcastic wits" rate high in influence. Apt humor in informative discourse establishes higher estimates of a speaker's character.

Gunnemann, Louis H.
"When Preaching Makes Sense." *Theological Markings* 2 (Win 1972):   **399**
22-24. Proposes that effective preaching must be faithful and responsible to
Jesus.

Gustafson, Henry A.
"The New Testament, Preaching and Today's Mind." *Theological Mark-*   **400**
ings 2 (Win 1972): 7-12. Reprinted in *Journal of the Academy of Parish
Clergy* (May 1973): 16-20. Argues for preaching that is biblical and relevant to
contemporary society. The author says that a sermon does its job by bringing
"the Christian faith and the current situation together in such a way that the
full force of each is felt simultaneously."

Hadidian, Dikran Y.
"Preaching, Pulpit, and Evangelism." *New Pulpit Digest* 57 (July 1977):   **401**
37-39. Defines preaching as, first and foremost, evangelism, and explores
Paul's sense of evangelism to substantiate this thesis.

Hageman, Howard G.
"Liturgical Place." *Princeton Seminary Bulletin* 56 (Feb 1963): 29-39. A   **402**
general description of the architectural history of the church, which also
reveals the relationship of this history to preaching and the sacraments.

"The Need and Promise of Reformed Preaching." *Reformed Review* 28   **403**
(1975): 75-84. Reprinted in *Banner*, 17 October 1975, pp. 12-14. Defines and
debates the essence of Reformed preaching. In its first printing it is followed
by responses from E. Earle Ellis, Vernon H. Kooy, John W. Beardslee III,
Charles Jay Wissink, Michael Allen, and Tom Schwanda.

Halvorson, Arndt L.
"Preaching Is for People." *Lutheran Quarterly* 20 (1968): 359-63. Argues   **404**
that preaching is the catalyst that aids the encounter of God with man. Faith
is a matter of life and death, says the author, and it must be preached as such.

Harrison, Randall P., and Knapp, Mark L.
"Toward an Understanding of Nonverbal Communication Systems."   **405**
Journal of Communication 22 (1972): 339-52. Sketches current trends in the
field, and orients the audience to the importance of nonverbal communication.

Haselden, Kyle
"Not So Much Heard as Experienced." *Pulpit* 36 (Mar 1965): 3. A plea for   **406**
consistently good sermons, and a warning that, due to variations in listener
receptivity, the response will be varied rather than consistent.

Haugh, Joseph P.
"Importance of Preaching." *Homiletic and Pastoral Review* 47 (1947):   **407**

1000-1001. Points out the lack of good preaching in the Catholic church, and stresses the need for articulate, effective preachers.

Heerema, Edward
"The Foolishness of Preaching." *Torch and Trumpet* 20 (Oct 1970): 2-3.   **408**
The fourfold purpose commonly given for preaching is refuted. The author sees preaching's purpose as the proclamation of God's righteousness.

"This Debate About the Pulpit." *Torch and Trumpet* 12 (May 1962): 13-15.   **409**
Explores the implications of a divided chancel.

Helm, Paul
"Preaching and Grace." *Banner of Truth* (June 1973): 8-13. After discussing   **410**
preaching's relevance and aim, the author lists four key elements that make preaching unique and indispensable.

Hendry, G. S.
"The Exposition of Holy Scripture." *Scottish Journal of Theology* 1 (1948):   **411**
29-47. Outlines the problems of evangelical and neo-orthodox views of scriptural inspiration and the relationship of these views to preaching.

Hiltner, Seward
"The Minister as a Guidelines Writer." *Reformed Review* 26 (Autumn   **412**
1972): 171-77. Reprinted in *Princeton Seminary Bulletin* 65 (Dec 1972): 31-37. Argues that a minister should offer laymen guidelines, not rules; that these should be communicated in part through preaching; and that preaching is a descriptive, rather than hortatory, activity.

Hines, John E.
"Preaching in the Contemporary World." *Saint Luke's Journal of The-*   **413**
ology 19 (1975): 3-17. A vigorous call to the exercise of a prophetic ministry through preaching.

Hobart, Charles W.
"Less Noise in Solemn Assemblies." *Theology Today* 19 (1963): 474-83.   **414**
Asserts that in urban churches the minister's role as preacher is increasingly obsolete. The size of churches should be greatly reduced, contends the author, and most of the preaching should be done by the congregation's more mature members.

Hockman, William S.
"Public Address or Closed Circuit TV?" *Church Management* 47 (Mar   **415**
1971): 18-19. Discusses whether a church should use merely an audio system for the overflow congregation, or install closed-circuit television.

Hodges, Graham R.
  "Moral Pathologists and Preachers of Good News." *Pulpit Digest* 33 (Mar   **416**
1953): 11-14. Explains that to be effective, the preacher must emphasize the
redemptive message of the gospel. The author offers tips on how to do this.

Holland, Robert Cleveland
  "The Foolishness of Preaching." *Pulpit Digest* 43 (July 1963): 17-24. Shows   **417**
why preaching is the most vital of the minister's several tasks.

Homrighausen, Elmer G.
  "Preaching in the Reformed Tradition." *New Pulpit Digest* 57 (Mar 1977):   **418**
25-29. Delineates three criticisms of preaching; discusses the future of preaching; covers the why, what, who, and where of preaching; and explains the
necessary qualities of a preacher.

Hope, Norman V.
  "Humor in the Pulpit." *Church Management* 43 (Jan 1967): 15-16. Stresses   **419**
the importance of including in the sermon tasteful humor.

Horne, Chevis F.
  "What Is Pastoral Preaching?" *Search* 9 (Win 1979): 51-54. Defines pastoral   **420**
preaching as accepting, supportive, and nurturing, and describes three more
areas that make pastoral preaching possible.

Houtart, François
  "Homiletic Discourse and the Political Dimension of Faith." *Lumen Vitae*   **421**
28 (1973): 601-6. Explores how the preacher can effectively approach everything
that pertains to the "political dimension" of faith.

Howard, J. Grant, Jr.
  "Interpersonal Communication: Biblical Insights on the Problem and the   **422**
Solution." *Journal of Psychology and Theology* 3 (1975): 243-57. Analyzes the
effects of man's fall on his communication with God and with man, and
examines the solution of sanctification.

Howe, Reuel L.
  "Overcoming the Barriers to Communication." *Princeton Seminary Bul-*   **423**
letin 56 (May 1963): 44-52. Explores the advantages in communication of
dialogue over monologue.

Hudson, Thomas Franklyn
  "The Preparation and Delivery of the Sermon." *Pulpit Digest* 35 (Oct   **424**
1954): 15-19. Offers suggestions and warnings to the preacher concerning the
preparation and delivery of sermons.

Jaberg, Eugene

"Your Theology Is Showing." *Theological Markings* 2 (Win 1972): 13-21.   **425**
Shows how a preacher's theology is exposed by his style in the pulpit, and
recommends that the message be presented in the form of an on-going
conversation.

Jack, Adam

"The Preacher, the People, and God." *Expository Times* 57 (1945): 50-51.   **426**
Envisions the preacher as God's representative, conveying to His people a
message that includes judgment and salvation.

Jackson, Edgar N.

"Mediating the Faith That Makes Whole." *Southwestern Journal of*   **427**
Theology 5 (Apr 1963): 54-71. Discusses the relationship between faith and
true wholeness of being, the relevance of this to the task of preaching, and the
mode and method of preaching that best mediates wholeness of being.

Jamieson, Graham

"Communicating and Relating in Religion." *Theology Today* 16 (1959):   **428**
30-39. Argues that the most effective way of preaching or of teaching religion
is the nondiscursive (creative) expression found in the Bible's prophets,
parables, and poetry, as well as in creative writing, drama, music, painting,
and dance.

Jensen, Irving L.

"Fattening Geese or Training Athletes?" *Christianity Today,* 23 April 1965,   **429**
pp. 20-22. A plea for Bible teaching that does not stop with imparting content,
but trains the hearer to exercise godliness. The author also explains how to
study the Bible when preparing the sermon.

Jeske, John C.

"The Formal Aspect of Preaching." *Wisconsin Lutheran Quarterly* 71   **430**
(Apr 1974): 83-93. Discusses a number of principles to be followed by the
pastor who would have an effective pulpit ministry. The author recommends
that sermons be simple and interesting.

Johnson, W. Walter

"The Ethics of Preaching." *Interpretation* 20 (1966): 412-31. Singles out   **431**
the three major concerns of contemporary theology: church renewal, ethical responsibility, and preaching. The author proposes that the pastor's
life, shown through the sermon, should be the church's model of ethical
responsibility.

Johnston, George

"Christian Mission and Christ's Prevenience." *Theology Today* 20 (1963):   **432**
31-42. Opposes the view that the missionary meets Christ in the non-Christian

neighbor, and affirms that preachers are sent by God, who speaks through them.

Jones, Ilion T.
"The Church's Defection from a Divine Mission." *Christianity Today*, 24   433
May 1968, pp. 3-5. The church's task, says the author, is not social change, but preaching the gospel to all people.

Jones, Miles J.
"A Pattern for Particularity in Preaching." *Andover Newton Quarterly* 19   434
(1979): 167-75. Delineates proper white attitudes toward black preaching.

Jones, Stan
"Being Real in the Pulpit." *Faith at Work* 91 (Oct 1978): 45, 50. Suggests   435
practical ways to eliminate the "distance" between preacher and people.

Jorgenson, Rodger L.
"The Necessity of Contemporary Preaching." *Covenant Quarterly* 30 (Aug   436
1972): 18-30. Discusses reasons for preaching's decline, definitions of preaching, and its necessary ingredients.

Julien, Jerome M.
"The Sacrifice of Praise: VII, Hearing the Word." *Outlook* 26 (Sep 1976):   437
14-17. Examines the nature and importance of preaching, and stresses the need to preach the word.

Kaiser, Walter C., Jr.
"The Use of Biblical Narrative in Expository Preaching." *Asbury Semi-*   438
narian 34 (July 1979): 14-26. Analyzes current narrative preaching, suggesting a procedure for properly using narrative in expository preaching.

Kelly, Timothy
"Reflections on Preaching and Teaching." *Worship* 53 (1979): 250-64.   439
Focuses on the ministry of preaching in the lives of Jesus Christ and the apostle Paul, and compares their preaching to today's.

Kemper, Deane
"Must Your Preacher Change His Style?" *Eternity* 23 (Apr 1972): 18-21.   440
Preaching should be flexible. The content and function remain the same, the form changes. The author gives parameters for preaching in today's society, and he illustrates this from the ministries of Jesus and Paul.

Kennel, LeRoy E.
"The Ministry of Communication." *Christian Ministry* 3 (Jan 1972): 18-20.   441
Lists five communication guidelines for the preacher: (1) translating expe-

rience, (2) enabling, (3) serving, (4) using situational materials, and (5) utilizing various media.

Kettner, Elmer A.
"Are We Really Preaching the Gospel?" *Concordia Theological Monthly*   442
24 (1953): 321-29. Demonstrates how to present the gospel effectively.

Kik, J. Marcellus
"The Evangelical Pulpit." *Banner of Truth* (Mar 1966): 14-17. States the   443
need for strong, evangelical preaching of God's Word, identifies the preacher's
key functions as evangelism and edification, and explains that the sermon's
power depends on the preacher's heart relationship with God.

Killinger, John
"Existential Preaching." *Princeton Seminary Bulletin* 55 (Apr 1962): 44-52.   444
Asserts that preaching is for people, looks briefly at some leading tenets of
existentialism, and suggests their relevance to Christian preaching.

Kok, William
"Preaching as the Call to Arms." *Torch and Trumpet* 15 (Nov 1965): 3.   445
Points out that "the gospel is a declaration of war" and that preaching should
reflect zeal and power.

Kraemer, Hendrik
"The Problem of Communication." *Union Seminary Quarterly Review* 11   446
(Mar 1956): 19-22. Discusses the universal breakdown of communication due
to man's fall and the difficulty of communicating the Christian message due
to the secularization of both the world and the church.

Kuiper, R. B.
"Proclaimer of the Truth." *Torch and Trumpet* 1 (Oct 1951): 27. Discusses   447
the importance of preaching.

Lacour, Lawrence L.
"If Aristotle Could Hear You Preach." *Pastoral Psychology* 16 (Oct 1965):   448
9-17; (Nov 1965): 43-52. Contends that the preacher must know his audience,
the dynamics of groups, and the image of his profession; and that he
must recognize the importance of attention, suggestion, and motivation in
preaching.

Lamont, Daniel
"Evangelism in the Modern World." *Evangelical Quarterly* 15 (1943):   449
206-15. Asks if preachers are preaching the whole counsel of God and if they
do so with a sense of urgency.

LaRossa, Ralph
"Interpreting Hierarchial Message Structure." *Journal of Communication*   450
24 (Spring 1974): 61-68. Shows that mapping certain relationships helps to
build an epistemological model of communication inference.

Lauer, Robert H.
"The Problem with the Pulpit." *Christianity Today,* 26 April 1968,   451
pp. 9-10. Reprinted in *Christian Minister* 5 (Mar 1969): 15, 22. Decries the
ethical thrust of much modern-day preaching, favoring instead sermons that
possess simplicity, redemptive thrust, and biblical authority.

Lawrence, Emeric A.
"Preaching: You Never Finish Preparing." *Homiletic and Pastoral Review*   452
72 (Aug 1972): 26-30. A veteran preacher, "pouring out his heart," deals
with the preparation of the sermon, preaching style, and preacher-people
relationships.

Lazell, David
"A Long Way Behind Wesley." *Christianity Today,* 22 July 1966, pp. 11-12.   453
A lay preacher's look at the modernistic "advances" proclaimed from the
pulpit.

Leabel, Pius
"Teaching Sermon Reliving." *Proceedings of the Catholic Homiletic*   454
Society Charter Convention (1960): 13-22.

Le Roy, William R.
"Tongues of Fire." *Reformation Review* 20 (1973): 201-14. This commence-   455
ment address states the need for preaching.

Lewis, A. W.
"The Efficiency of Sermons." *Bibliotheca Sacra* 83 (1926): 312-15. Insists   456
that preaching is the most effective way to turn the souls of men to God.

Lievaart, G.
"Lord, Give Us Good Preachers!" Translated by John H. Piersma. *Outlook*   457
29 (June 1979): 20-22. Defines good preaching as being Christocentric and
reverent, and the preacher as being completely committed to his commission
to speak the Word of God.

Likins, William H.
"'For Christ's Sake, Preach the Gospel.'" *Pulpit* 39 (Sep 1968): 9-12.   458
Encourages gospel preaching, briefly surveys the alternatives, and explains
how to preach for a verdict rather than a hung jury.

Lindsey, Albert J.

"The Messenger and the Message." *Presbyterian Journal,* 8 May 1974, **459**
pp. 9-11. States the need for more biblical, evangelistic, and prophetic preaching. The author reaffirms the need for pastors to be called of God, to pray, and
to be empowered by the Holy Spirit.

Linsley, Kenneth W.

"First Aid for Spiritual Corpses." *Christianity Today,* 19 July 1968, pp. 14- **460**
16. Contends that the church should be preoccupied with bringing men to
spiritual life through the preached word.

Litfin, A. Duane

"In Defense of the Sermon: A Communicational Approach." *Journal of* **461**
Psychology and Theology 2 (1974): 36-43. Both commends the sermonic
approach to communication and encourages the use of supplementary
approaches that enable the flock to communicate directly with the pastor.

"The Perils of Persuasive Preaching." *Christianity Today,* 4 February 1977, **462**
pp. 14-17. Cautions the preacher against taking upon himself the responsibility for securing from his audience a response—something only the Spirit
should do.

Long, Thomas G.

"Therapeutic Preaching: Three Views." *Princeton Seminary Bulletin* 68 **463**
(Win 1976): 80-93. Looks at the views of Clement Welsh, H. Grady Davis,
and Karl Menninger. The author raises the question of therapeutic preaching's
theological validity and explores some implications of therapeutic preaching
for the teaching of preaching.

Louden, R. Stuart

"The Ministry of the Word." *Scottish Journal of Theology* 2 (1949): 163-73. **464**
The proper ministry of God's Word is fundamental in the work of the Christian ministry and provides the source for the sacramental ministry.

Lovette, Roger

"Partners in Preaching." *Pulpit Digest* 51 (Dec 1970): 7-12. Suggests that **465**
the sermon can be a more vital force in a congregation's life if it speaks to
life-and-death concerns.

Lowe, Arnold H.

"There Is No Escape from the Twentieth Century." *Pulpit* 36 (Feb 1965): **466**
16-17. Because he sees the church as the custodian of moral values, the author
urges preachers to employ terms understood particularly by young people.

Luccock, Halford E.

"He Opened the Book." *Pulpit Digest* 34 (Feb 1954): 11-18. Vital preaching, **467**
says the author, is always firmly rooted in the Scriptures.

Macartney, Clarence Edward
"Suggestions to Students of Homiletics." *Christianity Today*, 8 December   468
1967, pp. 24-25. Furnishes advice on preparation for preaching through reading, steps in composing a sermon, and sources of sermonic subjects.

McCleary, John Franklin
"Pulpit and Stage." *Princeton Seminary Bulletin* 59 (Mar 1966): 41-47.   469
Promotes the use of drama as a means of Christian proclamation.

McClellan, Albert
"Preachers on Preaching." *Baptist Program* (Dec 1976): 23.   470

McCroskey, James C., and Combs, Walter H.
"The Effects of the Use of Analogy on Attitude Change and Source Credi-   471
bility." *Journal of Communication* 19 (1969): 333-39. Examines ways in which a message is affected by the use of analogy.

McEachern, Alton H.
"God's Messenger and His Message." *Church Administration* 18 (Mar 1976):   472
8-9. Requires the messenger to have a calling from God, a love for his people, and personal integrity.

"Preaching in the Pastorate." *Search* 6 (Fall 1975): 14-18. Analyzes the   473
pastor's task of preaching. The author sees a need for more dramatic dialogue and other techniques for making the Bible live for people, and he explains why preaching has changed from narration to exhortation.

McIntyre, David M.
"Life's Battle Lost and Won: Ezekiel 37:1-10." *Evangelical Quarterly* 7   474
(1935): 318-27. Examines Ezekiel 37:1-10 as a picture of revival, discovering that two essentials are preaching and prayer. The dry bones in Ezekiel 37 are revived, the author notes, by the Holy Spirit.

McKelvey, John W.
"How to Use Humor in Sermons." *Church Management* 53 (Jan 1977):   475
11-12, 27. Encourages the use of humor to illustrate, provide contrast, aid theological comprehension, and increase attention span.

McLaughlin, Raymond W.
"The Ethics of Persuasive Preaching." *Journal of the Evangelical Theo-   476
logical Society* 15 (1972): 93-106. Describes the views of ancient Hebrew-Christians, of classical and contemporary rhetoricians, the means and ends used in persuasion, and the standards of man and the Bible for persuasive preaching.

"Intensional-Extensional Language as a Measure of Semantic Orienta-   477
tion." *Bulletin of the Evangelical Theological Society* 10 (1967): 143-51. A

linguistic study of a scholarly liberal preacher (Harry Emerson Fosdick) and a less-educated conservative one (Oral Roberts).

MacLennan, David A.
"Preaching." *Pulpit Digest* 32 (May 1952): 17-23. Pleads with pastors and churches to give preaching top priority.   **478**

"Priming the Preacher's Pump." *Church Management* 47 (Jan 1971): 10. Advises preachers to save their sermons and preach them again.   **479**

"Priming the Preacher's Pump." *Church Management* 47 (Apr 1971): 10. Encourages the mild use of humor in sermons.   **480**

"We." *Pulpit Digest* 34 (Mar 1954): 17-24. Demonstrates ways for preachers to prepare themselves and their congregations for the preaching of the Social Gospel.   **481**

Macleod, Donald
"Better Preaching." *Princeton Seminary Bulletin* 67 (Autumn 1975): 7-8. Lists James T. Cleland's seven guidelines to better preaching.   **482**

"The Creative Preacher." *Princeton Seminary Bulletin* 55 (Jan 1962): 26-39. Looks at three ways in which the preacher can be creative in his preaching.   **483**

"The Marks of Effective Preaching." *Princeton Seminary Bulletin* 52 (Jan 1959): 33-38. Proposes proclamation, interpretation, and prophetic accent as important criteria for effective preaching.   **484**

"Talk About Preaching." *Christian Century*, 1 February 1978, pp. 98-102. Responds to twenty assorted questions about preaching.   **485**

McNamara, Robert F.
"How Not to Preach: Some Lurid Examples, U.S.A." *Homiletic and Pastoral Review* 78 (May 1978): 27-32, 44-50. Reviews preaching styles among individual Catholic priests, adding suggestions for improvements.   **486**

McNulty, T. Michael
"Pauline Preaching: A Speech-Act Analysis." *Worship* 53 (1979): 207-14. Analyzes the entire sermon in accordance with the broad context of the preaching act itself, then compares the conclusions with the apostle Paul's approach to the Corinthians.   **487**

McReynolds, James E.
"Sensitivity Group Insights and Contemporary Preaching." *New Pulpit Digest* 56 (Jan 1976): 27-29. Advocates the use in preaching of techniques employed in sensitivity groups.   **488**

McTaggart, Bill
"About Those Sermons." *Priest* 34 (Feb 1978): 23-25. Discusses the dissatisfaction of Catholic laity with the Sunday sermon, and lists stereotypes of   **489**

priests who do not give their parishioners what they want and expect from the pulpit.

Madren, E. Dale
"Preaching and the Emotions." *Pulpit Digest* 59 (Nov 1979): 49-50. **490**
Encourages pastors to teach and preach emotional responses that are consistent with the Scripture passage being preached.

Malte, Eric C.
"Preaching from the Greek New Testament." *Concordia Theological* **491**
Monthly 25 (1954): 656-62. Demonstrates how one can increase the effectiveness of one's preaching through the use of the Greek New Testament.

Marshall, Peter J.
"The Preached Word." *Christianity Today*, 2 January 1970, pp. 24-25. A **492**
brief but pointed statement of preaching's importance.

Martin, Albert N.
"What's Wrong with Preaching Today?" *Torch and Trumpet* 19 (Feb 1969): **493**
2-7; (Mar 1969): 20-23. Reprinted in *Christian Minister* 5 (June 1969): 21-25.
Discusses both the man (his personal devotions, practical piety, use of time, and purity of motivation) and the message (its biblical and practical character).

Marty, Martin E.
"Perspective and Preaching: A Reflection Inspired by Ortega." *Encounter* **494**
37 (1976): 8-20. Applies some insights of Spanish philosopher José Ortega y Gasset to the act of preaching. Preaching, the author concludes, should have clear speech and comprehensibility as well as a textual foundation and a historical awareness.

Marvin, John E.
"The Primacy of Preaching." *New Pulpit Digest* 56 (Sep 1976): 34-35. **495**
Argues that preaching should hold a primary place in the life of the church.

Maupin, John G.
"Let's Hear You Speak." *Homiletic and Pastoral Review* 65 (1965): 581-87. **496**
Identifies the key to successful preaching as systematic evaluation, and discusses the marks of a successful preacher (thought, action, voice, and language).

Mayer, Herbert T.
"The Old Testament in the Pulpit." *Concordia Theological Monthly* 35 **497**
(1964): 603-8. Proposes ways to use the Old Testament properly and thus make one's preaching more effective.

Mead, Frank S.
"What Has Happened to Preaching?" *Pulpit Digest* 39 (May 1959): 17–20.   **498**
Offers reasons, taken from the audience's viewpoint, why sermons are ineffective, and suggests ways to change that. See entry 354 above.

Mechem, James L.
"Authority and Freedom in Preaching." *Theology Today* 29 (1972): 70–85.   **499**
Grapples with the age-old dichotomy of authority and freedom as a pastor might deal with it in sermon form. The nature of authority, its exercise, and its tensions are discussed, using Jesus and Paul as illustrations.

Metcalf, John Calvin
"Literature and Modern Preaching." *Review and Expositor* 6 (1909): 450–70.   **500**
Traces the influence of preaching on the various forms of literature; examines excerpts from poems, prose, and novels for religious and moral dimensions; and urges preachers to study literature.

Middleton, Robert G.
"What Is the Matter with Preaching?" *Religion in Life* 45 (1976): 296–307.   **501**
Responds to three problems of preaching today: the retreat from the Word, the retreat from reason, and the retreat from politics (vital issues of the day).

Migliore, Daniel L.
"What Do We Mean by the 'Gospel' Today?" *Princeton Seminary Bulletin*   **502**
63, 1 (1970): 13–20. Develops the idea that timeliness is essential to the right understanding and proclamation of the gospel, and that timeliness requires bold, new forms.

Miller, C. John, and Mains, David
"What's Wrong with Preaching? Two Preachers Go at It." *Eternity* 23 (Apr   **503**
1972): 22–24. Answers three questions: (1) Is preaching the pastor's main role? (2) What new communication techniques should be used in the church? (3) What are the weaknesses of evangelical preaching?

Miller, Gerald R., and Lobe, Jon
"Opinionated Language, Open- and Closed-Mindedness and Response to   **504**
Persuasive Communications." *Journal of Communication* 17 (1967): 333–41.
Shows that attitude change is most drastically affected by opinionated language used by highly credible sources, regardless of how open- or closed-minded the listener is.

Miller, Louis G.
"Must Homilies Be Dull?" *Homiletic and Pastoral Review* 77 (July 1977):   **505**
19–23. Discusses Edward C. Macauley's interest in helping priests improve their preaching and the program he has begun as a result.

Miller, Samuel H.
"But Find the Point Again." *Union Seminary Quarterly Review* 15 (Mar   **506**
1960): 221-34. Because of the slow evaporation of the biblical usage of reality,
says the author, the preacher needs a new vision of reality. World conditions
demand that preparation for the ministry include vigorous intellectual activity.

Mitchell, Henry H.
"Black Preaching." *Review and Expositor* 70 (1973): 331-40. Traces the   **507**
history of black preaching and religion, and analyzes its methods of sermon
preparation and its characteristics.

Moffett, Samuel H.
"What Is Evangelism?" *Christianity Today*, 22 August 1969, pp. 3-5; 12   **508**
September 1969, pp. 13-14. A biblical study that defines evangelism as preach-
ing with power, purpose (to turn men to Christ), and strategy.

Moiser, Jeremy
"The Laity on Today's Preaching." *Clergy Review* 56 (1971): 782-93.   **509**
Reports lay response to a questionnaire concerning the purpose, form, and
effectiveness of Catholic preaching.

Moseley, Danny P.
"Preaching Without Authority." *Christian Ministry* 3 (May 1972): 2-3.   **510**
Proposes inductive preaching and the shared life as means by which preaching
can have authority in the minds of the hearers.

Muckerman, Norman J.
"Free Throws from the Pews: How an Ex-Basketball Star Helps Priest-   **511**
Preachers." *Liguorian* 65 (Feb 1977): 10-14. Reports on a seminar conducted
by layman Edward C. Macauley for thirty-five priests on the subject of
preaching.

Muilenburg, James
"Faith Comes by Preaching." *Union Seminary Quarterly Review* 15 (Nov   **512**
1959): 13-18. Contends that faith presupposes hearing, which presupposes
preaching, which presupposes someone sent to preach. In sermon preparation,
writes the author, the preacher must wait, labor, wrestle, pray. How can he
speak unless he himself is spoken to?

Mumford, Robert W.
"The Content of Christian Preaching." *Princeton Seminary Bulletin* 68   **513**
(Win 1976): 94-99. Sorts out two strands of the kerygma: one to the Jewish
culture, the other to the Hellenistic. The author lists three qualities of kerygma
that might be linked to American preachers.

Murphy, David M.

"Inductive Preaching: Reaching People Where They Are." *Priest* 34 (June   514
1978): 11–14. Insists that good sermons today should follow the inductive
approach, which is especially effective in introducing the homily.

"Preaching for People Where They Are." *Religious Communication Today*   515
(Sep 1979): 1–4. An appeal for inductive need-oriented preaching that ministers
to people with their own particular set of problems.

Nederhood, Joel H.

"Dimensions of the Ministry in the First Century—Ours." *Calvin Theo-*   516
logical Journal 3 (1968): 162–75. Pinpoints several aspects of future society to
which preachers will minister, and discusses new dimensions the ministry
might possess.

Neville, William G.

"Imagine—And Get Going." *Presbyterian Journal,* 5 November 1969, pp.   517
13, 23. Appeals to preachers to depend on God and preach the gospel. The
author describes a perfect society and discusses what one would then preach
about.

Newman, Leslie

"The Future of Preaching." *Preacher's Quarterly* 11 (1965): 97–104. While   518
there will always be a need for preaching, says the author, it will be effective in
the future only if one evaluates the method of communication, the type of
person preaching, and the relevance of the message.

Nichols, J. Randall

"Towards a Theological View of Responsibility in Communication."   519
Princeton Seminary Bulletin 68 (Win 1976): 100–114. Lists five points that
give a methodological foundation for discussion of the purpose of religious
communication.

Nikonov, K. I.

"The Russian Baptists: An Atheist's View." Edited and translated by   520
William C. Fletcher. *Foundations* 18 (1975): 321–35. Titled in Russian "Certain
Tendencies in the Preaching Activity of Contemporary Baptists." Presents an
unusually accurate picture of a local Baptist congregation in the U.S.S.R.

Niles, Daniel T.

"The Preacher." *Preacher's Quarterly* 11 (1965): 170–73. Suggests that   521
preaching is an event within Christ's ministry to persons, and that within this
ministry, one's preaching must be owned by Him.

Noth, Martin

"The 'Re-presentation' of the Old Testament in Proclamation." *Interpreta-*   522
tion 15 (1961): 50–60. Believes the Old Testament can be preached today by

re-presenting or proclaiming God's saving acts in history, just as Israel proclaimed them.

Oates, Wayne
"Plato and Preaching." *Review and Expositor* 41 (1944): 270-77. Extols the   523
value of studying Plato, discussing four functional areas in which such a
study can benefit one's preaching.

Oberman, Heiko A.
"Preaching and the Word in the Reformation." *Theology Today* 18 (1961):   524
16-29. Observes that the Reformation rediscovered the truth that the sermon is
an event, an encounter, when the Word of God meets the faithful with
authority.

Oliphant, Charles H.
"Authority and the Pulpit." *Bibliotheca Sacra* 61 (1904): 232-47. Calls for   525
preaching to be declarative, certain, and forceful. This gives authority to the
message, contends the author, and this authority is based on the nature of the
message proclaimed and on the witness of the living church.

Palmer, Edwin H.
"Phooey on the Sermon and the Church Order." *Torch and Trumpet* 20   526
(May 1970): 14-16. Examines the worship service as a means of outreach. The
author contrasts informal gatherings and formal gatherings, suggesting that
member churches follow the directives of their governing bodies. He considers
preaching essential to church growth.

"Preaching the Word." *Torch and Trumpet* 10 (Feb 1961): 4. Advocates   527
biblically centered preaching.

Palms, Roger C.
"Punch Lines from the Pulpit." *Christianity Today*, 20 April 1979, pp. 28-   528
29. Guidelines and suggestions for the effective use of humor in the pulpit.

Park, John Edgar
"The Miracle of Preaching." *Pulpit Digest* 37 (Dec 1956): 95-114. A con-   529
densation of the book by the same title. See RHT[1], entry 102.

Parker, Joseph
"The Trumpeter Has His Place in the Church." *Torch and Trumpet* 1   530
(June 1951): 8. Presses preachers to warn clearly against evil.

Patton, John H.
"What Is Religious Communication?" *Homiletic* 3 (1978): 8-12. Discusses   531
form and content within contemporary rhetorical theory, including the
worship atmosphere, audience, and general situational approach to the
sermon.

Paxton, Geoffrey J.

"The Evangelical's Substitute." *Present Truth* 3 (Nov 1974): 6–12. Focuses 532
on three specific areas in which Satan exploits distorted preaching about
man's salvation and sanctification.

Peters, Frank C.

"Counseling and Effective Preaching." *Bibliotheca Sacra* 126 (1969): 99–108. 533
Shows the necessity of both preaching and counseling, and stresses the value
of preaching that functions therapeutically and hygienically.

Phillips, Harold C.

"The Gospel and the Preacher." *Review and Expositor* 50 (1953): 279–97. 534
Urges preachers to preach sermons that consist of the gospel and theology,
and calls on them to live in a manner consistent with their preaching.

Pietersma, Henry

"The Place of Preaching in the Christian Life." *Calvin Theological* 535
Journal 8 (1973): 62–79. Criticizes improper reasons for retaining the sermon
today, and offers some proper ones. The author suggests that preaching
portrays the perennial relation of all to God.

Pilch, Wenceslaus J.

"Scripture in Your Sermon." *Homiletic and Pastoral Review* 64 (1964): 536
487–95. Propounds the values and advantages of using Scripture in sermons.

Piper, Thomas S.

"To Bring the Message." *Good News Broadcaster* 34 (Sep 1976): 31. In 537
response to a question about Romans 10:15 and the place of preaching today,
the author explains the use of the word *preach* and ways to give a biblical
message.

Portasik, Richard O.

"Priests and the Homily." *Priest* 21 (1966): 114–16. Recommends regular 538
preaching as opposed to lengthy commentaries on the church bulletin or
reading official church letters previously published.

Prior, Kenneth F. W.

"The Minister as a Teacher." *TSF News and Reviews* (Autumn 1970): 2–6. 539
Discusses the importance of the teaching ministry, its demands, and a seven-
point method of exposition.

Prussner, Frederick C.

"Preaching from the Old Testament." *New Pulpit Digest* 55 (Sep 1975): 540
61–64. Outlines three viewpoints on the unity of the Bible, and encourages the
preacher not to limit himself to only one of them.

Ramm, Bernard
   "The Gospel According to 'It Seems to Me.'" *Eternity* 16 (Mar 1965): 48.   **541**
Asserts that the failure of contemporary Protestant preaching is its lack of an
authority other than personal opinion.

Ray, Richard
   "Plato as Homiletician." *Princeton Seminary Bulletin* 64 (Mar 1971): 48-52.   **542**
Disagrees with Plato's homiletical model of appealing only to people's
emotions and avoiding controversial issues. The author believes that an appeal
to logic will result in more positive responses.

Read, David H. C.
   "The Old Testament and Modern Preaching." *Union Seminary Quarterly*   **543**
Review 12 (Jan 1957): 11-15. Modern ecumenical theology's rediscovery of the
Bible's unity, says the author, has implications for preaching. It should lead
us to relate Old Testament texts to the gospel of Christ.

Rees, Paul S.
   "The Preacher-Expositor." *Asbury Seminarian* 8 (Fall 1954): 11-19. Defines   **544**
the art of expository preaching, and discusses its need and dangers.

Reid, George T. H.
   "Preaching and the New Teaching Methods." *Expository Times* 83 (1972):   **545**
100-103. Effective communication from the pulpit must be "common-man
centered," says the author. It should stimulate listeners to discover truth for
themselves, truth related to everyday living.

Reid, Mark K.
   "On Identifying the Word of God Today." *Lexington Theological Quar-*   **546**
terly 10 (Apr 1975): 7-18. Asks, not only with respect to preaching but also in
relation to our present cultural situation, how we may discern and recognize
the word God speaks to us today. Fourteen criteria are listed and illustrated.

Roach, Corwin C.
   "Preaching and the New Versions." *Anglican Theological Review* 36   **547**
(1954): 181-90. Evaluates the Revised Standard Version's stimulus to biblical
preaching. The author suggests ways preachers can find assistance in this and
other translations.

   "Preaching in a Major Key." *Anglican Theological Review* 35 (1953): 1-8.   **548**
Observes that too much preaching is based on the grim circumstances of the
world. The author suggests that in light of Isaiah 40ff., preachers should
strike a more positive note.

Roberts, Donald L.
   "A Famine of the Word." *Presbyterian Journal*, 18 September 1974, pp. 10-   **549**
11. Using Paul and Amos as examples, the author stresses the importance of

preaching the entire Bible. He points out the deficiencies of small groups, which are often experience oriented and not Bible centered.

Robertson, James E.
"Preaching in the Work of the Ministry." *Asbury Seminarian* 29 (July 550
1974): 3-5. Supports an argument for the importance of preaching with biblical passages, men in history, and contemporary theology.

Robinson, James H.
"Preaching the Inclusive Christ." *Pulpit Digest* 36 (Apr 1956): 11-17. 551
Analyzes the art of preaching from the vantage point of its aim. The author says that preaching should exalt the inclusive Christ and strike at the root of human need.

Robinson, Jonathan
"What Shall I Preach?" *Homiletic and Pastoral Review* 77 (July 1977): 552
10-18. Describes how and what every Catholic priest should preach in light of the Second Vatican Council.

Robinson, R. J.
"The 'Preach-It-Again' Idea." *New Pulpit Digest* 54 (July 1974): 24-26. 553
Suggests that the congregation select their pastor's favorite sermons and that he repeat those sermons during one month of each year.

Robinson, William D.
"The Hidden Congregation." *Preacher's Quarterly* 12 (1966): 50-55. The 554
hidden congregation (people who do not go to church but who hear about the sermons from those who do) is always asking what difference it makes to believe in God. The author motivates preachers to answer that question in every sermon.

Rodd, C. S.
"Preaching Today." *Expository Times* 88 (1977): 237-38. Suggests five 555
reasons why preaching is out of favor today and four things modern preachers should be doing about it.

Rossel, John
"The Problem of Communication." *Minister's Quarterly* 16 (Autumn 1960): 556
19-23. Considers some problems of communication peculiar to the minister, then compares these with techniques practiced by the poet and dramatist.

Routley, Erik
"Text for a Religious Aesthetic." *Theology Today* 17 (1960): 192-99. Criti- 557
cizes the church for Saul-worship (judging things by their immediate attractiveness), citing examples in the areas of architecture, evangelism, and preaching.

Roxburgh, Robert L.
"What's Holding the Layman Back?" *Eternity* 20 (Apr 1969): 10, 14–16.   558
Traces the immaturity of laymen to the clergy's failure to teach biblical
concepts. This results, the author asserts, in weaknesses in the church's
worship, preaching, fellowship, and evangelism.

Rupert, Hoover
"Woe Is Me If I Preach Not." *New Pulpit Digest* 56 (May 1976): 37–42.   559
Concludes that the pastor must proclaim God's Word for the purpose of
meeting his people's needs.

Rushdoony, Rousas John
"Contemporary Preaching: Biblical Preaching vs. Obfuscation." *Journal*   560
of Christian Reconstruction 2 (Win 1975): 129–32. Illustrates the deficiency of
today's preaching by discussing the traditionally orthodox preacher, the
modern evangelical, the modernist, and the reformational preacher.

Sanford, Jack
"The Preacher's Top Priority: Preaching." *New Pulpit Digest* 56 (May   561
1976): 33–36. Insists that the preaching ministry is central and is essential to a
church's good health. The author also considers the layman's responsibility in
the church.

Scherer, Paul
"The History That Becomes History: Preaching from the Old Testament."   562
Union Seminary Quarterly Review 15 (May 1960): 273–80. Criticizes the "character" approach to Old Testament preaching because it ignores God's purpose
in history. The author asks the preacher to see the Old Testament from where
he is, back to what God did, through what God has done.

Scotford, John R.
"Pulpit and Pew Converge." *Pulpit Digest* 39 (Oct 1958): 17–19, 66. Demon-   563
strates ways in which the preacher can speak effectively to both large and
small groups.

Scott, Charles Wheeler
"Preaching in the 70's." *Pulpit Digest* 51 (Oct 1970): 5–6. Answers the critic   564
who says the sermon is outmoded, and gives tips to the preacher to make his
sermons more effective.

Scott, R. B. Y.
"Biblical Research and the Work of the Pastor: Recent Study in Isaiah   565
1–39." *Interpretation* 11 (1957): 259–68. Uses Isaiah 1–39 to show how a pastor
can integrate the findings of modern critical scholarship with the proclamation of that Word to his people.

Scroggie, W. Graham

"Preaching the Bible." *Eternity* 2 (Oct 1951): 9-10, 44. Exhorts the preacher   **566**
to take into account the overall movement of Scripture, and asks the man who
does not believe in Scripture's validity not to preach.

Seifert, Harvey

"Preaching as the Impossible Possibility." *Christian Ministry* 4 (Nov 1973):   **567**
3-8. Dissatisfied with traditional preaching, the author analyzes the changing
context of the preacher's work and suggests several ways to regain the listener's
attention and continuing involvement.

Self, William L.

"How to Succeed in the Pulpit Without Really Boring." *Pulpit Digest* 46   **568**
(Dec 1965): 19-26. Contains numerous suggestions for maintaining creativity
and freshness in preaching.

Sheffield, DeWitt

"Minister of the Word." *Pulpit Digest* 51 (Mar 1971): 7-11. Preaching, the   **569**
author says, should be grounded in the Bible; it is vital to worship; it necessi-
tates study, prayer, love; and it should teach.

Shelley, William

"Three Major Causes of Poor Homilies." *Priest* 34 (Jan 1978): 46-48. Dis-   **570**
cusses three major causes of poor homilies: too little preparation, an under-
estimate of their importance, and the time-clock mentality of many laymen.

Siedell, Barry

"And Hearing by the Word of God." *Good News Broadcaster* 30 (Mar 1972):   **571**
12-13. Focuses on the importance of the preacher's knowledge of his hearers
and of their culture's viewpoint and vocabulary.

"Faith Cometh by Hearing." *Good News Broadcaster* 30 (Feb 1972): 4-6.   **572**
Stresses the importance of understanding principles of communication.

Simonson, Norman R., and Lundy, Richard M.

"The Effectiveness of Persuasive Communication Presented Under Condi-   **573**
tions of Irrelevant Fear." *Journal of Communication* 16 (1966): 32-37. Presents
evidence that a persuasive message is more likely to be accepted by an audience
that is influenced by an irrelevant fear.

Sinks, Perry Wayland

"New Testament Conceptions of Preaching." *Bibliotheca Sacra* 94 (1937):   **574**
197-206. Preaching is the primary, perpetual function of the minister, says the
author. Its goal is to convince men of the truth of the gospel and secure their
belief in it.

Sleeth, Ronald E.
"The Crisis in Preaching." *Perkins School of Theology Journal* 30 (Sum   **575**
1977): 1-41. An essay on the preacher under siege, the recovery of the Word,
and the future shape of the pulpit.

"Issues and Problems in Contemporary Preaching." *Princeton Seminary*   **576**
Bulletin 66 (Oct 1973): 65-75. Urges the analysis of (1) preaching's theological
basis, (2) its ontology, (3) the fallout from the "electronic revolution," and (4)
the concern of communication theorists to maintain the efficiency of the
spoken voice.

Smith, Burkett L.
"The Power of Preaching." *Christianity Today*, 9 April 1965, p. 15. Affirms   **577**
the priority of preaching the gospel today, and deals with excuses that the
message is no longer suited to our world.

Smith, Harmon L.
"Can the Church Renew Itself from Within?" *Theology Today* 21 (1964):   **578**
184-95. Claims that the church can renew itself from within and that it must
free the pastor from other responsibilities to concentrate on preaching.

Smith, Noel
"Preach or Perish." *Christian Life* 31 (Apr 1970): 20. Defines preaching,   **579**
and describes its importance and effect in history.

Sockman, Ralph W.
"Don't Preach to Me." *Pulpit Digest* 47 (Sep 1966): 16-22. Supplies reasons   **580**
why people no longer look to the pulpit for guidance, and explains how to
restore the pulpit's appeal and make the sermon enticing.

Soper, Donald
"The Future of Preaching." *Preacher's Quarterly* 11 (1965): 12-18. If preach-   **581**
ing is to have a future, says the author, it must relate to the circumstances of
today and tomorrow. It must first inform and then demand a response to that
information.

Spurgeon, Charles Haddon
"Earnestness in Pulpit Work." *Banner of Truth* (Mar 1971): 5. Exhorts   **582**
preachers to feed their congregations spiritually and to work heartily on
sermon preparation.

Starling, Ira C., Jr.
"The Sermon That You Preach." *New Pulpit Digest* 53 (May 1973): 48-51.   **583**
A call to preachers not for clever sermons but for faithful lives.

Steimle, Edmund A.

"The Problem of Motivation in the Contemporary Pulpit." *Union Semi-* **584** *nary Quarterly Review* 17 (Nov 1961): 3–19. Diagnoses the preacher's most pressing problem—motivating men to respond to God's redemptive action now present—and supplies a remedy.

Steinmetz, David C.

"'Woe to Me If I Do Not Preach the Gospel.'" *Duke Divinity School* **585** *Review* 39 (1974): 1–9. A brief for the importance of preaching.

Stevens, Clifford

"The Task of Preaching." *Priest* 31 (May 1975): 20–22. Lists a few laws of **586** effective preaching, and explains that a priest cannot help others to have a full encounter with the Word until he has had a personal encounter in the Word himself.

Stibbs, Alan M.

"In Defence of the Sermon; or, Why Preaching?" *Christian Graduate* 19 **587** (Sep 1966): 12–15. Surveys the place of preaching in both the Bible and history, concluding that preaching is essential to salvation and edification.

Stoll, John H.

"Is the Church's Formula Upside Down?" *Good News Broadcaster* 28 (Oct **588** 1970): 22–24. Shows the importance of a church being Bible centered, points out how ignorant Christians are of the Word, then prescribes truly expository preaching of the "whole counsel of God," not of salvation passages alone.

Strait, C. Neil

"Biblical Preaching for Contemporary Man." *New Pulpit Digest* 56 (Nov **589** 1976): 44. Defines biblical preaching with five propositions.

Sweazey, George E.

"Living Without Oratory." *Christian Ministry* 3 (Jan 1972): 5–7. Discusses **590** the lack of great orators, which results from too little life-gripping conviction, and states the profit of one-way communication.

Sweet, J. P. M.

"Second Thoughts: VIII, The Kerygma." *Expository Times* 76 (1965): **591** 143–47. A critique of C. H. Dodd's *The Apostolic Preaching and its Development* (see RHT[1], entry 157) and of his understanding of kerygma as the content of preaching.

Tangelder, Johan D.

"What Greater Excitement Can One Have?" *Outlook* 24 (Jan 1974): 11–12. **592** Advocates a return to biblically centered preaching and a move away from dramas, choirs, and similar contemporary presentations.

Tarver, Jerry L.
"A Lost Form of Pulpit Address." *Southern Speech Journal* 31 (1966): **593**
181-95. Examines direct, individual exhortation, and concludes that it is a
form of pulpit address locked in the past.

Tesser, Abraham; Rosen, Sidney; and Waranch, Ellen
"Communication Mood and the Reluctance to Transmit Undesirable **594**
Messages (the Mum Effect)." *Journal of Communication* 23 (1973): 266-83.
Contains the results of an experiment in which subjects "overheard" messages
containing either good or bad news.

Thielicke, Helmut
"What Makes Good Preaching?" Edited by Leslie H. Stobbe. *Eternity* 18 **595**
(May 1967): 21-23. An interview in which the author discusses what makes
sermons great, how a preacher learns about the world around him, and how
to preach for a decision.

Thomas, Martha
"'Contact': An Experiment in Radio Preaching." *Preaching Today* 7 (Jan **596**
1973): 9-12. Describes the background, objectives, topics, style, preachers of,
and response to, this radio program.

Thompson, Henry O.
"Prophetic Preaching Today." *Christianity Today*, 1 September 1967, **597**
pp. 20, 22. Appeals for relevance in preaching and for an element of prophet-
ism to aid in the divine-human encounter that begins with God.

Thompson, John
"Imagination in Preaching." *Pulpit* 37 (May 1966): 7-9. Discusses the **598**
nature of imagination and its function in preaching. The author advocates
imaginative approaches to interpretation, sermon construction, and delivery.

Thomson, John M. A.
"Let the Old Testament Speak." *New Pulpit Digest* 57 (Sep 1977): 25-27. **599**
Laments the lack of Old Testament preaching, then elaborates on the need for
a solid exegetical base and a good understanding of the relationship between
the testaments.

Tiller, Robert W.
"The Shape of Preaching." *Foundations* 9 (1966): 318-24. Discusses the **600**
purpose of preaching and some of its basic principles.

Tilley, W. Clyde
"Proclaiming the Truth and Preserving the Tension." *Pulpit Digest* 49 **601**
(May 1969): 10-12, 58. Explains how to proclaim the whole truth and at the
same time preserve the tension inherent within it.

Timmerman, John J.
"Modern Communications and the Sermon." *Outlook* 25 (Sep 1975): 5–6.   **602**
Argues that the changed attitudes of the congregation have caused changes in
the style and content of the sermon.

"The Sermon in Dispute." *Reformed Journal* 22 (Apr 1972): 5–6. Reprinted   **603**
in *Outlook* 22 (July 1972): 24. Examines the trend toward more audience
participation in the worship service and less preaching of prepared sermons.

Tinney, James S.
"The 'Miracle' of Black Preaching." *Christianity Today,* 30 January 1976,   **604**
pp. 14–16. Discusses elements common to the black sermon, such as the
antiphonal call and response, pacing, cadence, rhythm, sentence forms,
formulas, melody or chant, and dramatics.

Todd, George E.
"Worship in an Urban Parish." *Union Seminary Quarterly Review* 13   **605**
(May 1958): 43–53. Affirms that able, dedicated, consistent preaching, strongly
based in Bible study, powerfully influences members of urban churches to
worship and witness more fully.

Toombs, Lawrence E.
"The Problematic of Preaching from the Old Testament." *Interpretation*   **606**
23 (1969): 302–14. Tackles the major problem of preaching from the Old
Testament, showing the passage's relevance to contemporary man. The author
suggests a solution: using the human situation of the passage as the key.

Topolewski, Nancy
"A Hole in the Heavens: A Theological Framework for Inductive Preach-   **607**
ing." *Religious Communication Today* (Sep 1979): 33–37. Recommends
inductive, story-centered preaching as an exceptional tool for pastoral care.

Towne, Edgar A.
"Communicating a Message and Believing a Message." *Encounter* 37   **608**
(1976): 21–29. Thoughts on the communication process of preaching, relating
its content to its success or impact.

Trentham, Charles A.
"The Importance of Preaching: On the Recovery of Transcendence."   **609**
Southwestern Journal of Theology 10 (Spring 1968): 19–29. Urges a return to
preaching that builds up faith based upon God's Word, encourages the hearers,
and consoles them by focusing on eternity and God's transcendence.

Trimp, C.
"The Relevance of Preaching (in the Light of the Reformation's 'Sola   **610**
Scriptura' Principle)." *Westminster Theological Journal* 36 (1973): 1–30.

Surveys the ways in which modern Roman Catholic theology and current Protestant hermeneutics approach each other, then gives four ways that the "Scripture only" principle conveys, seals, and guarantees the relevance of preaching.

Unger, Merrill F.
"Expository Preaching." *Bibliotheca Sacra* 111 (1954): 324-37. Defines **611** expository preaching and outlines its benefits.

"The Need of Expository Preaching in the Twentieth Century." *Bibliotheca* **612** *Sacra* 111 (1954): 229-40. Outlines the causes of expository preaching's decline, in an attempt to halt that decline.

van Buren, Paul M.
"The Word of God in the Church." *Anglican Theological Review* 39 **613** (1957): 344-58. Contends that the church must have exegetical preaching, which is the first step in making the Bible God's Word in and to the church.

Vanden Heuvel, Henry B.
"Advantages of the Parish Ministry." *Banner of Truth* (Dec 1971): 37-39. **614** Urges graduating seminarians to consider the challenges and blessings of the parish ministry. Systematic preaching of God's Word is viewed by the author as the parish preacher's key challenge and responsibility.

Vander Ploeg, John
"How to Rekindle the Fire." *Outlook* 24 (Apr 1974): 9-10. Encourages the **615** preaching of the Bible as the means of revitalizing what has become drab.

"The Pulpit and the Pew." *Outlook* 25 (Aug 1975): 7-9. Exhorts the **616** preacher to preach the Bible and the audience to both hear and do what has been said.

Van Houten, Fred
"Make the Message Plain." *Outlook* 26 (Feb 1976): 11-14. Explores four **617** factors that have much to do with preaching in our day: the supernaturalism of Christianity, the place of the institutional church, the dislike of authority, and the difficulty of communicating to all kinds of cultures in our day.

Van Santvoord, George
"The Teacher." *Anglican Theological Review* 30 (1948): 156-58. Contends **618** that the ineffective teacher cannot accomplish his work as a Christian minister.

Voigt, Robert J.
"Your Sermon: A 'Many Splendored Thing.'" *Homiletic and Pastoral* **619** *Review* 64 (1964): 762-66. Presents the balance between, on the one hand, the mechanics of preparing short and simple sermons, and on the other, the knowledge of one's audience that is essential to maximum effectiveness.

Vos, Johannes G.
"How to Make the Church Attractive to Those Not Interested in Religion." **620**
Torch and Trumpet 3 (Aug 1953): 4-5, 29. The Rev. Smoothly Softpedal, D.D.,
reveals possible weaknesses in a message.

Wahlberg, Rachel Conrad
"3,896 Sermons . . ." *Christian Ministry* 4 (July 1973): 15-18. Preaching is **621**
archaic and should be replaced with dialogue or discussion groups, says the
author. She wants to remove from the church service its strict regimentation
and thus to meet people's needs.

Wallace, David H.
"This Is the Christ We Preach." *Christianity Today,* 22 July 1966, pp. 3-5. **622**
Appeals for a return to preaching based on what the Bible teaches about
Christ rather than what society teaches. The author emphasizes the need for
theology and exegesis.

Ward, Wayne E.
"Preaching and the Word of God in the New Testament." *Review and* **623**
Expositor 56 (1959): 20-30. Examines C. H. Dodd's concept of the kerygma
and Karl Barth's concept of the Word of God. The author shows their similar-
ity, makes applications to preaching, and defines preaching in light of Barth's
understanding of God's Word.

Warren, Max A. C.
"Preaching from the Bible." *Preacher's Quarterly* 14 (1968): 185-96. Dis- **624**
cusses the three forms of preaching: proclamation, prophecy, and teaching.

Warren, Paul C.
"The Word and Sacraments and Healing." *Princeton Seminary Bulletin* **625**
62 (Sum 1969): 51-63. Encourages ministers to utilize the word (preaching)
and the sacraments in the church's healing ministry to the congregation.

Watkins, Keith
"Banishing the Disease of Literacy." *Worship* 47 (1973): 482-88. The pulpit **626**
needs to regain its ability to move those who listen, says the author. For this to
take place, preaching needs to be an oral event. It must provide a structure of
meaning for life. The preacher and hearers must discover ways to deal with
each other at close range.

"A Table in the Presence of Enemies: Reflections on Evangelism." *Encoun-* **627**
ter 34 (1973): 191-214. Discusses the task of the preacher (to declare God's
self-disclosure in Christ) and of the sermon (to diagnose the human condition
and give the gospel remedy).

Waugh, R. M. L.
"The Preacher and His Greek New Testament." *Expository Times* 61 (1950): **628**

175-77. Cites numerous examples of crucial facts brought to light by a knowledge of the Greek text, facts that contribute to making sermons interesting.

Weatherspoon, J. B.
"The Evangelistic Sermon." *Review and Expositor* 42 (1945): 59-67. **629**
Analyzes qualities of evangelistic sermons, and suggests ways to improve them.

Weeks, Louis
"Preaching Seminar." *Christian Ministry* 10 (May 1979): 28-30. Assesses a **630**
self-initiated self-improvement project begun by several pastors in Louisville.

Wenzel, August
"Criticisms of Preaching in Current Writing." *Lutheran Quarterly* 20 **631**
(1968): 389-95. Analyzes seven categories of criticisms. Concerning the form of communication, the author looks at the irrelevance, overemphasis, and uninteresting nature of preaching. Regarding content, he considers the lack of courage, change, and communication effectiveness.

Wesson, Anthony J.
"New Life in New Theology." *Preacher's Quarterly* 12 (1966): 227-32. Tra- **632**
ditional theology is a theology of the Word of God, says the author, and it sees the preacher as a herald. New theology, however, is a theology of the acts of God in Christ. So preachers must now be willing to enter into dialogue with the world, leading the church in demonstrating through obedient love its belief in the lordship of Jesus Christ.

White, Richard C.
"Preaching the New Hermeneutic." *Lexington Theological Quarterly* 9 **633**
(1974): 61-71. Suggests that the new hermeneutic is not new, but "a new encounter with what responsible exegesis and interpretation have ever been at their best."

Wiersbe, Warren W.
"Who Needs Dictionaries?" *Moody Monthly* 75 (Mar 1975): 112-17. To **634**
assist preachers in improving their word and language skills, the author lists a variety of dictionary resources.

Wietzke, Walter R.
"The K Trilogy: A Preaching Critique." *Pulpit* 37 (June 1966): 22-25. **635**
Focuses on three primary ingredients in preaching: the preacher, the message, and the congregation. The author emphasizes the prerequisites in each category for relevance and effectiveness.

Williamson, Clark M.
"Preaching the Easter Faith." *Encounter* 37 (1976): 41-52. Defines preaching, **636**

lists in propositional form the Easter faith of the church, and examines the new vision of reality evoked by preaching from the perspective of this Easter faith.

Wroblewski, Sergius

"On Homilists and Homilies." *Homiletic and Pastoral Review* 72 (Apr **637** 1972): 65-68. Contends that the preacher must be careful not to increase modern man's indifference to the Bible and preaching. He must make clear that he shares their human condition.

Wuest, Kenneth S.

"The Greek New Testament and Expository Preaching." *Bibliotheca Sacra* **638** 117 (1960): 40-46. Gives tips on how to use the Greek language effectively in expository preaching.

Yeaworth, Irvin Shortess

"Preach Biblical Themes." *Christianity Today*, 1 April 1966, pp. 34-35. A **639** cry for preaching that is biblical, and a guide to preaching this way.

Zylstra, Helen

"The Preaching of the Word." *Outlook* 23 (Aug 1973): 18-19. Stresses the **640** importance of the sermon as a communicative tool, and exhorts both preacher and hearer to excellence.

Preaching and Theology

Anonymous

"Ghosts in the Pulpit." *Christianity Today*, 15 April 1966, pp. 24-25. An **641** analysis of the importance of the Holy Spirit's contribution to a successful pulpit ministry.

Auricchio, John

"Kerygmatic Theology." *Pastoral Life* 14 (1966): 469-76. States that the **642** goal of "kerygmatic theology" is the gospel's expression in more concrete language.

Beauchesne, Richard

"The Mystery of Preaching." *Pastoral Life* 14 (1966): 488. Because the **643** preacher's words become the words of God, the author writes, the preacher's life must bear testimony to his faith in Christ.

Bloesch, Donald G.

"Burying the Gospel." *Christianity Today*, 24 September 1971, pp. 8-11; 8 **644** October 1971, pp. 12-14. One of five areas in which advocates of the new theology have tended to bury the gospel is that of "cultural preaching," described in part 2.

Buege, William A.
"Calling Modern Man to Himself by Preaching." *Concordia Theological* 645
Monthly 40 (1969): 97-109. Starting with God the Father, the author relates
preaching to each member of the Trinity. This article provides a background
for understanding neo-orthodox preaching.

Clinard, Gordon
"Proclamation: The Biblical Context." *Southwestern Journal of Theology* 646
8 (Spring 1966): 15-24. Defines biblical proclamation as bearing testimony to
God's redemptive work in Christ, whether directed to unbelievers or to
believers.

Clowney, Edmund P.
"Preaching Christ." *Christianity Today,* 12 March 1965, pp. 5-7. A biblical 647
study showing that all Scripture finds its unity in Christ and identifying the
minister's task as preaching the Word of the Lord so as to reveal the Lord of
the Word.

Connolly, Patrick R.
"What Language Do Priests Speak?" *Preaching Today* 7 (Jan 1973): 19-22. 648
The twentieth-century priest must, the author insists, repackage the meaning
of Christianity in contemporary terms without losing the essence of the
message.

De Jong, Alexander C.
"The Sermon, the Sender, the Sinner." *Torch and Trumpet* 14 (Feb 1964): 649
7-9. Explores the theological implications of the offer of the gospel and of
God's working through the sermon.

Ellens, J. Harold
"A Theology of Communication: Putting the Question." *Journal of Psy-* 650
chology and Theology 2 (1974): 132-39. Explores the nature of Christian
communication and the question of a sound theology of communication.

Enright, William G.
"Theology and the Crisis in the Pulpit." *Foundations* 18 (1975): 107-14. 651
Gives two reasons for the demise of theology's influence on preaching, then
gives five theological criteria for the homiletical process.

Eppinger, Paul D.
"Be Occupied with Preaching!" *Christianity Today,* 9 June 1967, pp. 13-14. 652
Identifies the need today for a theology of preaching. The author insists that
this theology be rooted in New Testament concepts, and he discusses seven
New Testament words for preaching.

Evans, Eifion

"Preaching and Revival." *Banner of Truth* (Dec 1970): 11-20. Discusses the   **653**
diminishing interest in both preaching and revival, then reveals the intimate
relationship between the two, examining the characteristics, content, and
effect of preaching during revival.

Forstman, Jack

"What Does It Mean 'to Preach from the Bible'?" *Encounter* 27 (1966):   **654**
28-38. Discusses the relation of theological and practical studies to preaching.
All of these studies come together in biblical preaching, the author observes,
for its aim is to proclaim the implications of the Christian faith.

Fuchs, Ernst

"Proclamation and Speech-Event." *Theology Today* 19 (1962): 341-54.   **655**
Dismisses much preaching about Christ as empty words. True proclamation
should bring God "to speech," insists the author. Then God is heard and
becomes known to faith.

Gibson, Elsie

"The Word as Sacrament." *Christian Century,* 28 September 1966, pp. 1172-   **656**
75. Discusses the sacramental character of the Word as found in the written
Word, the spoken word (proclamation), and the personal word in holy communion. All convey sacramental grace, says the author, evoking the response
of faith.

Gifford, Millard M.

"Preach Christ." *Church Management* 43 (May 1967): 17-18. The mandate   **657**
to "preach Christ in all His glory" summarizes the author's philosophy of
preaching.

Gritter, George

"Preach the Word." *Banner,* 10 September 1976, p. 12. A meditation based   **658**
on Paul's exhortation to Timothy in II Timothy 4:2.

Hall, Thor

"Preaching and Theology." *Pulpit* 39 (Mar 1968): 16-18. Discusses three   **659**
ways in which preaching and theology are interrelated: (1) they clarify the
nature of the sermon; (2) they explain the current framework for preaching;
and (3) they affect the sermon content.

Harman, Allan

"The Reformed Confessions and Our Preaching." *Banner of Truth* (Apr   **660**
1973): 23-29. Outlines the influence of Reformed theology on the Reformers
and on us today, making us aspire to preaching that is biblical, doctrinal,
systematic, balanced, and applicable.

Hill, William J.
"Preaching as a 'Moment' in Theology." *Homiletic and Pastoral Review* **661**
77 (Oct 1976): 10-19. A philosophical discussion of the "word event"—the
meaning of words—in preaching. Meaning comes from an encounter with
God's action in history and a communication of that action, contends the
author.

Hoefler, Richard
"The 'Real Presence' of Christ in the Preaching Situation." *Lutheran* **662**
Quarterly 21 (1969): 173-78. Argues for making Christ's presence a reality
today rather than something that must be conjured up from the past.

Hunter, A. M.
"The Unity of the New Testament: The Kerygma." *Expository Times* 58 **663**
(1947): 228-31. Points out that the apostolic preaching underlies the entire
New Testament Scripture, and expounds on what it means to preach the
kerygma today.

Kennedy, Gerald
"Preaching and Theology." *New Pulpit Digest* 57 (Mar 1977): 53. Shows **664**
that theology is essential to preaching that reaches the lives of people.

Lewis, H. J.
"Theology in Relation to Preaching." *Expository Times* 41 (1930): 458-62. **665**
Due to application of the scientific method, the author writes, theology has
vastly broadened. He outlines the dimensions of theology and summarizes its
contents.

McCollough, Thomas E.
"Preaching's Rediscovery of Theology." *Review and Expositor* 56 (1959): **666**
43-55. Decries the lack of theological knowledge in church congregations,
and identifies doctrinal preaching as a necessity. The author calls for such
preaching to be related to actual life experiences, and he suggests ways to
learn to preach doctrinally.

Macrae, Kenneth A.
"Preaching and the Danger of Compromise." *Banner of Truth* (July 1964): **667**
8-13. Discusses ways to evaluate a message's success in representing all of
Scripture.

Montgomery, John Warwick
"An Exhortation to Exhorters." *Christianity Today*, 16 March 1973, pp. 9- **668**
11. An exhortation to consider the essential nature of the Word, the irreduci-
bility of law and gospel, and the centrality of Christ.

Northcutt, Jesse J.
"Proclamation: The Theological Imperative." *Southwestern Journal of* **669**
Theology 8 (Spring 1966): 7–14. Declares that proclamation of the gospel is a
theological imperative: God seeks to communicate with man; the gospel
demands proclamation; the redeemed heart is impelled to respond; and the
receptive heart recognizes its need for the gospel.

Parker, George Gerald
"For Christ's Sake, Say Something!" *Andover Newton Quarterly* 6 (Mar **670**
1966): 53–64. Relates the reason for, and importance of, preaching messages
that are content-centered and well communicated.

Pennington, Chester A.
"An Acoustical Affair." *Drew Gateway* 45 (1974–75): 88–92. Documents the **671**
central concern with preaching in the theology of Carl Michalson.

Reid, W. Stanford
"Preaching Is Social Action." *Christianity Today*, 4 June 1971, pp. 10–11. **672**
Argues that faithful preaching of the gospel is social action, for it is regenera-
tive, changing the whole man.

Richards, Larry
"Church Teaching: Content Without Context." *Christianity Today*, 15 **673**
April 1977, pp. 16–18. Founds a communication theology on Deuteronomy 6
and other passages, stressing the importance of human relationships as well
as content.

Rosenau, Graeme M.
"Heirs of the Reformation in the Pulpit." *Concordia Theological Monthly* **674**
33 (1962): 581–86. Suggests ways in which the three great principles of the
Reformation are significant for the preacher of the written Word.

Rust, E. C.
"Theology and Preaching." *Review and Expositor* 52 (1955): 145–65. **675**
Argues that a theological base is essential to preaching that matures believers,
and identifies crucial doctrines that need to be preached.

Ryle, J. C.
"Does It Matter What Preaching We Hear?" *Banner of Truth* (Nov 1967): **676**
1–2. Contends that biblical truth must be spoken from the pulpit. The congregation is responsible to examine and evaluate the doctrines preached and
to respond appropriately, the author insists. The preacher is responsible to
proclaim God's truth despite public disapproval.

Saldutti, Soccorso J.
"Preaching: Proclamation of the Word of God Through Men of God."   **677**
Dimension 6 (Spring 1974): 31-40.

Shedd, William G. T.
"A Chapter on Doctrinal Preaching." Edited by Henry J. Kuiper. *Torch*   **678**
and Trumpet 10 (Sep 1960): 6. From Shedd's *Orthodoxy and Heterodoxy.*

Skerry, Donald P.
"Faith Born of Preaching." *American Ecclesiastical Review* 158 (1968):   **679**
299-318. A study of Paul's reflection on preaching in Romans 10.

Sleeth, Ronald E.
"The Office of Preaching: A Theological Appraisal." *Perkins School of*   **680**
Theology Journal 19 (Fall 1965): 38-44. Discusses five theological books on
preaching under the categories of (1) the centrality of the Word, (2) the Word
and the Bible, (3) the Word and the church, (4) the Word and sacrament,
(5) the Word and the world, and (6) the existential Word.

Spurgeon, Charles Haddon
"Preaching to Sinners." *Banner of Truth* (Mar 1969): 20-22. Holds to both   **681**
distinguishing grace in election and the universality of the gospel command.

Starkey, Lycurgus M., Jr.
"Henrich Ott: Theologian of Preaching." *Pulpit Digest* 50 (Apr 1970):   **682**
7-10. A report on a seminar held at Garrett Theological Seminary on theology
and preaching in Ott's thought.

Stevenson, Dwight E.
"The Word of God Through the Words of Men." *Lexington Theological*   **683**
Quarterly 7 (1972): 1-10. Examines the meaning of *word* in the Word of God,
identifying the preacher's responsibility to speak the Word of God.

Strong, Robert
"The Preaching of Salvation." *Presbyterian Journal,* 30 October 1963,   **684**
pp. 7-8, 20. Bases a philosophy of preaching on I Corinthians 1:1, 21-24.

Stroup, George
"Preaching as a Theological Discipline." *Homiletic* 3 (1978): 3-8. Discusses   **685**
the integral relationship between preaching as form and theology as content,
and stresses the necessity of properly integrating the two.

Walhout, Edwin
"Covenantal Preaching." *Banner,* 16 May 1975, pp. 10-11. Criticizes the   **686**
theory of preaching based on the presupposition that there are two lines of
connection between God and man: power and truth.

Wedel, Theodore O.
"Bultmann and Next Sunday's Sermon." *Anglican Theological Review* 39   **687**
(1957): 1-8. Explains how Rudolf Bultmann's theology will affect the preacher
and his message.

Woodfin, Yandall
"The Theology of Preaching: A Search for the Authentic." *Scottish Journal*   **688**
of Theology 23 (1970): 408-19. Constructs a theology of preaching in response
to this question: "Upon what authority and with what hope may a man
claim Christian proclamation, even his own interpretative strivings alongside
and sometimes distinct from the words of Scripture, as the Word of God?"

Topics of Preaching

Achtemeier, Elizabeth
"The Theological Message of Hosea: Its Preaching Values." *Review and*   **689**
Expositor 72 (1975): 473-85. Argues that the Old Testament serves principally
as an illustration of the New, and that Old Testament texts can be preached
only if paired with New Testament texts. The author suggests themes in
Hosea and corresponding New Testament texts.

Ackland, Donald F.
"Preaching from Hosea to a Nation in Crisis." *Southwestern Journal of*   **690**
Theology 18 (Fall 1975): 43-55. Examines the love of God for His people
Israel as expressed in the Book of Hosea. The author calls preachers to tell
sinful Americans of a God who loves them and has provided a means of
restitution through Christ.

Allen, Charles L.
"Speak All the Words." *Pulpit* 36 (Mar 1965): 11-12. Urges the preacher to   **691**
include in his sermons *all* the "words" of the gospel, words such as social
justice, personal redemption, comfort, stewardship, outreach, judgment, and
mercy.

Ashcraft, Morris
"Preaching the Apocalyptic Message Today." *Review and Expositor* 72   **692**
(1975): 345-56. Suggests an approach to preaching the apocalyptic message,
shows how this message is best proclaimed, and selects some apocalyptic
themes in Revelation with contemporary significance.

Barackman, Paul F.
"Preaching from Numbers." *Interpretation* 13 (1959): 55-70. Suggests topics   **693**
and methods for preaching from Numbers, discusses preaching on the book
as a whole and in parts, and includes applications for today.

Bayly, Joseph T.
"Did We Make the Same Mistake?" *Eternity* 19 (Aug 1968): 39-40. Reports   **694**
that there was little pulpit response to the assassination of John F.
Kennedy, and exhorts preachers to be more relevant and flexible by responding to great
events.

Bell, L. Nelson
"Beware!" *Christianity Today*, 24 October 1969, pp. 24-25. Warns preachers   **695**
against substituting the social problems of society for true biblical content in
their sermons. The author distinguishes between the gospel and its fruit.

"Peripheral Christianity." *Christianity Today*, 26 September 1969, pp. 30,   **696**
32. Argues for a new emphasis on the basics of the Christian faith in the
church's preaching ministry.

Bennett, T. Miles
"Preaching Values in Deuteronomy." *Southwestern Journal of Theology* 7   **697**
(Oct 1964): 41-53. A professor of Old Testament urges ministers to preach
more often from the Old Testament, and he suggests several outlines for
Deuteronomy, four major themes, and a brief bibliography.

Blackwood, Andrew W.
"Preaching Values in I Corinthians." *Southwestern Journal of Theology* 3   **698**
(Oct 1960): 39-52. Uses a "case study" approach to a homiletic survey of
I Corinthians, including sixteen key sermon texts, titles, and preaching tips.

Breines, Andrew R.
"Organizing a Sermon Series on Social Responsibility." *Proceedings of the*   **699**
Catholic Homiletic Society Charter Convention (1962): 29-36.

Brooks, Thomas
"Preaching Christ." *Banner of Truth* (July 1967): 18-19. Explains why   **700**
preachers should preach Christ, how they should do it, and what prerequisites
enable one to do it.

Brown, H. C., Jr.
"Preaching Values in Mark's Gospel." *Southwestern Journal of Theology*   **701**
1 (Oct 1958): 63-73. Surveys possible sermon series, and offers numerous texts
for preaching on six basic areas of need: ethical, supportive or pastoral,
devotional, actional, doctrinal, and evangelistic.

Brown, Ronald
"Why Preach On Hell?" *Torch and Trumpet* 16 (Mar 1966): 16-19. Argues   **702**
that the doctrine of hell must be a part of preaching because it is a part of
Scripture.

Brownson, William C.
"Preaching Sanctification Today." *Reformed Review* 28 (Spring 1975): **703**
201-11. Reviews the Reformed understanding of sanctification. This is an
exercise in biblical theology with comments on preaching.

Bruster, Bill
"Problems and Potential in Bicentennial Preaching." *Southwestern Jour-* **704**
nal of Theology 18 (Spring 1976): 79-90. Identifies temptations a preacher
faces in preparing messages for the U.S.A.'s bicentennial year: to misunder-
stand American history, to reinterpret Scripture, and to promote civil religion.

Burghardt, Walter J.
"From Classroom to Pulpit: How to Preach Dogma." *Proceedings of the* **705**
Catholic Homiletic Society Charter Convention (1961): 23-35.

Buttrick, David G.
"Preaching on the Resurrection." *Religion in Life* 45 (1976): 278-95. Dis- **706**
cusses some problems with preaching resurrection and some techniques for
solving them.

Caird, George B.
"Expounding the Parables: I, The Defendant (Matt. 5:25f.; Luke 12:58f.)." **707**
Expository Times 77 (1965): 36-39. Discusses the meaning of the parable of
the defendant and how this parable can be used in modern preaching.

Candeland, Arthur
"Psalms and the Preacher." *Preacher's Quarterly* 11 (1965): 31-36. After **708**
suggesting ways to preach the imprecatory passages, the author focuses on
five preachable ideas in the Psalms.

Carlton, John W.
"Preaching from the Johannine Epistles." *Review and Expositor* 67 (1970): **709**
473-83. Traces major themes developed in the Johannine epistles, and suggests
sermon ideas and applications for each.

"Proclaiming the Incarnation." *Review and Expositor* 71 (1974): 85-94. **710**
Stresses the reality of the incarnation, giving some implications for a Christian
world outlook and for preaching.

Carney, Francis W.
"Preaching the Social Doctrine of the Church." *Proceedings of the Catholic* **711**
Homiletic Society Charter Convention (1962): 20-28.

Chantry, Walter
"The Need for Preaching the Character of God." *Banner of Truth* (July **712**
1970): 9-11. Calls for the preaching of God's holiness as a prerequisite to
evangelism, thus helping the sinner recognize his sin.

Clinard, Gordon
"Biblical Preaching on Suffering." *Southwestern Journal of Theology* 1   **713**
(Apr 1959): 17-25. Outlines one's obligation to preach on suffering, and reviews
several biblical solutions to the problem of suffering.

"Preaching on Stewardship Themes." *Review and Expositor* 70 (1973):   **714**
197-206. Insists that preaching on stewardship stress such proper Christian
motivations as the giving of oneself to God before giving one's wealth.

"Preaching Values in the Epistle of James." *Southwestern Journal of*   **715**
Theology 12 (Fall 1969): 71-82. Encourages the preacher to preach a series of
sermons that moves through a biblical book, providing exegetical insights,
outlines, and principles gained from his own study.

Cox, James W.
"Preaching on the Great Themes." *Pulpit Digest* 59 (Sep 1979): 26. Exhorts   **716**
preachers to preach thematically, and suggests some ways to introduce the
themes to the congregation. The author commends the narrative approach as
the most effective one in highlighting a biblical theme.

Davis, M. Vernon
"Preaching from Job." *Southwestern Journal of Theology* 14 (Fall 1971):   **717**
65-76. Discusses some hard questions that plague one who decides to preach
the Book of Job.

De Jong, Alexander C.
"Is Not My Son a Sinner?" *Torch and Trumpet* 12 (Oct 1962): 3-4. Exhorts   **718**
the preacher to preach the whole counsel of God, including the sinfulness of
men.

Downing, F. Gerald
"Preaching from the Gospels Today." *Preacher's Quarterly* 14 (1968): 208-14.   **719**
Argues for the necessity of preaching today from the four Gospels.

Drescher, John
"What Will I Preach Next Sunday?" *Church Management* 51 (Jan 1975):   **720**
16-18. The problem of selecting sermon topics is analyzed. In choosing a
topic, says the author, the pastor needs to follow three guidelines: (1) the topic
should arise out of the people's needs; (2) it must be biblical; (3) the sermon
requires hard work.

Ebner, James D. R.
"Topics for Boys' Sermons." *Homiletic and Pastoral Review* 49 (1948):   **721**
213-21. Gives some down-to-earth areas one must investigate if one would
communicate with boys.

Edwards, Glen
"Preaching from the Book of Acts." *Southwestern Journal of Theology* 17   **722**
(Fall 1974): 65-81. Discusses the literary nature of the Book of Acts and ways to
preach from it.

Ferris, Frank Halliday
"Reflections of a Retired Preacher." *Pulpit Digest* 46 (Apr 1966): 9-13.   **723**
Suggests subjects the preacher should select from. The author speaks from the
vantage point of one who has preached and who now listens to much
preaching.

Finneran, Joan B.
"A Bloody Religion." *Presbyterian Journal*, 12 September 1979, pp. 9-10.   **724**
Ascribes the weakness of many churches today to the pastors' failure to
emphasize in their preaching the blood of Christ.

Francisco, Clyde T.
"Expository Themes in the Book of Exodus." *Review and Expositor* 74   **725**
(1977): 549-61. Suggests sermon ideas and applications derived from the major
themes of the Book of Exodus.

"Preaching from Problem Areas of the Bible." *Review and Expositor* 72   **726**
(1975): 203-14. Discusses the creation accounts of Genesis, the sub-Christian
ethical tone of Old Testament narratives, miracles, and prophecy fulfillments.

Garrison, Gene
"Preaching from Exodus." *Southwestern Journal of Theology* 20 (Fall   **727**
1977): 80-88. Treats the themes, types, and topics of the Book of Exodus.

Gideon, Virtus E.
"Preaching Values in Matthew 5." *Southwestern Journal of Theology* 5   **728**
(Oct 1962): 77-88. A New Testament professor suggests numerous titles and
seed thoughts for sermons on the Beatitudes. He also probes the "salt" and
"light" metaphors and Christ's various ethical teachings.

Harbuck, Don B.
"Preaching from Ephesians." *Southwestern Journal of Theology* 22 (Fall   **729**
1979): 56-73. Explains how to study the Book of Ephesians and how to preach
through it with perspective and purpose.

Harris, James G.
"Preaching from Luke." *Southwestern Journal of Theology* 10 (Fall 1967):   **730**
37-43. Presents insights on the development of the Gospel of Luke and on the
best homiletical approach to it.

Haygood, E. Langston
"Preaching Christ from Proverbs." *Journal of Pastoral Practice* 3, 4 (1979):   **731**
113–35. Shows how the Book of Proverbs can be preached with relevance to
Christians.

Higgins, George G.
"Preaching and Social Development." *American Ecclesiastical Review* 167   **732**
(1973): 121–33. A summary and brief commentary on statements concerning
the method of preaching social justice and charity.

Hinrichs, Everard
"Are We Preaching a Gospel Free from Law?" *Concordia Theological*   **733**
Monthly 29 (1958): 401–20. Suggests ways a preacher might preach the rela-
tionship between law and grace.

Hope, Norman V.
"Present-day Preaching and the Life to Come." *Expository Times* 52 (1941):   **734**
417–20. Discusses the destiny of those who reject Christ, those who accept
Him, and those who have never heard of Him. The author presents a way for
the Christian preacher to handle the doctrine of last things.

Horne, Chevis F.
"Preaching the Cosmic Christ to Cosmic Man." *Pulpit Digest* 51 (Apr   **735**
1971): 7–10, 66. Stresses the importance of preaching the doctrines of creation,
resurrection, and reconciliation to people today, who are aware of their failures
and achievements, and who need the hope found in Christ.

Howington, Nolan P.
"The Ethical Element in Preaching." *Review and Expositor* 62 (1965):   **736**
335–50. Urges preachers to address moral and ethical issues from a biblical
perspective. The author argues that the love ethic is so much a part of Scripture that the diligent preacher cannot avoid it.

Hoyer, George W.
" 'The Law and the Prophets.' " *Concordia Theological Monthly* 42 (1971):   **737**
443–46. Discusses one method of preaching the law, a method that can use
and interpret many aspects of life, from individual to societal.

Jones, Peter Rhea
"Preaching from Romans." *Review and Expositor* 73 (1976): 465–76.   **738**
Suggests a plan for preparing sermons based on the Book of Romans, then
identifies some great themes in that book, showing how they can be used in
preaching. The author describes chapters 9–11 as a hermeneutical problem for
which he has no solution.

Kippley, John F.
"Preaching on *Humanae vitae*." *Homiletic and Pastoral Review* 78 (Mar   **739**
1978): 15-19. A Catholic layman exhorts priests to preach on the sanctity of
human life, birth control, and abortion.

Koller, Charles W.
"Critical Themes in the Pulpit." *Christianity Today*, 4 June 1965, p. 35.   **740**
Suggests ways to handle problematic themes such as immorality while main-
taining good taste.

Liske, Thomas V.
"Contemporary Problems in Sunday Morning Preaching." *Proceedings of*   **741**
the Catholic Homiletic Society Charter Convention (1958): 51-57.

McBeth, Leon
"Preaching Values in Baptist History." *Southwestern Journal of Theology*   **742**
6 (Apr 1964): 111-22. A professor of church history uses several incidents in
Baptist history to show how brief studies of past events can minister to people
in the present.

Macleod, Donald
"Preaching Stewardship." *New Pulpit Digest* 56 (Nov 1976): 7-8. Studies   **743**
the biblical words for "steward" and the biblical concept of stewardship, and
suggests preaching approaches for stewardship Sundays.

Matthews, C. DeWitt
"Preaching from Colossians." *Southwestern Journal of Theology* 16 (Fall   **744**
1973): 49-63. Provides guidelines for preaching in general and a homiletical
outline of the Book of Colossians.

Menzies, Robert
"The Apocalyptic Note in Modern Preaching." *Evangelical Quarterly* 17   **745**
(1945): 81-90. Deals with the apocalyptic aspect of preaching and its relationship to history, the moral struggle, comfort, and social hopes.

Michael, J. Hugh
"Why Don't We Preach the Apocalypse?" *Expository Times* 49 (1938):   **746**
438-41. Argues for more preaching from the Book of Revelation, which is rich
in imagery for the preacher, and explains the book's "six great convictions."

Miller, Donald G.
"Preaching the Resurrection." *Asbury Seminarian* 24 (Jan 1970): 7-24.   **747**
Examines three responses to death (denial, acceptance, and defiance), and
urges as an antidote the preaching of resurrection.

Murray, Francis
    "Preaching the Miracles." *Worship* 42 (1968): 364–68. Miracle accounts 748
must be placed in the total context of the Gospels and of the authors' intentions before the preacher can adequately understand their meaning, writes the author. These accounts teach us about Christ our example, and the preaching of them must stir listeners to selfless action toward others.

Murray, J. J.
    "The Preacher's Use of Ezekiel." *Expository Times* 50 (1939): 314–16. Gives 749
the historical background to the neglected Book of Ezekiel, then suggests ways the preacher can deal with it.

Neil, William
    "Expounding the Parables: II, The Sower (Mark 4:3–8)." *Expository Times* 750
77 (1965): 74–77. Discusses the meaning of parables, designed to direct us to the great harvest of the kingdom. Then the author focuses on the parable of the sower, and particularly on the soils, supplying a series of steps for preaching this parable today.

Nelsen, Hart M.
    "Why Do Pastors Preach on Social Issues?" *Theology Today* 32 (1975): 751
56–73. Utilizes Samuel W. Blizzard's study of clergy roles.

Ockenga, Harold J.
    "Preaching from Romans." *Southwestern Journal of Theology* 19 (Fall 752
1976): 70–80. Reveals the central and subordinate themes of the Book of Romans, and offers suggestions for expository, textual, and biographical sermons.

Palmer, Edwin H.
    "Relevancy." *Torch and Trumpet* 20 (May 1970): 19. Advocates a balance in 753
preaching between social issues and biblical doctrines.

Piersma, John H.
    "Preaching About Political and Social Issues." *Torch and Trumpet* 10 754
(Nov 1960): 4. Urges the preacher to speak boldly against social inequities.

Ratzinger, Joseph
    "Preaching About God Today." *Theology Digest* 22 (1974): 196–201. 755
Presents seven theses to bear in mind when preaching about God.

Robinson, William Childs
    "What Shall the Preacher Preach?" *Christianity Today*, 26 April 1968, 756
pp. 10–11. A compilation of answers to the title question from well-known writers and ministers.

Ryle, J. C.
"Preach Hell." *Presbyterian Journal,* 11 December 1963, p. 1. An appeal to **757** preach on hell and thereby to promote faith, defeat the devil, and save souls.

Scott, Charles Wheeler
"Preaching Themes from the Christian Year." *Pulpit Digest* 49 (Dec 1968): **758** 11–14. Explains the Christian year, and encourages its use in preaching. The author shows how this can result in balanced, comprehensive, and objective sermon topics.

Scudder, C. W.
"Preaching on Moral Issues." *Southwestern Journal of Theology* 7 (Apr **759** 1965): 67–76. Pleads with ministers to be "pastoral prophets," willing to preach on moral issues, even those that are controversial or unpleasant.

Sheerin, John B.
"Buried Treasure in the Psalms." *Homiletic and Pastoral Review* 49 (1948): **760** 177–81. The early church fathers, including Augustine, often drew their sermon texts from the Psalms, the author points out, urging preachers today to do the same.

"Ideas for Christmas Sermons." *Homiletic and Pastoral Review* 53 (1952): **761** 213–17. Presents different approaches to the Christmas message.

Shell, William A.
"The Whole Counsel of God." *Other Side* 7 (Jan 1971): 13–15, 20. Proposes **762** that the whole counsel of God should be preached and that this includes contemporary social issues. The author discusses the failure of ministers to do so, based on a recent study.

Smith, Hoke, Jr.
"Preaching Values in Ephesians." *Southwestern Journal of Theology* 6 **763** (Oct 1963): 81–92. A former professor of New Testament offers preaching ideas for the Book of Ephesians, including themes, outlines, and titles.

Stanfield, Vernon L.
"Preaching Values in Jeremiah." *Southwestern Journal of Theology* 4 **764** (Oct 1961): 69–80. Suggests a basic outline for the Book of Jeremiah, briefly surveys its leading ideas and great texts, and includes a bibliography.

"Preaching Values in the Gospel of Matthew." *Review and Expositor* 59 **765** (1962): 512–17. Gives sources that help an expositor study the Gospel of Matthew for sermonic material, and suggests some preaching ideas.

Stedman, Ray
"A Steward of Mysteries." *Moody Monthly* 78 (Jan 1978): 104–7. Exhorts **766**

preachers to expound carefully and prayerfully the themes in Scripture relating
to "the mysteries of God."

Stevenson, Dwight E.
"Communicating Biblical Myths and Legends." *Religion in Life* 41 (1972): **767**
536-42. Calls·preachers to preach from the Old Testament narratives, and
discusses the interpretative process to be used with such literature.

"Preaching from the Book of Acts." *Review and Expositor* 71 (1974): 511-19. **768**
Suggests a method of studying the Book of Acts for sermon ideas, then offers
some ideas for preaching.

Strait, C. Neil
"Man Can Have a Great Life." *New Pulpit Digest* 56 (July 1976): 23. **769**
Suggests a positive approach to preaching, particularly through emphasis on
three basic themes.

"Proclaim a Great God." *Pulpit Digest* 58 (Jan 1978): 17. Exhorts pastors to **770**
preach the greatness of God and to reemphasize this theme in pastoral
visitation.

Strange, John O.
"Preaching from Amos." *Southwestern Journal of Theology* 9 (Fall 1966): **771**
69-79. Examines the themes and topics for preaching in the Book of Amos.

Tenney, Merrill C.
"Eschatology and the Pulpit." *Bibliotheca Sacra* 116 (1959): 30-42. Deals **772**
with the motive, content, and method of preaching on eschatology.

Tolar, William B.
"Preaching from Galatians." *Southwestern Journal of Theology* 15 (Fall **773**
1972): 77-89. Identifies in the Book of Galatians doctrinal themes and sermon
topics, and includes a bibliography on selected passages.

Tuck, William P.
"Preaching from Ephesians." *Review and Expositor* 76 (1979): 559-67. **774**
Captures the key idea of Ephesians and describes and lists the ways this book
can be preached. The author discusses ways to begin a study of the book as a
whole.

Ward, Ronald A.
"The Power of the Cross." *Christianity Today*, 1 April 1966, p. 30. Explores **775**
reasons why the death of Christ is not emphasized in current preaching.

The Preacher

Alexander, James N.
"The First Seven Years." *Expository Times* 62 (1951): 178-81. Argues that   776
the first seven years of one's ministry are determinative. The author identifies
the pastor's task as one of communication and effective sermon production,
and he gives advice for meeting the challenge.

Alexander, James W.
"Ministerial Study." *Banner of Truth* (Aug 1957): 11-15. Stresses the impor-   777
tance to the preacher of study, and suggests ways to improve the time spent in
study.

Anonymous
"Be a Man of God." *Presbyterian Journal,* 19 February 1975, pp. 10-11.   778
Calls preachers to be men of God, evidenced in their prayer lives, inoffensive-
ness, witness, and convictions held courageously.

"The Danger of Sterile Professionalism." *Torch and Trumpet* 11 (Apr   779
1961): 9-10. Lists five steps to follow in preaching well but without falling
into mere professionalism.

"How Can I Preach with Power?" *Torch and Trumpet* 11 (Apr 1961): 9.   780
One achieves the goal of preaching with power, writes the author, by first
living the truth in one's own life.

"A Minister Is Encouraged." *Presbyterian Journal,* 9 March 1966, pp. 10-11.   781
A preacher finds encouragement in seeking quality rather than quantity, a
biblical foundation to his sermons, and a response from the hearts of his
listeners.

"Payday Someday: The Message and the Man." *Proclaim* 7 (Oct 1976): 6.   782

"Read, Minister, Read!" *Christianity Today,* 12 February 1965, pp. 32-33.   783
Asserts that serious reading and study are essential to the preacher, and discusses types of necessary reading.

Asquith, Glenn H.
"Slap! Thanks, I Needed That!" *Christian Herald* 95 (Oct 1972): 40-43.   784
Articulates the problem of the preacher wanting people to come and hear
him, and thus becoming self-centered. The author explains how he overcame
this ego problem and discusses two things people want to hear.

Ayer, William Ward
"The Pulpit Prophet." *Bibliotheca Sacra* 124 (1967): 291-302. Calls for the   785
revival of prophetic preaching characterized by discernment, boldness to
condemn sin, and a humility spawned by a close relationship with God.

Barclay, William
"Prophet and Craftsman." *Expository Times* 61 (1949): 13–14. Gives reasons   **786**
why the preacher cannot disregard elements of craftsmanship, elements that
belong to the essence of the preacher's task.

Bateman, C. Robert
"Peddlers, or Purveyors and Persuaders." *Presbyterian Journal*, 20 April   **787**
1977, pp. 10–11. Paints the preacher as a purveyor and persuader for the glory
of God. The author urges the preacher to preach for his hearer's conversion,
not for popularity or success.

Bell, L. Nelson
"Hearts That Burn." *Christianity Today*, 16 July 1971, pp. 27–28. Insists   **788**
that the pulpit be a channel for transmitting divine power to the pew. This is
possible, says the author, only when the message centers on Christ in the
power of the Spirit.

Blustein, Allan M.
"How to Preach like the Prophets." *Church Management* 55 (Nov 1978):   **789**
28. An overview of talmudic thought on ways to develop a prophetic ministry.

Bodo, John R.
"The Pastor's Role as Prophet." *Theology Today* 18 (1961): 172–79. Pleads   **790**
with ministers to share leadership responsibilities, give first priority to Bible
study, practice truly biblical preaching, and engage in a prophetic ministry,
speaking God's Word with power.

Bolus, Michael
"Pastoral Honesty." *Presbyterian Journal*, 17 November 1976, pp. 9–11.   **791**
Contends that one of the greatest needs in the church today is pastoral honesty
in general and particularly in the pulpit. The author defines this as the
ability to deal with one's own sinful nature and that of those in the
congregation.

Bounds, E. M.
"The Preacher and Prayer." *Banner of Truth* (Nov 1965): 1–2. An extract   **792**
from *Power Through Prayer*, encouraging preachers to be men of prayer.

Brack, Harold A.
"The Listening Preacher." *Religious Communication Today* (Sep 1978):   **793**
18–20. Highlights the need for preachers to listen to their own messages as
well as preach them.

Brokhoff, John R.
"Can the Pulpit Recover Its Authority?" *Princeton Seminary Bulletin* 65   **794**

(Dec 1972): 73–79. Discusses the preacher's authority to speak, establishing where the authority is and how it comes across to the hearers.

"What Great Preachers Have in Common." *New Pulpit Digest* 57 (May **795**
1977): 29–34. Shows that great preachers had a firsthand relationship with God, a faith in preaching, the Bible as their textbook, a willingness to work hard, and a deep love for people.

Brown, Bob W.
"Why Are So Many Pastors Leaving Their Pulpits?" *Eternity* 17 (June **796**
1966): 8–9. Details reasons for the exodus of seminary students and pastors from the pulpit ministry.

Brown, C. J.
"Ministerial Guilt." *Banner of Truth* (Mar 1962): 5–15. An address delivered **797**
in 1844 discussing six aspects of the preacher's life that can weaken his effectiveness.

Brown, Robert McAfee
"The Minister and Contemporary Literature." *Union Seminary Quarterly* **798**
Review 12 (Nov 1956): 9–19. Surveys reasons why the minister should read contemporary literature, showing that it can help him to understand his people better and to detect irrelevance in his preaching.

Burnett, Brewer L.
"The Congregation." *Pulpit Digest* 45 (Mar 1965): 12–16. Teaches young **799**
preachers how to maintain a proper relationship with their congregation, thus enabling them to have an effective ministry. The Scripture text is Luke 4:14–30.

"Ready to Preach." *Pulpit Digest* 45 (Jan 1965): 13–18. Derives from the **800**
Lukan narrative of the temptation of Jesus (4:1–13) principles by which the young man can determine if he is ready to begin a preaching ministry.

Cain, Lincoln S.
"If I Were a Minister." *Minister's Quarterly* 13 (June 1957): 5–9. A prominent **801**
layman tells why he believes preaching and sermon preparation should be of premier importance to the minister.

Carroll, Thomas P.
"Getting Through from Pulpit to Pew." *Homiletic and Pastoral Review* 64 **802**
(1964): 397–402. A look at preachers' attitudes toward preaching and how these attitudes affect their ministries.

Castagnola, Lawrence A.
"Preaching and Personal Faith." *Pastoral Life* 16 (1968): 501–5. Contends **803**
that effective preaching is only born of struggle with faith, hope, and love.

Coker, William B.
"Prophetic Succession." *Asbury Seminarian* 24 (Jan 1970): 3-6. Defends **804**
the preacher's prophetic role, then expands on these concepts: (1) a conscious
identification as a prophet, (2) a personal identification with the preaching,
and (3) a compassionate identification with the people.

Cook, Charles E.
"Paul the Christian: A Preacher's Devotional Study." *Expository Times* 60 **805**
(1949): 212-14. Draws attention to Paul as a Christian and as an exemplar of
the modern minister's own personal devotional life. The author simultaneously suggests ideas that may prove to be of value in sermonizing.

Cook, Finlay
"The Ministry That Reaches the Heart." *Banner of Truth* (Dec 1970): 40. A **806**
nineteenth-century English preacher, writing at the time of his retirement,
points out characteristics of a ministry that reaches people's hearts: love of
God's Word, understanding of doctrine, and much time spent in prayer.

Craghan, John F.
"Ezekiel: A Pastoral Theologian." *American Ecclesiastical Review* 166 **807**
(1972): 22-33. Looks at the prophet Ezekiel's methodology of preaching.

Crosser, Harold R.
"Preach, Pastor!" *Christianity Today*, 15 April 1966, pp. 11-12. Singles out **808**
the fearless preaching of God's Word as the pastor's greatest responsibility, and
analyzes the varied roles he must play.

Crum, Milton, Jr.
"Preaching: What I Am About." *Worship* 50 (1976): 194-206. Identifies the **809**
preacher's dual task as allowing God to teach him through the Scriptures and
communicating to his people what he has learned.

Culbertson, William
"The Preacher's Mind and Heart." Edited by Warren W. Wiersbe. *Moody* **810**
Monthly 76 (July 1976): 93-96. Instructs the preacher who wishes to be used
by God to do three things: study the Word, love God, and love his people.

"The Preacher's Preparation." *Moody Monthly* 71 (Feb 1971): 53-54. Con- **811**
siders the balance between the preacher's devotional life and scholarship,
contending that the sermon should affect the preacher's daily life as he prepares
it.

Cullom, W. R.
"The Minister as Student." *Review and Expositor* 36 (1939): 204-13. **812**
Appeals to preachers to be diligent in study, suggests a method of study, and
explains how to use good books and periodicals.

Dana, Daniel
"Importance of Seriousness to the Christian Minister." *Banner of Truth* **813**
(Aug 1957): 5-10. Stresses the seriousness of the minister's task, including his preaching, and cautions against levity.

Davidson, J. A.
"What's Wrong with the Sermon?" *Pulpit Digest* 58 (Sep 1978): 55. De- **814**
scribes pastors' great need for adequate time to prepare their sermons.

Dayton, Edward R.
"Hey, Pastor! Forget the World—Just Remember Us Sheep!" *Eternity* 20 **815**
(Apr 1969): 20-21. Pleads with pastors to pour themselves into meeting the needs of their congregations, rather than into "being relevant to the world."

"A Layman Speaks His Mind." *Christian Minister* 5 (June 1969): 19, 34. A **816**
layman gives four ways the preacher can help laymen to relate their beliefs to their lives.

De Jong, Peter Y.
"Declare It, Preacher, Declare It!" *Torch and Trumpet* 15 (Sep 1965): 21. **817**
Stresses the need for ministers to preach with conviction and clarity.

De Kruyter, John A.
"Sabbaticals for the Ministry." *Torch and Trumpet* 16 (Mar 1966): 11-12. **818**
Recommends a sabbatical to enable pastors to refresh themselves, especially for their pulpit ministries.

Delapp, Sim A.
"What a Layman Expects of His Minister." *Presbyterian Journal*, 23 April **819**
1969, pp. 7-8. Asserts that the layman expects his minister to be godly, practice what he preaches, and provide spiritual food from the Word of God.

deVries, Abraham
"Ignorant Preachers." *Christianity Today*, 2 January 1970, pp. 8-10. Affirms **820**
that the preacher who desires an enduring prophetic ministry must be an able exegete of Scripture, and that this requires facility in Greek and Hebrew.

de Witt, John Richard
"Letter from America, 3." *Banner of Truth* (Nov 1974): 16-20. Advises **821**
young preachers to take advantage of their precious beginning years to develop disciplined study habits and reading programs.

"Some Criticisms Considered." *Banner of Truth* (June 1975): 9-13; (July **822**
1975): 1-6; (Dec 1975): 15-21, 32. Calls the preacher to hold in balance a sensitivity toward the congregation's needs and a determination to continue preaching God's Word.

Dover, John
"The Preacher's Calling." *Preacher's Quarterly* 14 (1968): 113–19. Describes   **823**
the threefold function of the preaching ministry, emphasizing the two functions of kerygma and didache, and the necessary qualifications of a preacher.

Echlin, Edward P.
"The Priest Is a Preacher." *Homiletic and Pastoral Review* 73 (Mar 1973):   **824**
17–24. Defends historically and culturally the Second Vatican Council's
emphasis on the priest's work of preaching God's Word. The author includes
in preaching not only the proclamation of the gospel but also the explanation
to people of what it means to be a Christian.

Erickson, George V.
"What Is a Minister Supposed to Do?" *Eternity* 13 (Aug 1962): 26–27,   **825**
37–38. Lays down guidelines for an effective, significant ministry, guidelines
dealing with five areas of life ranging from the pulpit to the home.

Fant, Clyde E.
"A Prophet of Their Own: Literature and the Sermon." *Southwestern*   **826**
Journal of Theology 10 (Spring 1968): 63–71. Stresses the importance of
reading widely in literature for a grasp of man's dilemma and a wealth of
illustrations, and proposes a reading plan.

Farmer, Herbert H.
"The Preacher and Culture." *Review and Expositor* 44 (1947): 34–49.   **827**
Rehearses the need and reasons for the preacher to maintain a cultural life,
including a study of past and contemporary culture, and calls for a discrimi-
natory use of it.

"The Preacher and Persons." *Review and Expositor* 43 (1946): 403–18.   **828**
Stresses the need for a close personal relationship between pastor and congregation, suggests some attitudes to assist the pastor in developing love and
sympathy for people, and shows how this affects one's preaching.

Faulkner, Brooks
"Expectations of the Minister's Role." *Search* 8 (Win 1978): 30–36. Reflects   **829**
on the pastoral role, biblically and historically, and reviews two recent surveys
of pastors' views of their role and identity.

Flavel, John
"The Character of a Complete Evangelical Pastor Drawn by Christ."   **830**
Banner of Truth (Aug 1957): 16–23. Notes of a sermon delivered to an assembly
of ministers about 1688.

Flucke, Paul
"Not with Skillful Words." *Christian Ministry* 6 (Nov 1975): 37-38. De- **831**
scribes faults with today's preaching due to pastors' doubt, drought, and
hypocrisy.

Francis, David
"What Is a Local Preacher?" *Preacher's Quarterly* 11 (1965): 138-42. Records **832**
and comments on a statement issued by the Methodist Conference in England
on "The Place and Function of the Local Preacher."

Fulton, J. Wayte, Jr.
"Preparing to Preach." *Christianity Today,* 19 August 1966, pp. 23-24. **833**
Thoughts on spiritual and intellectual forms of preparation needed for
preaching.

Furgeson, Earl H.
"The Person of the Preacher." *Religion in Life* 39 (1970): 567-81. Argues **834**
that the quality of a man's preaching depends greatly upon his character. The
author examines the dynamics of the preacher's hermeneutics and ethos with
respect to interpretation and proclamation.

Gaebelein, Frank E.
"The Minister and His Work." *Christianity Today,* 1 January 1965, pp. 8- **835**
10. Views the minister's preaching-related responsibilities alongside his identity, burden, and overall purpose.

Garman, F. E.
"Wanted: More Pastors and Fewer Preachers." *Eternity* 18 (July 1967): 33, **836**
40. Argues that the pastor's work of shepherding is swallowed up by his work
of preaching, and examines the shepherd's duties.

Gesing, Alphonse J.
"Toward a New Pastoral Synthesis." *Pastoral Life* 15 (1967): 601-3. Exhorts **837**
beginning pastors to preach to people, not just souls, and to experience
himself what he preaches.

Gibson, A. M.
"Theology and the Parish Minister." *Expository Times* 69 (1958): 144-46. **838**
Contends for the necessity of preachers giving time to the study of theology.

Gilmour, S. MacLean
"How to Fail in the Ministry Without Really Trying." *Christianity Today,* **839**
16 September 1966, pp. 3-4. Lists ways to become ineffective in the ministry,
including preaching.

Gray, John R.
"The Preacher's Syndrome: A Ministerial Malaise." *Princeton Seminary*   **840**
Bulletin 65 (Dec 1972): 91–92. Many preachers, says the author, have a recurring
fear of the pulpit, a fear sometimes stemming from an experience in the
pulpit when ill. He gives advice on overcoming this fear.

Greene, Thayer A.
"Roots and Fruits: The History of a Document." *Union Seminary Quar-*   **841**
terly Review 16 (Mar 1961): 263–74. Discusses the changing image of the
minister, one that challenges the necessity of such traditional functions as
preaching, leading in worship, caring for souls, and presiding over the church.
This image, the author writes, calls for more direct participation in church
life by the laity.

Greenway, Leonard
"Occupational Diseases of the Ministry." *Torch and Trumpet* 2 (Dec 1952):   **842**
5, 31–32. Identifies three potential problems for the preacher: fear, softness,
and boastfulness.

Grier, W. J.
"Boldness in the Work of the Ministry." *Banner of Truth* (Apr 1972): 1–5.   **843**
Urges ministers to preach with boldness, then looks at examples of boldness,
its incentives, and its rewards.

Gurnall, William
"Ministerial Boldness." *Banner of Truth* (Aug 1957): 36. Advocates boldness   **844**
on the part of the preacher, and gives ways to achieve it.

Halvorson, Arndt L.
"The Formation of a Preacher-Pastor." *Luther Theological Seminary*   **845**
Review 13 (Spring 1974): 27–39. Poetically expresses the view that the ministry
is the preaching of God's Word so that men and women can understand and
obey it.

Havner, Vance
"What Kind of Preacher Do We Need?" *Proclaim* 6 (July 1976): 38.   **846**

Hill, William E., Jr.
"Men of Faith." *Presbyterian Journal*, 14 February 1968, pp. 7–8. Describes   **847**
the preacher as a man of faith who is unconcerned with human approval and
who, despite fear, lack of peace, and lack of prosperity, is obedient to God.

Hodges, Graham R.
"Shattering the Composite Pastor Image." *Pulpit Digest* 42 (Sep 1961):   **848**
39–40, 42. A plea for ministers to resist the pressure to conform to the "pastoral

image." The author includes the implications of this nonconformity for one's pulpit ministry.

Horne, Chevis F.
"Who Are These False Prophets?" *Search* 7 (Sum 1977): 47–50. Exhorts   **849**
preachers to remain true to their calling in the face of excessive institutionalism, excessive professionalism, evasive preaching, and cultural pressures.

Huissen, Christian
"Ministers, Counselors, and Quacks!" *Torch and Trumpet* 13 (July 1963):   **850**
4. Asks pastors to remember their responsibility to preach the word and avoid overinvolvement in counseling.

Irons, Joseph
"An Ordination Charge." *Banner of Truth* (Nov 1968): 7–10. A nineteenth-   **851**
century sermon charging preachers to preach with diligence and conviction, striving for a change in men's souls and depending on the Holy Spirit.

Johnson, Kurt E.
"The Human Touch in Preaching." *Pulpit Digest* 50 (Nov 1969): 12–14.   **852**
Expresses five things preachers should consider before stepping into the pulpit.

Johnson, Robert Inman
"Speech Personality in Effective Preaching." *Review and Expositor* 35   **853**
(1938): 391–408. Identifies the improvement of one's personality as the key to improving one's speech ability. The author also discusses the message and the effect of ethos on an audience.

Jones, William
"The Role of the Minister." *Presbyterian Journal,* 5 April 1967, pp. 7–8.   **854**
Argues that the pastor's key responsibility is to preach the Word of God for the purpose of equipping saints for ministry. Social action and political involvement, the author writes, should be secondary.

Kerr, Hugh T.
"The Pastor and the Prophet." *Theology Today* 33 (1977): 325–28.   **855**

Kistemaker, Simon
"The New Testament Portrait of the Minister: III, Proclaim the Word."   **856**
Outlook 21 (Jan 1971): 20–23. Encourages ministers to preach God's Word, using Paul as an example.

"The Servant of the Word: New Testament Portrait of the Minister." *Torch*   **857**
and Trumpet 20 (Oct 1970): 14–15; (Nov 1970): 19–22. Analyzes the minister's functions of pastoring, teaching, and preaching, and concludes that the best

description of the minister is "servant." The author employs Matthew 28:19-20 to suggest that the pastor should both baptize and teach.

Kort, Dick
"A Serious Word to Our Young Preachers." *Torch and Trumpet* 11 (Apr   **858**
1961): 22-24. Encourages beginning preachers to prepare themselves through study and other means.

Koyama, Kosuke
"Communication Is the Communicator." *Spectrum: Christian Communi-*   **859**
cations 1 (Fall 1975): 25. Contends that the message and the messenger must become one, the message becoming incarnated in the messenger as it was in Abraham, Jeremiah, and Paul.

Kruis, John G.
"Preachers Without Fear." *Outlook* 21 (June 1971): 15-17. Maintains that   **860**
preachers must speak the full truth regardless of the possible scorn of those who hear the message.

Kruithof, Bastian
"The 'New' Role of the Minister." *Presbyterian Journal,* 6 November 1968,   **861**
pp. 9-10. Examines the minister's "new" role, and reminds him of his first responsibility: to preach God's Word. If this is neglected, there remains no foundation for social action.

Kuiper, Henry J.
"The Minister as a Shepherd." *Torch and Trumpet* 8 (Nov 1958): 4-5.   **862**
Explores the demands placed on the minister, particularly their effect on his time for study and the preparation of sermons.

Kuiper, R. B.
"A Layman Lauds His Pastor." *Torch and Trumpet* 15 (July 1965): 14-17.   **863**
Stresses various ways the pastor can serve his people. Prominent among these, the author claims, is preaching on various subjects.

Lindbeck, George A.
"The Lutheran Doctrine of the Ministry: Catholic and Reformed." *Theo-*   **864**
logical Studies 30 (1969): 588-612. Discusses the traditional Lutheran doctrine of the ministry in the light of contemporary developments and of current Catholic thought.

Lindemann, Herbert
"The Pastor as Scholar." *Concordia Theological Monthly* 38 (1967): 69-76.   **865**
The pastor should be a scholar and preach like one, insists the author. Though Scripture does not require this, history demonstrates the sad consequences of

ignoring this principle. And the large number of educated laymen today makes it imperative.

Luccock, Halford E.
"What Literature Can Do for a Preacher." *Review and Expositor* 42 (1945):   **866**
255-65. An appeal for preachers to use good literature not as a mere instrument but to develop the mind and personality.

McAllister, F. B.
"What Did Preaching Get You?" *Church Management* 47 (Nov 1970):   **867**
30-31, 39. A retired preacher, reflecting on his ministry, concludes that despite all the sacrifices, his life was well invested and very happy.

Macartney, Clarence Edward
"The Preacher and His Reading." *Pulpit Digest* 25 (July 1945): 15-18.   **868**
Encourages the pastor to increase his outside reading for better sermon preparation.

McCord, James I.
"The Theological Dilemma of the Protestant Minister." *Princeton Semi-*   **869**
nary Bulletin 54 (Nov 1960): 3-10. Concludes that the office of ministry of the word must not be eclipsed by the role of pastor-director.

McDowell, Leonard O.
"The Minister's Priorities." *Pulpit Digest* 49 (Sep 1968): 16-18. Reports a   **870**
survey of pastors (conducted by the National Council of Churches) in which they ranked their functions (including preaching) and correlated them with the church's needs.

McFarland, John Robert
"Where Are the Great Preachers Today?" *New Pulpit Digest* 56 (Sep 1976):   **871**
63-64. Argues that the day of the "great preachers" is past, and follows with a description of another kind of great preacher that better fits today's world.

Machen, J. Gresham
"Machen's Challenge to Prospective Ministers." *Torch and Trumpet* 17   **872**
(Jan 1967): 10. A message to students at Princeton Theological Seminary, encouraging them to remain true to what they have been taught, in their preaching and in every other aspect of their lives.

MacLennan, David A.
"I." *Pulpit Digest* 34 (Feb 1954): 19-24, 26. Explains when and to what   **873**
extent a preacher should inject into his preaching his own personality.

"Priming the Preacher's Pump." *Church Management* 43 (Oct 1966): 28.   **874**
Explores the danger to a preacher of seeking personal popularity.

"Priming the Preacher's Pump." *Church Management* 43 (May 1967): 34.   875
Presents seven essentials for pastoral success, the first being strong, biblical,
relevant, and interesting preaching.

Macleod, Donald
"Ambassadors for Christ." *Banner of Truth* (May 1977): 5-12. Identifies the   876
preacher as a witness and defender of the kerygma, noting the manner of life
and presentation that the preacher should have.

"The Creative Preacher." *Southwestern Journal of Theology* 3 (Apr 1961):   877
7-24. Argues that modern culture demands creativity on the preacher's part,
and suggests what the creative minister must do to be effective.

Macquarrie, John
"The Church and the Ministry: I, Ministerial Functions." *Expository*   878
Times 87 (1976): 113-18. Reprinted. "The Function and Character of Ministry."
Theology Digest 24 (1976): 237-45. Classifies the functions of the ministry
under three headings: serving, proclaiming, and priestly. Proclamation, says
the author, is authoritative because its content comes from God.

Martens, Wilfred
"Portraits of the Preacher in American Fiction." *Christianity Today*, 3   879
December 1971, pp. 12-13. Describes the preacher's image in American novels
as negative, and explores the type of failures depicted by novelists.

Martin, Ralph P.
"The Authority of the Preacher." *Christianity Today*, 8 June 1973, pp. 10,   880
12, 14. A four-point explanation of the sort of authority belonging to the
preaching office and the need for this authority today. This article is based on
Ephesians 3:7-8.

May, Cecil, Jr.
"To Preachers, from a Preacher." *Presbyterian Journal*, 17 November 1976,   881
p. 11. A preacher admonishes fellow preachers not to use other men's sermons,
but to mine the Bible for themselves. Only in this way, he says, will their
hearts be in their message.

Meiburg, Albert L.
"The Preaching Pastor." *Review and Expositor* 50 (1953): 430-33. Insists   882
that preaching and pastoral work are mutually dependent. The author sees
the goal of preaching as salvation, unity, and application of religion to life,
and he contends that pastoral work contributes to these ends.

Mitton, C. Leslie
"Devotional and Pastoral Classics: George Herbert's *The Country Parson*."   883
Expository Times 69 (1958): 113-15. Recommends this classic for its high view
of preaching and its many "gems on the pulpit ministry."

Montgomery, John Warwick
"The High Calling." *Presbyterian Journal*, 25 April 1973, p. 10. The high **884**
call of preaching is attained with difficulty, the author writes, and it is lost
with ease. To rise to this calling the preacher must declare the Word of the
Lord.

"Preachers and Roosters." *Presbyterian Journal*, 23 May 1973, p. 10. **885**
Compares preachers to roosters, showing the danger of preachers' presenting
drivel boastfully rather than God's Word humbly.

Morgan, G. Campbell
"Fifty Years' Preaching." Edited by Warren W. Wiersbe. *Moody Monthly* 72 **886**
(May 1972): 61–63. Emphasizes the need to preach the whole truth of the Bible
and not speculate in the philosophical realm.

Morrison, James
"Prayer in the Life of a Minister." *Banner of Truth* (Apr 1968): 37–40. **887**
Declares the necessity of fervent prayer to the preacher's preparation of his
heart to communicate God's message.

Mueller, Charles S.
"Pastoral Preaching to People in the Parish." *Concordia Theological* **888**
Monthly 42 (1971): 48–53. Although proficiency in the pulpit is important,
the author says, only when the preacher is obviously committed to his faith
and his congregation will his preaching be effective.

Munzell, Adrian
"The Inside Influence." *Presbyterian Journal*, 16 September 1970, pp. 10–11, **889**
17. Exhorts preachers to function in the power of the Holy Spirit and prayer,
and describes the need for preaching Christ crucified and resurrected.

Murray, John J.
"Can We Have a Part-time Ministry?" *Banner of Truth* (Mar 1968): 7–9. **890**
Calls for churches to settle for nothing less than a full-time preacher, citing
scriptural support for this position.

Narramore, Clyde M.
"Tell It Like It Is!" *Psychology for Living* 13 (Feb 1971): 2. Explains why **891**
preachers are not proclaiming the full gospel, reasons related to the preacher's
own insecurity.

Norden, Rudolph
"In Perils in the Pulpit." *Concordia Theological Monthly* 25 (1954): **892**
449–55. Discusses pitfalls faced by the preacher.

Oates, Wayne
"The Preacher and His Relation to the Unconscious." *Review and Exposi-*   **893**
tor 42 (1945): 427-43. Shows how a study of psychology can be of practical
benefit to the minister not only in his pastoral work, but also in his preaching.

Olford, Stephen F.
"The Power of Preaching." *Christianity Today*, 7 December 1979, pp. 21-   **894**
25. Discusses key elements of preaching that is powerful and effective.

O'Neal, Glenn F.
"Making Preaching Relevant." *King's Business* 61 (1970): 32-33. Presents   **895**
four ways to effective preaching: (1) be aware of man's needs; (2) believe Christ
is the answer to man's need; (3) have a heart for the people; and (4) have a
sense of urgency.

Owen, John
"Why We Have Lost Powerful Preaching." *Banner of Truth* (Nov 1970): 16.   **896**
Explains that the lack of power in one's preaching is due to the preacher
speaking only with his mind and not with his heart.

Palmer, Edwin H.
"How Long a Vacation for Ministers?" *Torch and Trumpet* 10 (Nov 1960):   **897**
3. Advocates a four-week vacation for ministers, in part for the positive effect it
will have on their preaching.

Patterson, LeRoy
"Over-Exposure: The Dulling of a Minister." *Eternity* 22 (Sep 1971): 15,   **898**
39-40. A plea for pastors to share their pulpits with members and outside
speakers more often than they do.

Perry, Lloyd M.
"Preaching with Power and Purpose." *Christianity Today*, 2 February 1979,   **899**
pp. 21-25. A call for returning to powerful and effective preaching by recognizing its importance and purpose.

Rhodes, Terry J., and Wright, Joel S.
"Role Expectations of the Minister." *Search* 8 (Fall 1977): 14-16. Based on   **900**
research that reveals possible areas of divergence between minister and laity:
counseling abilities, preaching, teaching, and visitation.

Rhonemus, Sharon Ann
"What Does Authority Have to Do with a Woman Minister? A Look at   **901**
I Timothy 2:12." *Asbury Seminarian* 31 (July 1976): 11-18. An ordained Methodist examines the New Testament concept of authority, finding support for
the role of a female minister on both the lay and vocational levels.

Rohrbaugh, James L.
"First Pastorate." *Presbyterian Journal*, 19 February 1975, p. 9. When a man   **902**
knows that God has called him to preach, the author testifies, he can count on
God's assistance.

Schmidt, John
"Preaching: Hard Work, Plus." *Christianity Today*, 23 June 1967, pp. 26–   **903**
27. Emphasizes the preparation not of sermons but of the preacher. The
author, a Lutheran pastor, explains the advantages of preaching extempo-
raneously.

Sell, A. P. F.
"'The Christian's Great Interest'—and the Preacher's." *Evangelical Quar-*   **904**
terly 46 (1974): 72–80. Uses William Guthrie's classic, *The Christian's Great
Interest*, to pose fundamental questions to preachers of our day.

Shannon, Robert C.
"The Preaching Minister." *Seminary Review* 20 (1974): 73–82. Reprinted   **905**
in *New Pulpit Digest* 55 (Jan 1975): 60–63. A plea for more and better preaching, and a description of many preachers past and present.

Shelton, Robert M.
"Freed to Preach." *Austin Seminary Bulletin* 91 (Nov 1975): 7–36. Lists   **906**
three causes for the fear of preaching, then discusses ways to experience
authentic freedom to preach.

Stacey, David
"Clues from the Old Testament." *Preacher's Quarterly* 11 (1965): 110–17.   **907**
Finds points of contrast and agreement between Old Testament prophets and
modern preachers.

Stacey, John
"Truth Through Personality." *Preacher's Quarterly* 13 (1967): 180–84.   **908**
Focuses on the meaning of personality and the relationship between a
preacher's personality and his preaching.

Starenko, Ronald C.
"Preaching and Counseling." *Concordia Theological Monthly* 42 (1971):   **909**
633–37. Argues that a pastor should specialize in neither preaching nor counseling, since the exposure to counseling helps him determine the content and
form of the sermon.

Stevenson, Dwight E.
"Giving Voice to Faith." *Lexington Theological Quarterly* 3 (1968): 75–84.   **910**
Insists that a preacher must expect results from his preaching, and that he
must preach each sermon through his own personality.

Strait, C. Neil
"I Wish I Had Studied More." *Pulpit Digest* 58 (1978): 18. Gives practical   **911**
suggestions for improving and increasing one's study time. The author, a
veteran preacher, wishes he had studied more and preached less.

"Summer Checkup." *New Pulpit Digest* 55 (July 1975): 13. Suggests that   **912**
the preacher use the time after a vacation to plan for the upcoming year and
to review what needs to be changed, particularly in the area of preaching.

Stratman, Gary D.
"Of Preaching and Preparation." *Church Management* 52 (Apr 1976):   **913**
27-29. Discusses several disciplines necessary to the preparation and delivery
of sermons week after week: reading theological works, communicating person
to person, writing down thoughts, and keeping a journal.

Strong, Robert
"The Making of a Minister." *Presbyterian Journal*, 23 April 1969, pp. 8-10.   **914**
Affirms that the minister's primary responsibility is preaching; his secondary
responsibility, pastoring.

Stuart, Alexander Moody
"The Spiritual Condition of the Ministry and Its Influence on the People."   **915**
Banner of Truth (Sep 1961): 25-28. Identifies essentials to a pulpit ministry
that is spiritual.

Sugden, Howard F.
"A Ministry of Power." Edited by Warren W. Wiersbe. *Moody Monthly* 72   **916**
(Apr 1972): 77-81. Describes the nature of the preacher's ministry, dangers to
avoid, and the need to identify with the people.

Tennent, Gilbert
"The Danger of an Unconverted Ministry." *Presbyterian Journal*, 13 April   **917**
1966, pp. 9-10. First preached in 1740, this famous sermon urges preachers to
examine their worth as communicators of God's Word.

Thompson, John
"Is There a Prophet in the Land?" *Christianity Today*, 24 June 1966,   **918**
pp. 3-4. Argues that only when ministers take a prophetic stance can the
church fulfill her true mission, being the voice of God in a hostile world.

Tolman, George L.
"The Minister as Prophet." *Christian Ministry* 9 (May 1978): 34-36.   **919**
Analyzes the ministry of biblical prophets and its implications for preachers
today.

Torgersen, Gordon M.

"Peace Activity in a Local Congregation and How It Affects a Ministry." **920** *Foundations* 15 (1972): 319–32. Relates a pastor's involvement in peace activities in the 1970s and its adverse effects on his ministry and congregation. The author includes references to his sermons during this period.

Torry, Peter

"The Mystery and Power of Preaching." *Christianity Today*, 22 September **921** 1978, pp. 30–31. Deals with the mystery of preaching, which, because God speaks through the preacher, should be done with power and confidence.

Turner, John Munsey

"The Consecration of a Bishop." *Expository Times* 85 (1973): 9–11. A **922** sermon that explores the bishop's roles of pastor, teacher, prophet, and administrator. The pastor must help people see their little part in God's bigger design, says the author.

Vander Ploeg, John

"Dynamite in the Pulpit." *Outlook* 24 (Nov 1974): 5–7. Examines the **923** essentials of powerful preaching, and exhorts the reader to preach the Bible.

"Pulpits Without Power." *Presbyterian Journal*, 17 April 1968, pp. 11, 19. **924** Identifies prerequisites for pulpit power as a continual, thorough study of God's Word and a thoughtful consideration of problems today.

Van Houten, Fred

"Preaching: We Can't Quit!" *Outlook* 24 (Feb 1974): 8–9. Exhorts preachers **925** to remain at their pulpits preaching God's Word, no matter how difficult the task.

Wallace, Horace F.

"The Emphasis in the Work of the Ministry." *Expository Times* 52 (1941): **926** 296–99. Questions the dictum that preaching is the minister's prime task. The author would make it teaching instead.

Wiersbe, Warren W.

"Discouragement: An Occupational Hazard." *Moody Monthly* 75 (Sep **927** 1974): 67–71. Examines discouragement in the life of the preacher, and reveals what the Bible and great preachers of the past have said about it.

"The Pastor and Prayer." *Moody Monthly* 72 (Nov 1971): 47–51. Insists that **928** a vital prayer life is essential to preaching the Word of God effectively.

Williams, Daniel Day

"Authority and Ministry." *Union Seminary Quarterly Review* 14 (Nov **929** 1958): 17–23. The divine source of their authority requires preachers and teachers of God's Word, the author contends, to exercise a patient acceptance of human problems.

Wilson, Marvin R.
"A Question for Rabbis, Pastors, and Teachers." *Christianity Today*, 14   **930**
February 1969, pp. 5-7. Argues that pastors must set a time to study if they are
to preach more effectively, and looks at Jewish practices that bear on the task
of preaching.

Wood, Arthur
"The Preacher and Nature." *Preacher's Quarterly* 13 (1967): 47-53. Lists   **931**
three advantages of becoming a student of nature: it provides a treasury of
illustrations, exalts the mind and character, and promotes bodily health.

Wood, Frederic C., Jr.
"Kerygma and Therapy: The Pastor's Dilemma." *Union Seminary Quar-*   **932**
terly Review 18 (Jan 1963): 123-34. Surveys the roles of pastoral care and
preaching, asking which should be primary.

Zavitz, Lance
"Clergymen I Have Known." *Christianity Today*, 24 June 1966, pp. 14-16.   **933**
Recounting personal experiences as a journalist, the author exposes types of
ministers who cheapen their profession.

The Congregation

Adams, Henry B.
"The Role of Feedback in Preaching." *Pulpit* 37 (Dec 1966): 17-18.   **934**
Suggests that feedback from those who hear the sermon is the primary means
for growth in preaching. Thus the author urges preachers to create a preaching
context conducive to constructive feedback.

Anonymous
"Memos to My Pastor." *Eternity* 20 (Apr 1969): 11-14. Letters to a new   **935**
pastor explaining why his sermons are not gaining a hearing (e.g., using old
sermons and dropping names).

App, Austin J.
"Do Collegians Like Your Sermons?" *Homiletic and Pastoral Review* 62   **936**
(1962): 600-604. This survey of college students showed that students almost
unanimously prefer sermons on moral topics to disciplinary or dogmatic
sermons.

Atkinson, W. T.
"A Discriminating Ministry." *Banner of Truth* (Feb 1961): 10-14. Exhorts   **937**
the preacher to appraise the spiritual condition of his audience and to preach
accordingly.

Bartlett, Gene E.
"Preaching in Suburbia." *Andover Newton Quarterly* 11 (1971): 192-201. **938**
Acquaints the preacher with the spiritual needs of suburbia, and advises him
on how he can meet these needs from the pulpit.

Belgum, David
"Preaching and the Stresses of Life." *Lutheran Quarterly* 20 (1968): 352-58. **939**
A religion professor asks preachers to deal with the actual stresses of life,
helping people ask the questions that will lead to the right answers.

Bird, George L.
"The Real Crisis in Communication." *Christianity Today,* 10 June 1966, **940**
pp. 16, 18. Analyzes forces that have broken down man-to-man and man-to-
God communication.

Blackwood, Andrew W.
"Getting the Layman to Read His Bible." *Southwestern Journal of* **941**
Theology 4 (Apr 1962): 67-77. Calls for a pastoral ministry of cooperative
gospel preaching and lay Bible reading, including seventeen sermon topics
from Mark.

"Preaching to the Man in the Pew." *Asbury Seminarian* 10 (Spring 1956): **942**
12-19. Views preaching from the vantage point of the man in the pew, and
offers ways to make sermons more relevant to laymen.

Caemmerer, Richard R., Sr.
"Preaching and the Recovery of the Church." *Concordia Theological* **943**
Monthly 37 (1966): 146-57. Argues that preaching should stimulate the hearers
to minister to one another.

Curran, Charles A.
"The Psychology of Audience Reaction: Personal Change Through Ser- **944**
mons." *Proceedings of the Catholic Homiletic Society Charter Convention*
(1960): 33-46.

Davidson, J. A.
"How to Listen to a Sermon." *Expository Times* 86 (1975): 335-36. Gives **945**
laymen, who will be held accountable for the sermons they have heard, four
tips on listening more attentively.

De Jong, Peter Y.
"Praying for the Preacher." *Torch and Trumpet* 13 (Feb 1963): 20. Explains **946**
Charles Haddon Spurgeon's conviction that a congregation's prayers for its
preacher are indispensable.

Dillman, Charles N.
"'He Preaches over Our Heads' Is No Compliment." *Christian Ministry* 6   947
(Sep 1975): 26. Exhorts the preacher to communicate his message so that the
congregation can understand it.

Eakin, Mary M.
"Sermon Seminar in a Parish Church." *Christian Century*, 19 January   948
1966, pp. 75-77. Describes and evaluates a weekly discussion group in which
laymen discuss with the pastor the sermon he will preach the following
Sunday.

Fitch, William
"Preaching amid Smog." *Christianity Today*, 18 December 1970, pp. 6-8.   949
Lists obstacles the preacher faces in society: permissiveness, syncretism, lack
of expectant faith, ignorance of the Bible, and ignorance of the Holy Spirit.

Galle, Joseph E., III
"How to Locate Your Listeners' Needs." *Proclaim* 6 (July 1976): 47-48.   950

Guild, Austin W.
"I Enjoyed That Sermon, Pastor." *Church Management* 45 (Dec 1968): 34,   951
41. A preacher acknowledges the indifference of many in his congregation to
his sermons, and he presents ideas for solving this problem.

Gulledge, Jack
"The Perplexity of the Pew." *Church Administration* 18 (Mar 1976): 10-11.   952
Lists four problems of people in churches today (they feel guilty, confined,
and confused, and they are gullible), and tells how to overcome them through
preaching.

Harnish, J. Lester
"Preach the Word." *Christianity Today*, 7 January 1966, p. 27. An auto-   953
biographical sketch of how this preacher moved the Bible to the center of his
pulpit ministry and induced his congregation to study Scripture.

Hatch, Leonard J.
"Let Your Laymen Help You Preach." *New Pulpit Digest* 57 (Nov 1977):   954
27-28. Suggests that the preacher have a group from the congregation help
develop the sermon, and discusses contributions that such groups can make.

Heusser, Douglas-Bruce
"Preaching as Part of the Educational Event." *Spectrum: International*   955
Journal of Religious Education 5 (Fall 1975): 10-12. Describes educational
preaching, then lists and discusses ten specific ways to involve the congregation in preaching.

Hockman, William S.
"Preaching Under Criticism." *Church Management* 52 (Sep 1976): 10.   **956**
Suggests that the preacher have a committee of average church members meet
at least monthly to discuss the content, structure, delivery, and impact of his
sermons.

Howe, Reuel L.
"The People's Part in Preaching." *Minister's Quarterly* 16 (Sum 1960):   **957**
18–20. Outlines the necessary role in the church's preaching ministry played
by the layman.

Johnson, Paul G.
"News from the Pews." *Lutheran Quarterly* 26 (1974): 275–80. Concludes   **958**
that congregations listen to sermons only selectively.

Kleinhans, Theodore J.
"Preaching to the Military." *Pulpit* 37 (Mar 1966): 7–8. Offers insights into   **959**
the unique preaching requirements of the chaplaincy, showing the composition of the congregation and their needs.

Kok, William
"The Preaching of the Word." *Torch and Trumpet* 5 (Jan 1956): 16–17.   **960**
Deals with points the audience should remember when listening to a sermon.

Kolb, Robert
"Parents Should Explain the Sermon: Nikolaus Von Amsdorf on the Role   **961**
of the Christian Parent." *Lutheran Quarterly* 25 (1973): 231–40. Notes the
importance of parents' using sermons to teach their children Christian truth.

Krieger, Wilfred L.
"They Understand and Respond to What They See and Hear." *Chaplain*   **962**
30 (Win 1973–74): 53–59.

McKenna, David L.
"The Jet-Propelled Pulpit." *Christianity Today,* 4 June 1965, pp. 5–9.   **963**
Argues that the direction and character of American life make it imperative
that a person's pulpit ministry be up to date, and supplies parameters for such
a ministry.

McLaughlin, John
"Shared Preaching." *America,* 22 March 1969, pp. 342–43. Describes inter-   **964**
actional preaching, its benefits, and the problems with it—theological,
canonical, practical, and clerical.

MacLennan, David A.
"They." *Pulpit Digest* 34 (Apr 1954): 23–30. A look at preaching from the   **965**

viewpoint of the layman, and suggestions on how to make preaching more effective in meeting the congregation's needs.

"Thou." *Pulpit Digest* 34 (Jan 1954): 15-22. Demonstrates ways a congre- **966** gation may acquire an awareness and knowledge of God through preaching.

Martin, W. B. J.
"Modern Poetry and the Preacher." *Expository Times* 69 (1958): 110-12. **967** Advocates the study of modern poetry as a way the preacher can gain insight into man's predicament and contemporary times. The author cites examples from the works of modern poets.

Mitchell, W. Fraser
"Preaching and the Techniques of Contemporary Culture." *Expository* **968** *Times* 63 (1952): 305-8. Defines preaching as the proclamation of the gospel using current rhetorical devices, then discusses changes in the novel, poetry, and modern media.

Moellering, Ralph L.
"Preaching to the Intellectual." *Concordia Theological Monthly* 40 (1969): **969** 308-16. Describes most laymen today as people who think critically and scientifically, arguing that sermons must therefore reflect changes in terminology, show integrity, and be relevant to social issues.

Mueller, Charles S.
"Pastoral Preaching in the Parish." *Concordia Theological Monthly* 42 **970** (1971): 117-23. Insists that a pastor can get to know his people. The author forbids him to stereotype people according to ethnic and educational backgrounds, requiring him instead to see each one as an individual with unique spiritual needs.

Murray, Iain H.
"Children and the Sermon." *Banner of Truth* (Sep 1972): 1-6. Maintains **971** that it is scripturally improper to remove children from the preaching service and provide them with a substitute.

Murray, John J.
"Why Have a Pastor?" *Banner of Truth* (May 1966): 24. Recommends that **972** preachers beware of preaching occasionally to groups that refuse to organize themselves into a church in accord with New Testament principles.

Ozinga, Tom
"Listening to Sermons in the Mass-Media Age." *Banner*, 12 December **973** 1975, p. 7. Contrasts the communication process of television with that of the sermon, suggesting ways for the preacher to enliven the sermon and entice the congregation to listen more attentively.

Paul, Winston
"A Voice from the Pew." *Pulpit Digest* 41 (Nov 1960): 22. Demonstrates the   **974**
importance of the preacher knowing his people and their needs.

Scotford, John R.
"The Credibility Gap in Preaching." *Church Management* 45 (June 1969):   **975**
14–15, 26. Advises the preacher to respect the people and preach truths they
have proven in their lives, and in this way to overcome their lack of trust in
the sermon.

"How Many Determines What?" *Church Management* 48 (Feb 1972): 18–19.   **976**
Analyzes (in part from the preacher's standpoint) the advantages of small
churches (they have more intimacy) and large ones (they can reach more
people).

Smith, Hilary Dansey
"Feedback or Echo?" *Pastoral Life* 21 (1972): 20–23. Explains the mechanics   **977**
of feedback and how the pastor can use it effectively to improve his preaching.

Spooner, A. Boyce
"Charge to the Congregation." *Presbyterian Journal*, 5 December 1973,   **978**
pp. 11, 22. A departing pastor directs his congregation to watch their new
minister, listen to him, support him, work for him, and (most importantly)
pray for him.

Stackel, Robert
"Pastoral Preaching." *Lutheran Quarterly* 20 (1968): 364–72. Suggests that   **979**
the pastor, in his preaching, show that he knows the hurts of people, relate
Christianity to science, speak to individual needs, and seek feedback.

Starkey, Lycurgus M., Jr.
"Preaching in a Pop Culture." *Religion in Life* 41 (1972): 196–204. Analyzes   **980**
the influence of television, paperback books, comic strips, and radio on
American life, and stresses the need for preaching that is up to date in light of
this influence.

Steingruber, Paul
"Preaching Plus!" *Pulpit Digest* 52 (Feb 1972): 7–9. Describes the system   **981**
used in the author's church: a forty-five–minute sermon followed by forty-five
minutes of congregational feedback.

Stevenson, Dwight E.
"A Layman's Guide to Listening." *Pulpit Digest* 46 (Apr 1966): 14–16.   **982**
Gives the layman twelve tips on how to listen to a sermon more effectively.

Walton, Andrew K.
"Some Aspects of War-Time Preaching." *Evangelical Quarterly* 16 (1944):   **983**
241-50. Discusses the effects of war on the faith and theology of the congregation, and suggests ways in which the preacher should respond.

Watkins, Keith
"Second Thoughts on a Monday Morning." *Worship* 47 (1973): 30-37.   **984**
Reflections on an unsuccessful preaching interim in a suburban church.

White, J. Melville
"Desperate to Communicate." *Christianity Today*, 26 February 1965, pp. 6,   **985**
8-9. Examines areas of development in youth ministry, including preaching, in light of a survey of "hundreds of typical American young people," asked to tell why they are not in church.

Williams, Michael Ray
"A Model for Lay-Listening Education." *Journal of the Academy of Parish*   **986**
Clergy (Dec 1973): 12-14.

Willimon, William H.
"How to Improve Your Preaching." *Christian Ministry* 7 (May 1976): 22-23.   **987**
Offers a "Sermon Reaction Questionnaire" for use in the pew during and following the sermon, and cites several benefits of this approach.

Winegarden, Neil
"How to Listen to a Sermon." *Eternity* 10 (Dec 1959): 17-19. Gives the   **988**
elements that should be present when the preacher (God's ordained spokesman) preaches the message.

Young, J. Terry
"Pastor, What Was That You Said?" *Christianity Today*, 20 November   **989**
1970, pp. 26-27. Lists six characteristics of the society to which the pastor preaches, and in the light of these gives several ways to build a sermon.

The Setting—Liturgical

Babin, David E.
"Toward a Theology of Liturgical Preaching." *Anglican Theological*   **990**
Review 52 (1970): 228-39. Identifies and defines the theological ground for liturgical preaching.

Berg, Darrel E.
"Is the Sermon a Happening?" *Church Management* 44 (Mar 1968): 20-21,   **991**
26. A preacher calls for a break from dead ritual in the worship service, urging instead a spontaneous atmosphere.

Bolton, Robert H.
"No Lectionary for Me!" *Pulpit Digest* 52 (Nov 1971): 7-9. Argues against   **992**
the use of the lectionary and the church year in planning sermon topics.

Brand, Eugene L.
"Preaching and the Lord's Supper in the Liturgy of the Church." *Lutheran*   **993**
Quarterly 20 (1968): 342-51. Promotes a balanced approach to preaching and
the Lord's Supper, suggesting that the sermon deal specifically with the
meaning of the sacrament.

Brannon, T. Leo
"Creating the Atmosphere for Preaching." *New Pulpit Digest* 56 (July   **994**
1976): 55-57. Describes four stages essential to a good worship service, and
characterizes the kind of preacher who can conduct such a service.

Brokhoff, John R.
"The Advent Season." *Pulpit Digest* 58 (Nov 1978): 23-25. Hints on pre-   **995**
paring messages for the Advent season.

"Liturgical Preaching." *New Pulpit Digest* 57 (Sep 1977): 44-47. Discusses   **996**
differences between liturgical and nonliturgical preaching, and sets forth
several values of the former.

Carlton, John W.
"Preaching and Worship." *Review and Expositor* 62 (1965): 319-34. Insists   **997**
that all parts of the worship service, including the sermon, be unified in
purpose and closely interrelated.

Cocks, H. F. Lovell
"The Place of the Sermon in Worship." *Expository Times* 49 (1938): 264-68.   **998**
Argues that preaching, because it is the proclamation of God's Word, is
sacramental, not symbolic. The author believes the sermon to be at the center
of worship.

Coleman, John J.
"The Priest and the Word of God." *American Ecclesiastical Review* 158   **999**
(1968): 19-28. Considers two broad directives regarding preaching from the
Constitution on the Sacred Liturgy, and concludes that the homily is an
esteemed part of liturgy, benefiting people and possessing a purpose in the
context of the Mass.

Couratin, A. H.
"The Book of Common Worship: I, Critique of the Service for the Lord's   **1000**
Day." *Princeton Seminary Bulletin* 61 (Win 1968): 38-45. A critique of the
service for the Lord's Day, part of which is the sermon.

Cox, James W.
"Worship and Preaching." *New Pulpit Digest* 56 (Mar 1976): 35. Affirms 1001
the importance of uniting worship and the sermon. All of the worship service
is to be an introduction to the sermon, says the author. Worship is the creature's
affirmative response to the person and work of the Creator.

Ebner, Mark S.
"The Liturgy and Preaching." *Proceedings of the Catholic Homiletic* 1002
Society Charter Convention (1958): 17–23.

Esbjornson, Robert
"Preaching as Worship." *Worship* 48 (1974): 164–70. States that preaching 1003
should be an act of worship, which always involves work. While preaching is
God's work, it must, as an act of worship, involve work on the part of both
preacher and congregation.

Farmer, Herbert H.
"Preaching and Worship." *Review and Expositor* 43 (1946): 243–60. Sees 1004
worship as a temporary withdrawal from the world, a turning of one's whole
being toward God. One goal of preaching, then, is to help people turn from
the world to God, a process the author calls "otherworldliness."

Ford, D. W. Cleverley
"Preaching in the Context of the Eucharist." *Clergy Review* 55 (1970): 1005
175–79. Analyzes the purpose, form, content, and effects of an expository
sermon.

Grant, Frederick C.
"Preaching the Christian Year." *Anglican Theological Review* 30 (1948): 1006
227–30; 32 (1950): 33–39; 33 (1951): 18–23; 36 (1954): 93–99. Discusses, from the
point of view of New Testament theology and exegesis, questions that ought
to be faced by one preparing to preach on Christmas, Palm Sunday, Trinity
Sunday, and Advent.

"Preaching the Easter Message." *Anglican Theological Review* 28 (1946): 1007
53–59. Contends that Easter preaching is sometimes tentative and apologetic
because the preacher has not availed himself of the results of modern New
Testament research. The author then presents some of these results and identifies relevant bibliography.

Haig, Frank R.
"Why Not a Daily Sermon?" *Homiletic and Pastoral Review* 65 (1964): 1008
209–11. Argues for daily preaching as another step in the improvement of
Christian worship, a process that has stemmed from the liturgical movement.

Lahrson, Gordon R.
"Preaching and the Lord's Supper." *Foundations* 12 (1969): 19-33. Discusses **1009** the relationship between preaching and the Eucharist. The author covers both Protestant and Catholic views.

McFarland, John Robert
"The Sermon Within the Context of Contemporary Worship." *Pulpit* **1010** *Digest* 50 (Oct 1969): 13-20. Criticizes the traditional preaching service, advocating instead such contemporary worship forms as drama, dialogue, and popular music.

Macleod, Donald
"The Dialogue of the Sanctuary." *Princeton Seminary Bulletin* 56 (May **1011** 1963): 15-32. Observes the "rebirth in liturgical concern," much of it due to the effects on worship of preaching.

"Epiphany Preaching." *New Pulpit Digest* 54 (Jan 1974): 23-25. Discusses **1012** the season and feast of Epiphany, suggesting a fitting series of sermons.

"Multi-Faceted Presentation." *New Pulpit Digest* 54 (Sep 1974): 37-38; **1013** (Nov 1974): 53-54. Advocates the use of A. Allan McArthur's trinitarian format for the Christian year, concluding with an outline and a description of an actual series.

"Preaching During Holy Week." *New Pulpit Digest* 54 (Mar 1974): 28-29. **1014** Discusses the history of Holy Week, furnishing suggestions for successful worship services.

"Preaching in Advent." *New Pulpit Digest* 53 (Nov 1973): 39-42. Discusses **1015** the history of, significance of, and format for Advent.

"Preparing Your Lenten Preaching." *New Pulpit Digest* 56 (Jan 1976): **1016** 39-40. Discusses the use of a series for the Lenten season, and includes a bibliography of sources for such a series.

"The Sermon During Holy Communion." *New Pulpit Digest* 54 (July **1017** 1974): 47-48. Treats the sermon's role in communion, and suggests ways it can be used effectively.

Miller, Charles E.
"What Is a Homily?" *Homiletic and Pastoral Review* 66 (1966): 505-11. **1018** Views the homily as not simply a sermon but a type of preaching integrally woven into the Catholic liturgy. The author gives a form for the homily that could be used for a sermon as well. A sample homily demonstrates this form.

Nes, William Hamilton
"Liturgical Preaching." *Anglican Theological Review* 38 (1956): 201-4. **1019** Reviews several concerns of preaching within the context of the liturgy.

O'Shea, William
"The Sermon Is Part of the Mass." *Homiletic and Pastoral Review* 60   **1020**
(1960): 517-26. Recognizes the sermon's role in the liturgical service of the
Mass.

Scott, Gideon G.
"The Unity of Word and Sacrament." *Expository Times* 78 (1966): 72-76.   **1021**
Discerns in worship two movements: the downward movement of God's Word
to us and the upward movement of our response to Him. Preaching is an act
of God, the author writes, and it is He who transforms it into a sacrament.
Preaching's sacramental character prevents it from being mere public speaking
or empty ritual.

Stacey, John
"Putting the Sermon in Its Place." *Preacher's Quarterly* 14 (1968): 77-79.   **1022**
Gives three reasons why the sermon ought to be part of the total act of
worship rather than the climax toward which the rest of the service moves.

Starenko, Ronald M.
"Preaching and Liturgical Life." *Concordia Theological Monthly* 40   **1023**
(1969): 591-99. Sees preaching as an event, as an act of God in the Christian's
worship, as a sacrament by which God communicates His love and grace, as
God's ordained method to redeem men.

Steichen, Alan J.
"A Look at Homily Services." *Worship* 48 (1974): 236-41. Deals primarily   **1024**
with Rudolf Bultmann's thinking about kerygma. The author concludes
with observations about the setting in which the sermon is delivered.

Tripp, David
"'Liturgical Preaching': What Can Methodists Make of It?" *Preacher's*   **1025**
Quarterly 14 (1968): 11-16. Asserts that Methodist preachers should preach
liturgically because such preaching links the sermon with the Collect and
Lessons for the day, and because it fits tightly into the framework of the
liturgy.

Viviano, Robert L.
"The Presentation of the Word." *Torch and Trumpet* 20 (June 1970): 24.   **1026**
Advocates biblical preaching as the center of the worship service.

Weems, Lovett Hayes, Jr.
"The Lectionary as an Aid to Biblical Preaching." *New Pulpit Digest* 53   **1027**
(May 1973): 52-53. Sets forth several arguments for using a lectionary of the
Christian year.

The Setting—Special Occasions

Blackwood, Andrew W.
"The Demands of Special Occasions." *Pulpit Digest* 35 (Sep 1954): 65, **1028**
68–70, 72–73. Suggests ways to preach biographical sermons on the special
days in the Christian year.

Cleland, James T.
"Preaching at Christmas." *Pulpit Digest* 42 (Dec 1961): 9–11. Stresses the **1029**
importance of preaching the incarnation of Christ, and suggests ways to make
sermons on this subject more effective.

Harrod, Allen F.
"Personalizing the Funeral." *Pulpit Digest* 58 (Nov 1978): 22. Hints on **1030**
preparing funeral messages.

Horne, Chevis F.
"Using Community Opportunities for Proclamation." *Church Adminis-* **1031**
tration 18 (July 1976): 37.

McCaul, Thomas V.
"My First Funeral." *Christianity Today*, 1 April 1966, p. 14. A personal **1032**
account of the author's first funeral service as a pastor.

Noyes, Henry Drury
"The Future of the Parish Mission." *American Ecclesiastical Review* 154 **1033**
(1966): 320–27. Maintains that the parish mission is of enduring value and
fills a permanent need in the church, then discusses the content and setting of
missionary preaching.

Owen, Franklin
"Funeral Preaching." *New Pulpit Digest* 54 (July 1974): 57. Discusses the **1034**
significant opportunity offered by the funeral sermon.

Sanford, Jack
"Memo to Commencement Speakers." *Christianity Today*, 8 May 1970, **1035**
pp. 14, 16. Urges speakers to cease giving empty platitudes of optimism, and
to look at the world that awaits the graduate with more realism.

Scott, Charles Wheeler
"Preaching Themes for Good Friday." *Pulpit Digest* 49 (Mar 1969): 14–16. **1036**
Discusses the importance of and ways to use the passion narratives in preach-
ing Christ's crucifixion.

Thebeau, Duane H.
"Are We Burying the Gospel at the Grave?" *Christianity Today*, 17 March   **1037**
1967, pp. 7-8. Argues that Christian funeral messages ought to distinguish
between the faithful saint and the unbelieving man.

Thomas, Milton
"The Ministerial Workshop." *Pulpit Digest* 25 (May 1945): 65-67. Encour-   **1038**
ages ministers to become involved in memorial services, then gives scriptural
foundations, quotations usable in memorial messages, illustrations, pertinent
ideas, bits of verse, and outlines.

"The Ministerial Workshop." *Pulpit Digest* 26 (May 1946): 71-76. Encour-   **1039**
ages pastors on Mother's Day to preach on the foundations, opportunities,
and responsibilities of Christian parenthood, and on principles of the Christian home.

The Sermon

Abbey, Merrill R.
"Strategies for a Program of Biblical Preaching." *Review and Expositor* 72   **1040**
(1975): 149-59. Reviews several strategies of programmed preaching: using
lectionaries, preaching through Bible books, and dealing with biblical and
practical topics in series.

"Tapping the Potential of Programmed Preaching." *Church Management*   **1041**
47 (May 1971): 22-24. Stresses the need for devising a preaching calendar for
the year, and for using the congregation to help assemble the calendar, thus
ensuring that it meets their needs.

Ackley, Charles W.
"Preaching: Preparation and Practice." *Christian Ministry* 7 (Mar 1976):   **1042**
22-23. Explains the steps the author takes in preparing his sermon for the
coming Sunday. The author recommends that one plan one's sermon topics
in advance.

Adams, Jay E.
"Make Your Preaching Live." *Journal of Pastoral Practice* 2 (Win 1978):   **1043**
171-75. Encourages preachers to spruce up their word choice and illustrative
material.

"Making Preaching a Pleasure." *Journal of Pastoral Practice* 3, 3 (1979):   **1044**
161-67. Argues that preparing each sermon six months in advance will make
preaching a pleasure.

"More—on Purpose." *Journal of Pastoral Practice* 1 (Sum 1977): 157-61.   **1045**
Examines the role of the preaching purpose in determining what the passage

should be, how it should be outlined, and whether or not to announce one's outline.

"Outlining." *Journal of Pastoral Practice* 2, 2 (1978): 165–69. Discusses the **1046** relationship between the preacher's outline and his "preaching stance," and counsels preachers to stay away from the "lecture stance."

"Preaching with Purpose." *Journal of Pastoral Practice* 1 (Win 1977): **1047** 135–38. Emphasizes the function of, and importance of having, a clear purpose in preaching.

Alexander, James N.
"Preaching on the Positives: A Study on Sermon Construction." *Expository* **1048** *Times* 68 (1957): 180–82. Explains why preachers should be more positive, and proposes steps for letting the positives have priority.

Alston, Wallace M., Jr.
"On Discerning Good Faith from Bad Religion: From Text to Sermon?" **1049** *Interpretation* 26 (1972): 451–68. Stresses the need for theological preaching, and gives three ways in which preaching can function in the church as a theological discipline. A sermon by the author illustrates this emphasis.

Anderson, Bernhard W.
"The Contemporaneity of the Bible." *Princeton Seminary Bulletin* 62 **1050** (Sum 1969): 38–50. Offers to teachers and preachers suggestions for bridging the gap between the historical situation of the biblical texts and the present.

Anonymous
"Expository Preaching." *Banner of Truth* (Sep 1963): 9–28. Offers seven **1051** reasons why expository preaching is preferable to preaching on isolated texts. This article first appeared in *Princeton Review* in 1847.

"How to Make the Sermon a Living Message." *Torch and Trumpet* 11 (Apr **1052** 1961): 13–14. Provides seven steps toward improving one's presentation of a message.

Awalt, William J.
"Some Premises for a Homily." *Homiletic and Pastoral Review* 79 (Aug **1053** 1979): 52–59. Offers guidelines for preparing a homily more carefully, stressing the importance of diligence and prayer.

Baker, Donald
"Hear Me Talking." *Preacher's Quarterly* 12 (1966): 207–13. Encourages the **1054** preacher to use, not conversational language, but dignified language, "a style appropriate to the occasion and to the speaker."

Barclay, William
"Guidance for the Preacher from the Greek Literary Critics." *Expository*   1055
Times 65 (1953): 67–71. Provides a random list of advice, including analysis,
attention to detail, persuasion, and lucidity.

Barrett, Thomas van B.
"College Preaching." *Anglican Theological Review* 30 (1948): 1–9. Covers   1056
several aspects of good sermon development. The author believes the art of
preaching must be practiced on a high level in the college setting.

Beaman, Robert S.
"Selecting Sermon Titles." *Pulpit* 38 (Apr 1967): 26, 28. Discusses reasons   1057
for and ways to create a good sermon title, as well as suggestions for using the
title to greatest advantage.

Berry, Harold J.
"A Plea for Spiritual Scholarship." *Good News Broadcaster* 27 (May 1969):   1058
3, 31–32. Exhorts preachers to make application to people's lives only after
expounding the meaning of the sermon text. People need to know, says the
author, that the application is based on proper exposition of the Word.

Bieze, Gerrit
"What Preaching Do We Need?" *Torch and Trumpet* 16 (Nov 1966): 12–13.   1059
Examines what laymen mean when they request that preaching be more
practical, and offers a possible solution to the problem.

Blackwood, Andrew W.
"The Selection of a Bible Passage." *Pulpit Digest* 33 (June 1953): 11–16.   1060
Discusses a primary step in preparing an expository sermon: the thoughtful
choice of biblical material.

Blair, Burton F.
"Preaching as Biblical-Deductive and Biblical-Inductive." *Pulpit Digest*   1061
58 (Sep 1978): 41–43. Shows the difference between an inductive sermon and a
deductive one.

Blake, Richard A.
"Visual Rhetoric for the Word of God." *Worship* 42 (1968): 292–98. Defends   1062
the use of audio-visuals to communicate the sermon, and gives two examples
of multimedia sermons.

Bolton, Robert H.
"Our Friend the Enemy: A Sermon in Process." *Christian Ministry* 3 (Jan   1063
1972): 30–36. A sermon critiqued line by line by a journalism professor.

"Sermon Titles Should Sparkle." *Pulpit* 39 (Feb 1968): 24-25. Contends **1064**
that a sermon title should attract attention, entice, create expectancy, and aid
in the recall of the sermon's content.

Borreson, Glenn L.
"Making Words Live." *Christian Ministry* 7 (Mar 1976): 35-37. Describes a **1065**
variety of methods to enhance the verbal message. The author recommends
slide-tape presentations, which he calls metaphorical words.

Boyd, William
"Applications That Hit the Mark." *Christianity Today,* 24 October 1969, **1066**
pp. 26-27. Gives six guidelines for sermon application, which the author
believes to be the aspect of evangelical sermons in greatest need of improvement.

Brannon, T. Leo
"Expository Preaching and the Modern Scene." *New Pulpit Digest* 56 (Sep **1067**
1976): 44-47. Advocates expository preaching because people need to hear
what God says about eternal values.

Brown, H. C., Jr.
"Proclamation: The Kerygmatic Act." *Southwestern Journal of Theology* **1068**
8 (Spring 1966): 25-31. Identifies the need for truly biblical preaching with
kerygmatic emphasis, and explains the procedure for developing a biblically
based sermon.

Brownson, William C.
"The Sermon's Grand Theme." *Christianity Today,* 2 September 1966, **1069**
pp. 22-23. Shows how preaching can be affected when Christ becomes the
center of attraction. Describes the steps from studying the Bible to asking
questions that sharpen the preaching idea.

Burtness, James H.
"Sharing the Suffering of God in the Life of the World: From Text to **1070**
Sermon on I Peter 2:21." *Interpretation* 23 (1969): 277-88. A sermon followed
by the author's discussion of the principles he follows and his goal in preaching God's Word.

Burton, C. Emory
"Making Preaching Practical." *Christian Ministry* 1 (July 1970): 12-13. **1071**
Proposes that the effective preacher will be pointed and practical, and suggests
ways to reach those objectives.

Carlson, N. Gene
"The Best Way to Preach." *Christianity Today,* 4 June 1965, pp. 9-11. A **1072**

reexamination of the nature of expository preaching, in which the author argues for the primacy of this type of sermon.

Carter, Nancy
"Words Aren't Enough." *Christian Ministry* 3 (Jan 1972): 8, 10–12. Analyzes   **1073**
the adequacy of today's preaching, and recommends the use of audio-visuals or recordings to improve communication.

Cassels, Louis
"A Consumer of Sermonology Speaks Out." *Christian Herald* 97 (Apr   **1074**
1974): 26–29. Urges the preacher to make his main point clear and to begin with an interesting sentence or story. The author discusses the proper use of anecdotes and the advantage of sermons that are brief.

Castagnola, Lawrence A.
"Of Sacraments and Sermons." *Priest* 21 (1965): 835–38. Advises homilists   **1075**
to make sermons relevant to the audience, using experience gained in the confessional, in counseling, and in general observation.

Chappell, Clovis G.
"Preparing the Sermon." *Pulpit Digest* 31 (Feb 1951): 11–15, 88–92. Discusses   **1076**
the art and steps of sermon preparation.

Clasper, Paul D.
"Glib or Graceful?" *Pulpit Digest* 47 (Dec 1966): 9–12. Offers principles for   **1077**
making a sermon both direct and clear.

Cleland, James T.
"Go for the Jugular." *Pulpit Digest* 39 (Mar 1959): 17–18, 90. Argues that   **1078**
preaching can be more effective through concentrating on the biblical passage's central idea.

"Someone There Is Who Doesn't Love a Wall: From Text to Sermon on   **1079**
Ephesians 2:11–22." *Interpretation* 21 (1967): 147–57. Demonstrates the author's procedure for developing a sermon, from exegesis to delivery.

Clinard, Turner N.
"Preaching the Sermon Series." *Pulpit Digest* 47 (Feb 1967): 14–16. Explains   **1080**
how the sermon series can be an effective tool, and suggests types, length, and sources of effective series.

Connors, Charles
"The Sermon Hatched on Saturday Night." *Homiletic and Pastoral Review*   **1081**
57 (1957): 1094–99. Preachers often put off sermon preparation because of their inability to select a good topic, says the author, who explains why this should not happen and how to prevent it from happening.

Conrad, F. Leslie, Jr.

"Preaching to Sports-Minded People." *Pulpit Digest* 36 (July 1956): 15-18. **1082**
A professor of systematic theology, showing how Paul used the language of
classical games to communicate more effectively, argues that today's preacher
can do the same in today's sports-minded culture.

Cox, James W.

"Are Illustrations the Answer?" *Pulpit Digest* 58 (Jan 1978): 56. Explains **1083**
how to determine the kind of illustrations to use in a sermon.

"Dialogue in Preaching." *Pulpit Digest* 59 (May 1979): 52. Christian **1084**
preaching has always had the character of conversation, says the author, and
he lists several ways a contemporary preacher can incorporate dialogue.

"Figures of Speech." *Pulpit Digest* 59 (Jan 1979): 30-31. Illustrates how **1085**
metaphors and similes, scattered throughout a sermon, can create images and
thus illuminate the entire message.

"Forming the Pattern of the Sermon." *Princeton Seminary Bulletin* 58 **1086**
(June 1965): 31-38. Abridged in *New Pulpit Digest* 55 (Mar 1975): 19-22.
Discusses three rules for composing the sermon: (1) the outline should grow
out of the text; (2) it should have unity; (3) it should achieve suitable climax.
The author also lists eight cautions in using these guiding principles.

"How Good Is Your Expository Preaching?" *Pulpit Digest* 59 (Nov 1979): **1087**
45-48. Describes the relationship between expository preaching and biblical
preaching. The author includes a self-evaluation test to measure the quality
of one's own expository sermons.

"The Hypothetical Example." *Pulpit Digest* 58 (Sep 1978): 10-11. Suggests **1088**
a good source of sermonic illustrations—the hypothetical example—and
explains how to develop and use illustrations drawn from this source.

"The Illustrative Story." *Pulpit Digest* 58 (Nov 1978): 41-42. Defines the **1089**
illustrative story, and encourages its use in the pulpit.

"On Being Particular." *New Pulpit Digest* 55 (July 1975): 60. **1090**

"A Plea for Redundancy." *Pulpit Digest* 58 (Mar 1978): 23-24. Urges the **1091**
preacher to restate ideas in a sermon for the sake of clarity, communication,
and impressiveness.

"Truth in General." *New Pulpit Digest* 55 (July 1975): 60-61. Advocates the **1092**
use in preaching of the general proposition.

"The Use of Examples." *Pulpit Digest* 58 (May 1978): 34-35. Describes two **1093**
kinds of examples to be used in preaching, general and specific.

"The Value of Definition." *Pulpit Digest* 58 (Jan 1978): 56-57. Urges **1094**
preachers more frequently to define theological terms.

"Where Does a Sermon Begin?" *New Pulpit Digest* 54 (July 1974): 24. **1095**
Discusses sources for sermon ideas.

"Writing Sermons." *New Pulpit Digest* 55 (Sep 1975): 25. Describes pros **1096**
and cons of writing sermons.

Criswell, W. A.
"How I Prepare My Sermons." *Moody Monthly* 71 (June 1971): 84, 86–87. **1097**
Gives an overview of how the author prepares his sermons, emphasizing the
importance of depending on the Holy Spirit.

"The Preacher in His Study." *Moody Monthly* 78 (Feb 1978): 119–20. **1098**
Encourages pastors to preach expositionally through books of the Bible.

"Preaching Through the Bible." *Christianity Today*, 9 December 1966, **1099**
pp. 22–23. Explains the blessing, method, and success of preaching through
the Bible.

Curley, Francis X.
"Preachers Are Shorn Sheep, Dewdrops and Locusts." *Homiletic and* **1100**
Pastoral Review 59 (1959): 724–31. Calls for imagery, used by many great
preachers of the past, to become once again a vital part of sermons.

Davidson, J. A.
"A Formula for Writing a Sermon." *Pulpit Digest* 51 (Oct 1970): 7–10. **1101**
Presents a sermon-preparation method that utilizes the writing-rewriting
process.

"Rehabilitating the Sermon." *Church Management* 42 (June 1966): 7. Calls **1102**
for a return to the sermon as the basic means of communicating spiritual
truth. The author warns fellow ministers of the cost in time and effort that
this will involve.

Day, Thomas F.
"Expository Preaching." *Banner of Truth* (Oct 1973): 11–14. Explains why **1103**
expository preaching is important; gives four prerequisites for doing it and
five characteristics of an expository sermon.

De Jong, Alexander C.
"Preaching the Catechism." *Torch and Trumpet* 13 (Feb 1963): 10–11. **1104**
Explores both advantages and problems in preaching regularly through a
catechism.

DeJong, Jerome
"Preaching by the Calendar." *Moody Monthly* 79 (Oct 1978): 143–45. De- **1105**
scribes a planned preaching program that synchronizes topically with seasons
in the church year.

De Jong, Peter Y.

"How Not to Preach." *Torch and Trumpet* 12 (Dec 1962): 10–11. Evaluates a preacher's sermon outline, and exhorts him to stay true to his chosen text. **1106**

"Structuring the Sermon." *Banner of Truth* (June 1974): 21–32. Considers three aspects of sermon development: reasons for adapting structure in the sermon, patterns for arranging it, and ways to develop this structure. **1107**

"We Ought to Tell the *Whole* Truth." *Torch and Trumpet* 14 (Mar 1964): 3. Exhorts preachers to give in their messages a full representation of their beliefs. **1108**

De Koekkoek, Paul

"Response to Gospel Preaching." *Outlook* 29 (July 1979): 13–14. An appeal for preaching that is sound exegetically and that includes pertinent application for all ages. **1109**

Di Blasi, Augustine J.

"Etymology: An Aid to Preaching." *Homiletic and Pastoral Review* 75 (Dec 1974): 64–68. Shows how a knowledge of the derivations of English phrases and terms can make sermons more lucid. **1110**

Di Gangi, Mariano

"The Recovery of Expository Preaching." *Evangelical Recorder* 82 (Mar 1976): 10–11. Covers the need for expository preaching, its indispensable elements, and the practical implementation of homiletical training. **1111**

Dinter, Paul E.

"Preaching and the Inquiring of God." *Worship* 52 (1978): 223–36. A Catholic priest and counselor suggests ways to replace monotonous moralizing in the pulpit with revelational preaching of the biblical text. **1112**

Dixon, Ian

"The Use of Modern Fiction in Preaching and Pastoral Care." *Expository Times* 85 (1974): 277–80, 298–302. Suggests that films, plays, and novels can be a great aid to the preacher in search of an understanding of the human situation, and that the use in sermons of storytelling will best relate the gospel to real-life situations. **1113**

Durken, Daniel

"The One-Point Sermon." *Homiletic and Pastoral Review* 72 (Mar 1972): 11–15. Calls for sermons to have just one idea, and to support it with explanation, comparison, illustrations, and visual material. **1114**

"St. Luke's Paradigm of Sermon Preparation." *Priest* 33 (Apr 1977): 30, 32–33. Describes essential characteristics of Christian preaching and sermon preparation. The author uses the Emmaus account in Luke's Gospel as an illustration and paradigm. **1115**

Elftmann, M. V.
"A Preacher's Card System." *Church Management* 51 (Apr 1975): 11–12.   1116
Explains an index system that puts in order and makes accessible the illustrations and ideas one has accumulated.

Elson, Edward L. R.
"A Washington Pulpit." *Christianity Today,* 10 June 1966, pp. 32–34.   1117
Explains how this preacher plans a year's pulpit work, adhering closely to the liturgical calendar.

Epp, Theodore H.
"From My Study." *Good News Broadcaster* 30 (Feb 1972): 2–3. Lists four   1118
stages in the preparation of a message: read the book through several times; choose commentaries on the book; organize the information; and meditate on the message just before delivering it.

Evans, Christmas
"Christmas Evans on Preaching." *Banner of Truth* (July 1971): 17. Calls   1119
preachers to preach Christ evangelistically and with compassion for the congregation. The author deals with how to prepare both the sermon and the preacher's heart.

Faber, Warren H.
"Does the Preacher Need Rhetoric?" *Proceedings of the Catholic Homiletic*   1120
Society Charter Convention (1962): 101–5.

Farra, Harry
"The Preacher Among the Rhetoricians." *Christian Ministry* 7 (Jan 1976):   1121
22–24. Analyzes the use of rhetoric in preaching.

Fickett, Harold L., Jr.
"Preaching in Series." *Christianity Today,* 14 October 1966, pp. 37–39.   1122
Demonstrates how a series of sermons helps to communicate biblical truth effectively.

Fink, Michael
"Hit the Mark with Your Preaching." *New Pulpit Digest* 57 (July 1977):   1123
63–66. Gives five steps for structuring a sermon: attention, need, satisfaction, visualization, and action. These steps are based on Alan H. Monroe's "motivated sequence."

Fitch, William
"A Plea for Expository Preaching." *Christianity Today,* 10 November 1967,   1124
pp. 29–30. Despite the attitude that preaching is obsolete, the author makes a plea for restoring preaching—and particularly expository preaching—to its rightful place.

Fitzgerald, Edward

"The Medium and the Message." *Homiletic and Pastoral Review* 70 (1970): 1125
433-37. The difference between Christian and non-Christian preachers, the author contends, is in experience and the message.

Folprecht, William

"Five Ways to Sharpen Your Sermons." *Church Management* 42 (Sep 1966): 1126
18-19. A retired preacher suggests that humor, love, and illustrations be used by preachers more often.

"Lessons from Literature." *Pulpit Digest* 48 (Feb 1968): 12-14. Demonstrates 1127
how the preacher can present Bible truths more effectively through the proper use of good literature.

Fortin, Ernest L.

"Augustine and the Problem of Christian Rhetoric." *Augustinian Studies* 1128
5 (1974): 85-100. Interacts with Augustine's ideas in book 4 of *De doctrina christiana*, "the first handbook of Christian rhetoric."

Foster, John

"The Preacher's Use of Church History, with Special Reference to the Early 1129
Centuries." *Encounter* 26 (1965): 48-64. Urges the use of church history in the pulpit, and offers three suggestions for doing this.

Francis, D. Pitt

"Prepare Your Sermon with a Tape-Recorder." *Preacher's Quarterly* 12 1130
(1966): 63-65. Encourages the preacher to use a tape recorder in place of a written manuscript when preparing a sermon, explaining how this will remove from the preacher the fear of forgetting the sermon.

Francis, David

"The Preacher's Plan." *Preacher's Quarterly* 13 (1967): 27-33. Preaching 1131
plans, writes the author, ensure that one will preach the whole counsel of God and take advantage of significant holidays and observances.

Fraser, Duncan

"The Preacher's Task in the Modern World." *Evangelical Quarterly* 20 1132
(1948): 241-51. Explores and analyzes declaratory, evangelistic, expository, and doctrinal preaching.

Fritz, John H. C.

"The Limitations of Christian Preaching." *Concordia Theological* 1133
Monthly 17 (1946): 94-99. Reveals the sense in which the biblical message and its application constitute the limitations of Christian preaching, and suggests ways to overcome this.

"What Makes for Effective Preaching?" *Concordia Theological Monthly* 1134
13 (1942): 684-91. Outlines the ingredients of an effective sermon.

Fuller, Reginald H.
"Preparing the Homily." *Worship* 48 (1974): 442-57. In preparing the 1135
sermon, the author insists, the first step is exegesis. Most of the article deals
primarily with exegesis in light of biblical criticism, secondarily with ways to
move from exegesis to preaching. This article was reprinted in Reginald H.
Fuller, ed., *Preaching the New Lectionary: The Word of God for the Church
Today* (Collegeville, Minn.: Liturgical, 1974): pp. xvii–xxxii.

Galle, Joseph E., III
"The Power of the Particular." *Homiletic and Pastoral Review* 76 (July 1136
1976): 57-61. Contends that cliches and stale illustrations do not confront
listeners with the reality of Christ, and that preachers must speak specifically,
concretely, and with illustrations drawn from their own lives.

Gilmore, John Lewis
"Sermons: Forestalling Fizzles." *Christianity Today*, 15 February 1974, 1137
pp. 36-37. Discusses the text, title, introductions, body, digressions, and conclusions. The author also reviews reasons for failure.

Goslin, Thomas S., II
"A Time for Dialogue." *Christian Ministry* 9 (Jan 1978): 27-28. Tells how a 1138
dialogue sermon began in a church, and gives pros and cons for this kind of
sermon.

Grabowski, Stanley M.
"Preaching and Mass Media Techniques." *Priest* 29 (Apr 1973): 26-28. 1139
Draws upon patterns of the mass media, particularly television commercials,
for broad principles of sermon construction.

Green, F. Pratt
"The Preacher and the Hymn-Writer: Hymns on the Transfiguration." 1140
Expository Times 83 (1972): 329-32. Compares the hymnologist's task of
composing a hymn on a specific subject to the preacher's task of writing a
sermon, and illustrates the point with various hymns on the transfiguration.

Greet, Brian A.
"Dialogue Preaching." *Expository Times* 78 (1967): 148-50. Explains why 1141
one church began to use dialogue preaching, how they went about it, and
some points to remember when using dialogue preaching.

Hageman, Howard G.
"Listen Before You Speak." *Christianity Today*, 25 November 1966, pp. 22- 1142

23. If a sermon is to be heard, says the author, it must be heard first in the study by the preacher as he prepares it.

Hall, Thor
"Let Religion Be Religious: From Text to Sermon on II Corinthians   1143
5:14-17." *Interpretation* 23 (1969): 158-89. A sample sermon is preceded by a discussion of the steps that lead to a sermon and of the importance of a preacher studying both the Word of God and his congregation.

Halverson, Richard C.
"The Privilege of Preaching." *Christianity Today*, 4 February 1966, pp. 24-   1144
25. Makes suggestions for proper sermon planning and preparation.

Hammerton, H. J.
"The Art of Illustration." *Expository Times* 71 (1959): 84-86. Defines and   1145
discusses the use of illustrations in preaching, and supplies examples from
seventeenth-century sermons.

Hansen, C. D.
"Preaching Takes Work." *Christianity Today*, 19 December 1975, p. 25.   1146
Discusses the importance of a quiet study place, discipline, adequate prepara-
tion, and relevant illustrations.

Harcus, A. D.
"Listening to Sermons." *Expository Times* 64 (1953): 209-11. Covers struc-   1147
ture, variety, illustrations, unknown factors, and the worshiper.

Heetland, David
"Have I Preached the Wrong Sermon?" *Pulpit Digest* 59 (May 1979): 24-26.   1148
Moralizing, commanding, and judgment, the author insists, must never be
preached in place of grace.

Helm, Paul
"Plain Speaking." *Banner of Truth* (Mar 1971): 1-5. A plea for freshness   1149
and clarity in speech. The author believes that jargon often fails to convey
what the speaker intends, is not biblical, and could be put more simply.

Hendricks, William L.
"Biblical Interpretation, the Pastor, and the Contemporary Scene." *South-*   1150
western Journal of Theology 2 (Apr 1960): 17-26. Encourages the preacher to
study principles of biblical interpretation, the history of the discipline, and
current trends.

Hendriksen, William
"Catechism Preaching." *Torch and Trumpet* 10 (Nov 1960): 4. Provides   1151
pointers on preparing a catechism message.

Hensley, Wayne
"Suggestion as Sermon Strategy." *Christianity Today,* 27 March 1970, **1152**
pp. 28-29. Offers an alternate, more indirect form of persuasive speech, and
discusses types of suggestion and their use in the pulpit.

Hersey, Norman L.
"Watch Your Language!" *Church Management* 42 (Feb 1966): 24-25. Urges **1153**
pastors to evaluate carefully the terms they use in the pulpit to insure that
their audiences understand them.

Hollenweger, Walter J.
"Preaching Dialogically." *Concordia Theological Monthly* 42 (1971): 243- **1154**
48. Using illustrations from different cultures and denominations, the author
suggests that the pastor and congregation communicate with each other
through a discussion format.

Holmer, Paul L.
"Indirect Communication: Something About the Sermon with References **1155**
to Kierkegaard and Wittgenstein." *Perkins School of Theology Journal* 24
(Spring 1971): 14-24. Discusses the mode of the sermon.

Homrighausen, Elmer G.
"The Actual World and the Biblical World." *Theology Today* 13 (1957): **1156**
535-36. Notes E. H. Robertson's view that when Bible passages are read we
must ask: Is it true? What does it mean? Am I involved? Without the third
question, the author says, Bible reading or preaching becomes mere intellectual exercise.

Hope, Norman V.
"Illustrations Are Where You Find Them." *Church Management* 44 (Oct **1157**
1967): 18, 22. Contends that any preacher willing to work diligently can find
sermon illustrations through invention, observation, and experience.

Hovda, Robert W.
"A Pastoral Case for the Dialog Homily." *American Ecclesiastical Review* **1158**
159 (1968): 331-36. Observes that in the dialogue sermon the preacher unfolds
the Word of God and invites people to contribute their witness and insight.
The author discusses the rationale and technique of the dialogue homily.

Howard, Thomas
"Good Preaching, Good Prose." *Christianity Today,* 4 July 1975, pp. 19-20. **1159**
Ponders the importance of quality homiletical preparation, considering the
author's view of preaching as an art form.

Howington, Nolan P.
"Expository Preaching." *Review and Expositor* 56 (1959): 56-65. Defines **1160**

expository preaching, stressing the author's intent and practical application, and deals with objections to and advantages of expository preaching.

Hudson, R. Lofton

"The Dynamics of a Sermon." *Review and Expositor* 45 (1948): 169-77. **1161**
Argues that sermons should address "felt" needs, speak to the audience's experience, and include proper motivational appeals.

Hugo, John J.

"Audio-Visuals in Divine Worship." *Homiletic and Pastoral Review* 74 **1162**
(Jan 1974): 54-60. Questions the use of audio-visuals in any part of the worship service, even the sermon.

Huie, Janice Riggle

"Biblical Preaching." *Perkins School of Theology Journal* 26 (Spring **1163**
1973): 26-33. Discusses definitions of biblical preaching, its importance, and its method. The author encourages the preparation and delivery of sermons that expose the hearers to the Scriptures.

Huie, Wade P., Jr.

"The Poverty of Abundance: From Text to Sermon on Luke 16:19-31." **1164**
Interpretation 22 (1968): 403-20. A sermon accompanied by an explanation of the steps taken in developing the sermon text. The author emphasizes the importance of a preacher understanding his text, himself, and his congregation.

Huxhold, Harry N.

"On Homiletical Method." *Encounter* 37 (1976): 73-74. Discusses the **1165**
author's technique and method of organizing and preparing sermons.

Ingles, James Wesley

"The Place of Poetry in Preaching." *Review and Expositor* 54 (1957): **1166**
264-79. Urges the use of poetry as a source of illustrative material, as well as of inspiration and renewal. The author suggests ways it can be used and calls for preachers to develop poetic imagery and imagination in their style.

Johnson, Alan

"Letting the Bible Speak Today: I, The Bible and Your Preaching." *Moody* **1167**
Monthly 67 (Feb 1967): 28-30, 50-51. Argues that powerful preaching results from a conviction of the authority of God's Word, a clear grasp on the meaning and central theme of the passage, and an application of the passage to the lives of the hearers.

Johnson, Paul G.

"Digesting the Sacred Cow." *Encounter* 39 (1978): 77-84. Contends that the **1168**
sermon motif is ineffective, and proposes a sermon-response setting.

"The Pulpit Word and the Great Unsaid." *Dialog* 13 (1974): 305-8. A plea **1169**
for allowing the congregation to "digest" the sermon by verbalizing it in
small groups, assembled in the sanctuary.

"The Sunday Morning News." *Christian Ministry* 7 (July 1976): 30-32. **1170**
Discusses the problem of one-way communication in sermons and the advantage of the two-way sermon.

Jones, Milton William
    "Can Exegetical Preaching Change Your Church?" *Moody Monthly* 70 **1171**
(Jan 1970): 38-40, 42. Discusses the need for exegetical preaching and some
principles for doing it. The author illustrates it from John 3:16 and contrasts
it with topical preaching.

Julien, Jerome M.
    "Catechism Preaching." *Outlook* 23 (Feb 1973): 27-28. Examines the **1172**
preaching of a catechism, and suggests that this provides order in preaching
on difficult subjects.

Justice, William G.
    "Do You Preach in an Unknown Tongue?" *Church Administration* 18 **1173**
(July 1976): 30-31. Describes a survey of church people that shows their ignorance of theological terms, and discusses the resulting communication problem
in sermons using this jargon.

Keck, Leander E.
    "Listening to and Listening for: From Text to Sermon (Acts 1:8)." *Interpre-* **1174**
tation 27 (1973): 184-202. A professor of New Testament argues that attention
to exegesis is critical in sermon preparation, and then discusses his exegesis of
Acts 1:8. His sermon on this text follows.

Kehl, D. G.
    "Have You Committed Verbicide Today?" *Christianity Today*, 27 January **1175**
1978, pp. 18-21. Discusses Christian semantic distortion, including rhetorical
overkill, euphemism, and jargon, and reminds the preacher that the Holy
Spirit seeks to diminish such doubletalk.

Kerr, Hugh T.
    "Poetry and Preaching." *Theology Today* 21 (1964): 347-49. Charges con- **1176**
temporary preachers with using unimaginative language and simplistic solutions to the world's problems, thus failing in both technique and epistemology.

Kirkland, Bryant M.
    "Expository Preaching Revitalized." *Pulpit Digest* 45 (July 1965): 9-14. **1177**
Gives several hints on how to make expository preaching more effective.

Kolbe, Henry E.
"Preaching with the Bible." *Pulpit Digest* 50 (Dec 1969): 9–10. Helps the **1178**
preacher to make the Bible more meaningful to his congregation.

Koller, Charles W.
"So What?" *Christianity Today*, 9 April 1965, p. 40. Insists that sermonic **1179**
thrust, a response requested by the preacher, is an essential part of the sermon.
A printed sermon is given by way of illustration.

Krieger, Wilfred L.
"Visual Aids in Your Homily: Bridging the Boredom Gap." *Homiletic* **1180**
and Pastoral Review 69 (1969): 708–16. A military chaplain discusses advantages of using the overhead to help communicate the sermon, and he suggests
ways to prepare transparencies.

Lantero, Erminie Huntress
"Sermons Too Christian: A Complaint." *Pulpit Digest* 50 (Feb 1970): 9–14. **1181**
A call for creative originality in preaching, and some ways to achieve this.

Lauer, Robert H.
"Wise and Foolish Words." *Christianity Today*, 4 March 1966, pp. 18–19. **1182**
Shows the various extremes in word usage in preaching, and offers a balanced
view of the place of words in preaching.

Lay, Thomas
"Words Made Flesh." *Worship* 42 (1968): 337–41. Insists that communica- **1183**
tion of spiritual truth requires the preacher to make the Christian vocabulary
interpret the hearers' experience through visual, auditory, verbal, and tactile
channels.

Leps, Charles
"A Matter of Words." *Lutheran Quarterly* 26 (1974): 52–57. Challenges **1184**
preachers to use words that engage listeners at the deepest levels of their
experience, aiding them in making sense of life, that is, in reconciling their
experience with their convictions.

Levinson, Harry
"The Trouble with Sermons." *Journal of Pastoral Care* 22 (1968): 65–74. A **1185**
look at some psychological reasons why certain types of sermons fail to
motivate listeners, and three principles for preparing sermons that do motivate
them.

Lewis, Ralph L.
"Four Preaching Aims of Amos." *Asbury Seminarian* 21 (Apr 1967): 14–18. **1186**
A concise evaluation of Amos and his message, focusing on his four purposes:

attention, authority, audience appeals, and action. The author shows that Amos's preaching was visual, vital, vivid, and varied.

Lockerbie, D. Bruce
"We Use Great Plainness of Speech." *Christianity Today*, 24 October 1969, 1187
pp. 12, 17–18. Directs the preacher to a study of rhetoric, and particularly of persuasion, style, and message construction.

Lowry, Eugene L.
"The Homiletical Bind." *Christian Ministry* 6 (Jan 1975): 20–22. A five-step 1188
approach to building sermons, related to building plots and resolving conflict. The sermon idea, writes the author, is that "discrepancy," the gap between what is and what can be in the light of the gospel. The sermon theme should touch the congregation's needs.

Luecke, Richard Henry
"Renaissance Rhetoric and Born-Again Preaching." *Theology Today* 35 1189
(1978): 168–77. A discussion of eloquence and style, as treated by rhetoricians of the pre-Renaissance and Renaissance periods.

McBride, Alfred
"Preaching and Conversion." *Pastoral Life* 16 (1968): 497–99. Preaching 1190
must, the author contends, call men to a change of heart and urge them onward with rational appeals.

McKelvey, John W.
"How to Develop Varieties and Series of Sermons." *Church Management* 1191
54 (Apr 1978): 28–30. Gives thumbnail sketches and potential benefits of expository, textual, topical, biographical, narrative, and dialogue sermon series.

"How to Improve Your Sermons." *Church Management* 52 (Aug 1976): 1192
26–27. Argues that the key to effective sermons is good illustrative material, and discusses several resources to build up one's illustration file.

"How to Prepare a Sermon." *Church Management* 54 (Feb 1978): 21–23, 28. 1193
First defines a sermon, then speaks to such areas of sermon preparation as preparing oneself, one's mind, delivery, mechanics of sermon preparation, the sermon outline, and openness to God's Spirit.

McKeown, Robert E.
"Preaching and Poetic Vision: A Response to Dr. Willimon." *Worship* 50 1194
(1976): 110–15. Contends that the preacher can get too simple in his vocabulary and then be unable to express the paradoxes of the Christian faith. The preacher must, writes the author, view the world with "poetic vision" and express this vision with an appropriate vocabulary. See entry 1313 below.

MacLennan, David A.

"Priming the Preacher's Pump." *Church Management* 43 (Nov 1966): 30.　**1195**
Identifies as a key in the communication of a sermon the disciplined study of
God's Word in preparation.

"Priming the Preacher's Pump." *Church Management* 43 (July 1967): 42.　**1196**
Encourages preachers to touch the emotions of the audience, deliver spiritual
content that may be remembered, and make applications that are concrete.

"Priming the Preacher's Pump." *Church Management* 43 (Sep 1967): 22.　**1197**
Suggests ways to maintain the attention of the audience during the worship
service.

"Priming the Preacher's Pump." *Church Management* 49 (Feb 1973): 8.　**1198**
Describes the author's method of filing illustrations, and touches on the
process of sermon preparation.

"Words." *Pulpit Digest* 34 (Dec 1953): 13-21, 84. Analyzes the effect on a　**1199**
sermon of the choice of language.

Macleod, Donald

"Great Texts." *New Pulpit Digest* 57 (Nov 1977): 9-10. Points out advan-　**1200**
tages to the preacher and listener of a "great text" for the sermon, and defines
a "great text."

"The Homily and the Sermon." *New Pulpit Digest* 55 (Jan 1975): 14.　**1201**
Discusses the differences between a homily and a sermon, and suggests that
the homily be used more frequently.

"The Language Gap." *New Pulpit Digest* 57 (Jan 1977): 56-57. A plea to　**1202**
use words that "touch our lives" rather than ecclesiastical words strange to the
average man. The author gives four methods to improve communication in
the sermon.

"The Preacher and His Illustrations." *New Pulpit Digest* 57 (July 1977):　**1203**
58-59. Covers three aspects of illustrations: their importance and timing in a
sermon, their appropriateness, and the sources of illustrations.

"Topics, Titles, and Themes." *New Pulpit Digest* 56 (July 1976): 49-50.　**1204**
Defines sermon topics, titles, and themes; demonstrates the importance of a
good topic; and gives three characteristics of one.

McNamara, Robert F.

"What Is a Homily?" *Homiletic and Pastoral Review* 79 (Aug 1979): 40-46.　**1205**
Defines the homily as "a sermon that takes its departure from the text or
context of the liturgy being celebrated, and by applying the message of salvation . . . to the needs of the listeners, prepares them to participate fruitfully in
the Eucharist that follows."

MacNutt, Sylvester
    "How to Judge a Sermon." *Proceedings of the Catholic Homiletic Society*   **1206**
Charter Convention (1959): 30-39.

Madson, Norman A.
    "Homemade Homiletics." *Concordia Theological Monthly* 14 (1943):   **1207**
33-39. Describes a sermon born in the pastor's heart and mind as he studies
the Word, and explains the steps to preparing this kind of sermon.

Matthews, C. DeWitt
    "The Sermonic Grasshopper." *New Pulpit Digest* 56 (Mar 1976): 49. Argues   **1208**
for the use of the Bible's larger themes and passages rather than of random
Scripture passages. The author also promotes the diligent study of a text and
the preaching of its central idea.

Mavis, W. Curry
    "Preaching from the Depths." *Sunday School Times and Gospel Herald*, 1   **1209**
August 1974, pp. 30-31. Shows how one may formulate new insights to truth
through the Holy Spirit's working and one's own research.

Meadley, Thomas D.
    "How Sermons Come." *Preacher's Quarterly* 12 (1966): 11-16. Identifies   **1210**
three creative and power-filled methods for preparing sermons: the discipline
of concentrating, the ability to look at the subject in a fresh way, and the need
to get one's sermons through prayer. This is the third of a three-part article
(see RHT[1], entry 1150).

Merrill, Arthur L.
    "The Biblical Context of Preaching." *Theological Markings* 2 (Win 1972):   **1211**
36-39. Identifies three hermeneutical features in three sample sermons. The
author relates the multidimensional nature of Scripture and the way it
expresses the community's response to the revelatory event.

Mickey, Paul A.
    "Strength in Weakness: From Text to Sermon on II Corinthians 12:7-9."   **1212**
Interpretation 22 (1968): 288-300. Presents a sermon and explains how it was
prepared. The author emphasizes the preacher's responsibility to address
current problems clearly and aid the hearer in applying scriptural principles.

Miller, Philip V.
    "A New Hearing for the Allegorical Method." *Perkins School of Theology*   **1213**
Journal 29 (Win 1976): 25-34. Asserts that by interpreting "some" Scripture
passages allegorically, one can enhance preaching.

More, Robert, Jr.
    "Charles Finney and the 'Altar Call.'" *Banner of Truth* (July 1970): 29-34.   **1214**

Discusses the "altar call," which originated with evangelist Charles G. Finney and developed from his soteriology.

Morton, Richard K.
"What Makes a Sermon Today?" *Church Management* 51 (Aug 1975): 16, 1215
24. Attributes the decline of sermons to their having become news commentaries, entertainment, or artistic exhibitions. The author suggests that sermons should include scholarly research as well as pastoral talent.

Mounce, Robert H.
"What Makes Good Preaching?" *Eternity* 25 (Dec 1974): 47, 50. Discusses 1216
the need for preaching God's Word and making it relevant to the people, and contrasts this with merely modernizing the sermon.

Müller-Schwefe, Hans-Rudolph
"How Full of Promise Is Our Preaching?" *Lutheran Quarterly* 20 (1968): 1217
172-82. Treats the various effects of preaching, the language and the proclamation, the sermon and the text, and the meaning of "proclamation" in the course of preaching.

"The Sermon and Its Form." *Lutheran Quarterly* 20 (1968): 161-71. Dis- 1218
cusses three primary forms of public address, applies them to the sermon form, and analyzes the characteristics, strengths, and weaknesses of the various types of sermons.

Murphey, Cecil B.
"Personal Experience Adds Punch." *Christianity Today*, 25 May 1979, 1219
pp. 36-37. Suggests guidelines for the positive use in sermons of personal illustrations.

Murray, Iain H.
"Some Thoughts on Our Preaching." *Banner of Truth* (May 1975): 20-29. 1220
Outlines some weaknesses of contemporary Scottish sermons, finding them too intellectual and heavy, lacking sufficient application, and too often read from a manuscript.

Nelson, Wesley W.
"Practical Guidelines for Sermon Preparation." *Covenant Quarterly* 32 1221
(Feb 1974): 25-35. Defines preaching, and gives specific steps in the development of a sermon, discussing the research of the text and the structuring of the sermon.

Nixon, Leroy
"All Scripture Is Profitable." *Christianity Today*, 7 July 1967, pp. 24-25. 1222
Exhorts pastors to preach entire Bible books, and explains how to choose and prepare a series of sermons on a book.

Nord, Kermit J.
"Sermon Illustrations." *Pulpit Digest* 34 (Mar 1954): 77–80. Offers seven helps for illustrating sermons. **1223**

Northcutt, Jesse J.
"How to Prepare a Biblical Sermon." *Southwestern Journal of Theology* 2 (Apr 1960): 33–48. Defines biblical preaching, and offers guidance in selecting and interpreting a text, determining its relevance, and selecting the sermon's aim, central idea, and structure. **1224**

Ockenga, Harold J.
"The Metropolitan Pulpit." *Christianity Today*, 4 March 1966, pp. 36–37. An overall composite of the author's pulpit ministry, including the acquisition of material, yearly planning, and weekly schedule. **1225**

Ogilvie, Lloyd J.
"Relational Preaching: I, Speak from Your Life." *Faith at Work* 84 (Apr 1971): 21. Contends that relational preaching should convey not only ideas, but a good quality of life based on dynamic relationships to God and people. **1226**

"Relational Preaching: II, Direct and Flaming." *Faith at Work* 84 (June 1971): 21. Discusses how the author related his preaching to the immediate needs of his congregation. **1227**

"Relational Preaching: III, How Personal Can You Be?" *Faith at Work* 84 (Aug 1971): 21. The author believes that relating his own struggles to his congregation has improved his preaching. **1228**

"Relational Preaching: IV, How Do You Feel About People?" *Faith at Work* 84 (Oct 1971): 21. Emphasizes that how the preacher feels about his congregation is readily communicated through his preaching. **1229**

"Relational Preaching: V, Are You Excited by Christmas?" *Faith at Work* 84 (Dec 1971): 25. Relates the author's experience of Christ's indwelling, which improved his preaching. **1230**

Olford, Stephen F.
"Preaching the Word." *Christianity Today*, 18 August 1967, pp. 32–33. Insists that expository preaching is essential to the proper communication of biblical truth in a world that has lost the Word of God. Ordination, preparation, and declaration, says the author, are determinative in preaching. **1231**

Orr, J. M.
"Dialogue Preaching and the Discussion Service." *Expository Times* 82 (1970): 10–13. Explains why the author tried dialogue preaching and how it worked in his church. A sample dialogue sermon is included. **1232**

Owen, Robert L.
"Is the Cliché Here to Stay?" *Christianity Today*, 24 June 1966, p. 16. Cites   1233
common clichés that preachers should avoid, and provides some alternatives
to make preaching more interesting.

Palms, Roger C.
"Invest Your Illustrations." *Christianity Today*, 21 June 1974, pp. 31-32.   1234
Explains how to invest illustrations in each sermon, making a productive
piece that is remembered and reflected upon by congregations for the entire
week.

Paxton, Geoffrey J.
"The Gospel as the Power of God." *Present Truth* 5 (Aug 1976): 6-11. Gives   1235
four characteristics of poor sermons, and discusses three ingredients for biblical
preaching.

Pearson, Roy M.
"Choosing the Ideas." *Pulpit Digest* 43 (Feb 1963): 10-20. Enunciates five   1236
questions one should address to the sermon idea in determining its worth. A
chapter from *The Preacher: His Purpose and Practice* (see RHT[1], entry 264).

Peterman, Kenneth O.
"Principles of Expository Preaching." *Good News Broadcaster* 32 (Dec   1237
1974): 20-22. Examines three distinctives of expository study and the teaching
of God's Word: content centered, audience aimed, and Holy Spirit controlled.

Peterson, Eugene H.
"Kittel Among the Coffee Cups." *Princeton Seminary Bulletin* 66 (Oct   1238
1973): 33-36. Preaching requires a commentary at the levels of both exposition
and exegesis, says the author. He describes how to have a group of pastors
involved in the process of biblical exegesis.

Pfitzner, V. C.
"The Hermeneutical Problem and Preaching." *Concordia Theological*   1239
Monthly 38 (1967): 347-62. Deals with the definition and history of hermeneutics, formulates the central principles of biblical hermeneutics, and draws
some practical conclusions for preaching. The author then explicates six
steps in the process of going from text to sermon.

Poovey, W. A.
"Preaching and Drama." *Lutheran Quarterly* 20 (1968): 373-80. Suggests   1240
reasons why drama should be used in preaching, and surveys the history of
religious drama.

Pouncy, A. G.
"What Is Evangelistic Preaching?" *Christian Graduate* 20 (June 1967): 1-6.   1241

A summary of the place of evangelism in the context of the sermon, considering terminology, deficient gospel preaching, consecutive textual preaching, the teaching/evangelism balance, and results.

Reed, John W.
"How to Prepare a Message." *Moody Monthly* 75 (Apr 1975): 51-53. A   1242
step-by-step process of composing a sermon from start to finish. Included are resources to assist the preacher.

Rees, Paul S.
"Declare It, Preacher, Declare It!" *Christianity Today*, 16 July 1965, p. 30.   1243
Argues that to be true to Christ and His church, preachers must strike in their messages a declarative, affirmative note. A sermon illustrates the principle.

"A Homiletical Checkup." *Christianity Today*, 7 May 1965, p. 41. Urges   1244
the preacher to evaluate his pulpit ministry in terms of authenticity, specificity, and catholicity.

Rhys, T. Tudor
"The Technique of Preaching." *Expository Times* 58 (1947): 144-47.   1245
Affirms that form in preaching facilitates preaching and that the basic form is exposition, development, and recapitulation. The author includes examples.

Rice, Charles R.
"The Preacher as Storyteller." *Union Seminary Quarterly Review* 31   1246
(Spring 1976): 182-97. A definition and description of a sermon as a story. The author sees the preacher entering into the text as a person and visualizing the congregation as he composes the sermon.

"The Expressive Style in Preaching." *Princeton Seminary Bulletin* 64 (Mar   1247
1971): 30-42. A plea for the sermon to stay close to the preacher's human experience, thus illuminating the message rather than obscuring it with formalism.

Riddell, J. G.
"A Question of Words." *Scottish Journal of Theology* 1 (1948): 73-85.   1248
Analyzes the problem of pastors and evangelists communicating in terms understandable to congregations, and offers two principles for employing recognizable terms.

Riegert, Eduard Richard
"'Parabolic' Sermons." *Lutheran Quarterly* 26 (1974): 24-31. Distinguishes   1249
between the usual kind of sermon and the parabolic sermon, and offers a methodology for creating parabolic sermons. An example of a parabolic sermon is also given.

Riel, Arthur R., Jr.
"Why Do I Remember So Few Sermons?" *Homiletic and Pastoral Review* **1250**
76 (Nov 1975): 55-56, 58-62. Sermons are seldom remembered, says a speech
professor, because so little time is spent in preparing them. He suggests ways
to make the best use of one's time in preparing sermons.

Robinson, Haddon W.
"Preaching with an Impact." *Good News Broadcaster* 35 (Dec 1977): 31-32. **1251**
Defines expository preaching, then explains the definition.

"What Is Expository Preaching?" *Bibliotheca Sacra* 131 (1974): 55-60. After **1252**
explaining why preaching has been discredited, the author defines expository
preaching and then analyzes the definition part by part.

Rossell, William H.
"Preaching Values in Hebrew Words." *Southwestern Journal of Theology* **1253**
2 (Oct 1959): 19-25. A professor of Old Testament, employing Psalm 23 as an
example, illustrates how to use a concordance in preparing a sermon and
shows how many helpful sermon ideas can come from the Hebrew text.

Rossetti, A. Thomas
"In Search of the Sermon Topic." *Pulpit Digest* 58 (Mar 1978): 45-47. **1254**
Explores ways to choose sermon topics in light of individual experience, the
congregation, the text, and the "life situation."

Rueter, Alvin C.
"Isn't Preaching the Work of the Holy Spirit?" *Christian Ministry* 6 (Mar **1255**
1975): 24-26. Argues for the study and effective use of method in preaching.
The author supplies seven elementary steps for improving one's preaching
skill.

Rutledge, Wiley I.
"Good News from the Market Place." *Faith at Work* 89 (Sep 1976): 6. **1256**
Explains the author's techniques of devising meaningful applications by
polishing his sermons in local cafés.

Ryle, J. C.
"Simplicity in Preaching." *Banner of Truth* (July 1967): 1-7. Presents the **1257**
necessity of communicating God's Word truthfully yet simply, and offers five
hints in attaining simplicity: understand the subject, use simple words,
compose simply, use a direct style, and illustrate each point.

Sassaman, Dick
"How to Give a Successful Children's Sermon." *Church Management* 46 **1258**
(Mar 1970): 15. Provides guidelines on the composition and delivery of effective
children's sermons.

Scherer, Paul
"A Gauntlet with a Gift in It: From Text to Sermon on Matthew 15:21-28   1259
and Mark 7:24-30." *Interpretation* 20 (1966): 387-99. Examines the text,
presents a sermon on it, and explains the process through which the author
gained his sermon idea.

"A Great Gulf Fixed." *Pulpit Digest* 46 (Oct 1965): 9-16, 66. Offers ways the   1260
preacher can make his message more effective through better communication.
This is chapter 1 from *The Word God Sent* (see RHT[1], entry 117).

Schiavone, Jeldo
"A Modern View of the Homily." *Priest* 35 (Oct 1978): 37-39. Describes   1261
dialogue preaching as an excellent supplement to monologue preaching,
describes several types of dialogue preaching, discusses its advantages and
disadvantages, and suggests other methods for parish priests to improve their
preaching.

Schum, Henry
"You Can Minister Effectively to Children." *Journal of Pastoral Practice* 2   1262
(Win 1978): 153-56. Contains ideas for the preparation and delivery of sermons
intended for children.

Schweizer, Eduard
"From the New Testament Text to the Sermon." Translated by James W.   1263
Cox. *Review and Expositor* 72 (1975): 181-88. Discusses the process of exegesis
and sermon preparation, illustrating it with Mark 4:1-20 as a sermon text.
Exegesis consists of analysis, exposition, and construction of the sermon,
writes the author, and it is based on form criticism.

Scofield, C. I.
"Discovering Sermons in the Bible." Edited by Wilbur M. Smith. *Moody*   1264
Monthly 68 (Jan 1968): 35-36, 56. Contends that good sermons are the by-
product of good Bible study. The true preacher, says the author, comes to the
Scriptures not primarily for sermons but for the truth of God. If the preacher
would study, sermons would leap out at him.

Scotford, John R.
"Preaching Is Self-Exposure." *Pulpit Digest* 49 (Apr 1969): 15-18. Shows   1265
how much more effective sermons can be through the use of illustrations
from personal experience.

"Writing: The Preacher's Sport!" *Pulpit Digest* 39 (July 1959): 15-18.   1266
Outlines the benefits of writing out each sermon, and gives tips on how to
make this practice more profitable.

Shaw, Arthur
"Planning and Filing Sermon Material." *Christian Minister* 5 (Sep 1969):   **1267**
9–10. Proposes a card system for planning a schedule of sermon topics.

Shaw, Henry K.
"Preaching in the Imperative Mood." *Encounter* 28 (1967): 368–73. Reviews   **1268**
the lack of imperatives in today's preaching. Showing the imperative mood at
work in the Scriptures, the author argues for including the imperative mood
with other forms of homiletic expression.

Sherman, W. Goddard
"Preaching with Persuasion." *Pulpit Digest* 46 (June 1966): 12–14. Gives   **1269**
three basic rules for maintaining effectiveness in a sermon.

Skoglund, John E.
"Towards a New Homiletic." *Princeton Seminary Bulletin* 60 (Feb 1967):   **1270**
55–58. Insights into a possible new approach to homiletics, perhaps best
characterized as the world-word. The author advocates a confrontation of the
world with the Word of God.

Skublics, Ernest
"The Word Proclaimed and Applied." *Worship* 42 (1968): 627–34. Argues   **1271**
from the Catholic viewpoint that the gospel of salvation must be preached
every Sunday in the church service, the sermon must be limited to the facts of
the gospel, and the hearers should be left to make the applications for
themselves.

Slemp, John C.
"Principles and Methods of Bible Interpretation and Exposition." *Review*   **1272**
and Expositor 34 (1937): 452–69. Argues for an honest, historical, and objective
approach to Scripture. The author decries allegorizing, spiritualizing, and
making claims for the Bible it does not make for itself.

Smith, C. Ralston
"One Man's Way of Working." *Christianity Today*, 5 November 1965,   **1273**
pp. 26–27. One man's method for planning, preparing, and preserving
sermons.

Smith, Hilary Dansey
"Finding a Medium for Your Message." *Pastoral Life* 23 (1974): 20–23.   **1274**
Explains the meaning of style, tells why it is important, and suggests some
ways to develop an effective homiletic style.

Smith, Neil Gregor
"What Is a Sermon?" *Evangelical Quarterly* 30 (1958): 152–60. Discusses   **1275**
the nature of a sermon and its goal in communicating.

Snow, Arthur J.
"The Modern Novel in Preaching." *Minister's Quarterly* 16 (Sum 1960): 1276
7-10. Articulates the advantages of using the modern novel as a working tool
in the preparation of sermons.

Southard, Samuel
"Illustrations for Everybody." *Pulpit Digest* 42 (June 1962): 11-16. Asserts 1277
that the sermon's effect can be heightened by varying the content and length
of the illustration according to the listeners' ages, occupations, and social
status.

Sperry, Willard L.
"Sermon Illustrations." *Pulpit Digest* 32 (Sep 1951): 11-18. 1278

Spurgeon, Charles Haddon
"Long Sermons." *Banner of Truth* (Feb 1972): 35-40. Discusses the length 1279
of sermons, stating reasons why sermons should be short and why they are
sometimes too long.

Spurgeon, [Susannah] Mrs. C. H.
"Sermon Preparation at 'Westwood.'" *Banner of Truth* (Oct 1969): 29-32. 1280
Explains that throughout the week, Charles Haddon Spurgeon pondered the
subject and passage on which he would preach. On Saturday night he made
his final decision, then with his wife's help put his material in order.

Stacey, John
"Controversial Preaching." *Preacher's Quarterly* 14 (1968): 203-7. Contends 1281
that sermons purged of all controversy are like vegetables and potatoes without
salt. After urging preachers to tackle issues in politics, theology, ecclesiology,
or ethics, the author gives five guidelines for preparing a controversial sermon.

Steimle, Edmund A.
"The Fabric of the Sermon." *Luther Theological Seminary Review* 17 1282
(Spring 1978): 45-55. A plea for relevant preaching characterized by secularity,
dialogue, dramatic story form, and leanness.

Stephan, Paul G.
"Pulpit Payoff." *Christianity Today*, 8 July 1966, pp. 27-28. Ten steps for 1283
preparing sermons.

Stevenson, Dwight E.
"Eleven Ways of Preaching a Non-Sermon." *Lexington Theological Quar-* 1284
terly 10 (July 1975): 19-28. Explains eleven common sermon types that are in
fact "nonsermons," including the moralistic harangue, the aesthetic artifact,
the pontifical pronouncement, and the ecclesiastical commercial.

Strait, C. Neil
"Encouragement Is the Word." *New Pulpit Digest* 54 (Nov 1974): 7. Argues **1285** for a positive emphasis in the sermon rather than a guilt-producing emphasis.

"Take Saturday Night Off." *New Pulpit Digest* 56 (Mar 1976): 50. Offers **1286** practical ideas for sermon preparation, including ways to use the week wisely for sermon preparation.

Surfleet, Florence
"Speak with Ease." *Preacher's Quarterly* 14 (1968): 175-79. Describes a **1287** method designed to free the speaker of notes so that he can speak more spontaneously, combining the inspiration of the moment with careful thought and preparation beforehand.

Thomson, Ronald W.
"The Detective Novel and the Preacher." *Expository Times* 55 (1943): 69-71. **1288** Asserts that much within the realm of detective literature is pertinent to the preacher, such as the tone and style of the suspense writer.

"Modern Poetry and the Preacher." *Expository Times* 56 (1945): 164-67. **1289** Modern poetry satisfies two interests of the preacher: to give insight into his times and to be a source of quotation.

Timmerman, John J.
"In Praise of the Sermon." *Outlook* 22 (Dec 1972): 6-7. Examines the **1290** sermon as an example of the art of oratory and rhetoric. The author says that because the sermon is a "highly effective medium" of communication, it should continue to be part of worship.

Toohey, William
"Is Preaching Merely Sacred Rhetoric?" *Proceedings of the Catholic* **1291** *Homiletic Society Charter Convention* (1962): 94-100.

Towne, Edgar A.
"The Preacher's Languages." *Encounter* 37 (1976): 30-40. Comments on **1292** several "languages" the preacher employs in preaching: religious language, the language of everyday, the language of theology, and the language of feeling and value.

Toycen, Dave
"The Pewholder's Nightmare: Cotton Candy Preaching." *World Vision* 19 **1293** (June 1975): 18. Speaks of the need for preaching that touches the direct needs of the church, and discourages cotton-candy preaching, which makes simplistic observations.

Tuininga, Simon
"Clowns in the Pulpit?" *Torch and Trumpet* 14 (Dec 1964): 18–19. Exhorts 1294
preachers to keep their messages Christ-centered and to avoid mere moralizing.

Vines, Maxwell L.
"Discoveries Among Homiletical Meanderings." *Foundations* 21 (1978): 1295
82–90. Gives four basic principles of sermon development, and discusses the
role of dialogue, the use of illustrations, incongruity in sermons, and practical
considerations of preaching.

Vos, Johannes G.
"Are Bones a Luxury?" *Torch and Trumpet* 4 (June 1954): 9. Argues that 1296
sermons ought to be both based on doctrine and vitally related to life.

Ward, Ronald A.
"Pin-Points and Panoramas: The Preacher's Use of the Aorist." *Expository* 1297
Times 71 (1960): 267–70. Contends that a knowledge of the picturesque nature
of Greek, and particularly of the aorist tense, can give the preacher added
insight into the text and its vivid description of events.

Watson, Richard G.
"What's Wrong with Preaching Today?" *Christianity Today*, 25 October 1298
1974, p. 27. An appeal for sermons that contain subjects and substance directly
from the Word of God.

Watts, John D. W.
"The Methods and Purpose of Biblical Interpretation." *Southwestern* 1299
Journal of Theology 2 (Apr 1960): 7–16. Surveys three principles of hermeneutics, and identifies four kinds of biblical interpreters: the theologian, the
preacher, the worship leader, and the pastor in counseling.

Webber, Robert
"Content: A Priority for Communicators." *Spectrum: Christian Communi-* 1300
cations 1 (Fall 1975): 26–27. Discusses the necessity of communicating effectively not only in style and technique, but also in content. "Having something
to say," writes the author, "is an absolute imperative."

Westermann, Claus
"From the Old Testament Text to the Sermon." Translated by James W. 1301
Cox. *Review and Expositor* 72 (1975): 169–79. Proposes a hermeneutic to help
one preach from the Old Testament. The author relies on historico-
philological exegesis, making use of literary and form criticism. He demonstrates his method in a study of Psalms 42 and 43.

Westhoff, Alponse; Gavaler, Campion; Scannell, Anthony; and Toohey, William
"Let's Look at the Homily: A Panel Discussion." *Homiletic and Pastoral*   **1302**
Review 65 (1965): 832-36. A panel of priests discuss their views on the homily and how they prepare it.

Weyermann, Andrew M.
"Process of Preparation: Genesis 22:1-14: From Text to Proclamation."   **1303**
Concordia Theological Monthly 43 (1972): 752-65. Explains how the author developed a sermon (included in its entirety), from his basic assumptions about preaching to the application and the delivery.

White, J. Melville
"Media, from the Pulpit Hotseat." *Eternity* 25 (Dec 1974): 49-50. Illustrates   **1304**
a variety of methods for preaching, taken from the author's own experience.

White, M. Jackson
"How to Light Up a Sermon." *Christianity Today*, 26 May 1967, pp. 30-31.   **1305**
Highlights the importance of illustrations, different sources for them, and cautions to remember when using them.

Whitesell, Faris D.
"Achieving Simplicity in Preaching." *Sunday School Times and Gospel*   **1306**
Herald, 15 April 1976, pp. 30-31. Discusses how to prepare and deliver a simplified sermon. The author covers such things as the theme, simple language, and delivery, and he uses John 3:16 as an illustration.

"Evangelistic Preaching." *Sunday School Times and Gospel Herald*, 1   **1307**
February 1976, pp. 30-31. Arguing that evangelistic preaching is the most important kind, the author lists five steps in doing it.

"The Plea for Relevance in Preaching." *Sunday School Times and Gospel*   **1308**
Herald, 15 November 1975, pp. 30-31. Discusses the need for biblical sermons, for knowing the people's needs, for appropriate illustrations, for easy language, and for relevant applications.

"Using the Imagination in Preaching." *Sunday School Times and Gospel*   **1309**
Herald, 1 September 1975, pp. 30-31. Shows the importance of imagination in preaching, and lists four types: historical, sympathetic, creative, and futuristic. The author also tells how to develop one's imagination.

"The Values of Expository Preaching." *Sunday School Times and Gospel*   **1310**
Herald, 15 July 1976, pp. 30-31. Defines expository preaching and delineates its value to the congregation and the preacher.

Wiersbe, Warren W.
"Humor in the Pulpit." *Moody Monthly* 74 (Sep 1973): 65-69. Considers   **1311**

the place of humor in preaching, concluding that it should be in accord with the preacher's personality and the sermon topic.

Williams, John H.
"Diversity in the Format of the Sunday Sermon." *Proceedings of the Catholic Homiletic Society Charter Convention* (1961): 36–49. **1312**

Willimon, William H.
"Kierkegaard on Preachers Who Become Poets." *Worship* 49 (1975): 107–12. **1313** Agrees with Kierkegaard that the preacher must avoid his tendency to be poetic when delivering the sermon, and that he must try instead to be realistic. The author argues that the preacher is to stir listeners to action, not, like the poet, to stimulate their emotions. See entry 1194 above.

"Must We Devastate to Deliver?" *Christianity Today,* 18 June 1976, pp. 10– **1314** 12. Ponders ways to preach to the person who is strong and "at the top."

Wilson, C. Ronald
"Illustrations Make the Difference." *New Pulpit Digest* 57 (Sep 1977): **1315** 68–70. Argues for the use of illustrations in preaching, mentions sources of illustrations, and suggests a system for filing them.

Wolf, Carl Umhau
"The Continuing Temptation of Christ in the Church: Searching and **1316** Preaching on Matthew 4:1–11." *Interpretation* 20 (1966): 288–301. Precedes the text of a sermon with the preparatory steps taken in building it.

Wood, John Edwin
"A New Testament Pattern for Preachers." *Evangelical Quarterly* 47 (1975): **1317** 214–18. Examines the many excellent preaching techniques in the Book of Hebrews.

Woodbridge, Barry A.
"Preaching as Subversive Activity." *Christian Century* 6 February 1974, **1318** pp. 142–50. Considers conceptual problems of the new hermeneutic, and explains the need for authentic language or subversive language that overthrows everyday language from underneath.

Wuest, Kenneth S.
"The Holy Spirit in Greek Exposition." *Bibliotheca Sacra* 118 (1961): 216–27. **1319** Discusses the work of the Holy Spirit in inspiration, teaching, and controlling the believer, as these relate to sermon preparation.

"Preparation Technique for Greek Exposition." *Bibliotheca Sacra* 118 **1320** (1961): 123–32. Describes and demonstrates a simple method of doing exegesis in the preparation of sermons, and suggests tools to use. The procedure is basically one of doing word studies on each major word in the verses studied.

Delivery

Adams, Jay E.
"Bodily Action in Preaching." *Journal of Pastoral Practice* 3, 1 (1979): **1321**
143-46. Suggests practical ways to improve the use of the body.

Botti, Anthony
"The Speaking Voice." *Proceedings of the Catholic Homiletic Society* **1322**
Charter Convention (1959): 42-55.

Cooper, Morton
"Vocal Suicide Among the Clergy." *Church Management* 46 (July 1970): **1323**
42-43. Advocates more voice training for preachers. The author discusses
typical voice problems and voice control.

Cox, James W.
"Preaching Without Notes." *New Pulpit Digest* 56 (May 1976): 53-54. **1324**
Argues for preaching without notes, and suggests ways to do it.

de Witt, John Richard
"Preaching, Today and Yesterday." *Banner of Truth* (Mar 1975): 1-6. **1325**
Stresses the need for contact with the audience and freedom from a manuscript.

Ekman, Paul, and Friesen, Wallace V.
"Hand Movements." *Journal of Communication* 22 (1972): 353-74. Groups **1326**
hand movements into three classes, and explains how each may be used.

Haggai, W. A.
"Practical Points for Preachers to Ponder." *Sunday School Times and* **1327**
Gospel Herald, 15 September 1973, pp. 30-31. Reviews fourteen areas preachers
should watch, dealing mainly with general appearance and sermon delivery.

Hope, Norman V.
"Is a Read Sermon a Dead Sermon?" *Christianity Today*, 28 April 1967, **1328**
pp. 30-31. Discusses three major types of sermon delivery, suggesting ways to
preach with no notes whatever.

Hostetter, Richard
"Let's Polish Our Delivery." *Christianity Today*, 2 March 1979, pp. 47-48. **1329**
Designed to give immediate help on basic problems in delivery.

Johnson, Ben E.
"Use Gestures Wisely." *Church Management* 43 (Aug 1967): 45, 47. An **1330**
English teacher gives guidelines to preachers on the proper use of natural
gestures for effective communications.

Lass, Norman J., and Prater, C. Elaine
"A Comparative Study of Listening Rate Preferences for Oral Reading and 1331
Impromptu Speaking Tasks." *Journal of Communication* 23 (1973): 95–102.
Demonstrates that the preferred listening rate for both oral reading and
impromptu speaking is between 175 and 200 words per minute.

Lewis, Ralph L.
"Speech Training for the Minister." *Asbury Seminarian* 16 (Fall 1962): 1332
29–38. Discusses the importance of speech training to the pulpit ministry.

McCarthy, David S.
"Mind Your Mannerisms." *Christianity Today,* 26 October 1973, pp. 52, 54. 1333
Lists and describes a variety of bad mannerisms, especially those involving
the hands, that arise in sermon delivery.

Martin, Albert T.
"'Paper-Geniuses' of the Anglican Pulpit." *Quarterly Journal of Speech* 1334
51 (1965): 286–93. Examines the phenomenon of Anglican preachers reading
their sermons from manuscripts, reviewing the defense of this practice, oppo-
sition to it, and the effect of the controversy upon eighteenth-century delivery.

Reilly, Godfrey
"What Is He Talking About?" *Homiletic and Pastoral Review* 48 (1948): 1335
440–44. Stresses the importance of accompanying the spoken word with
gestures.

Schork, R. J.
"The Sung Sermon." *Worship* 47 (1973): 527–39. Explains the "sung 1336
sermon," which was part of the Eastern church. Included are the lyrics of a
"kantakion" (metrical homily set to music) written and delivered by Ramanos
the Melodist.

Scotford, John R.
"Watch Your Listeners." *Church Management* 46 (Feb 1970): 24–25. A 1337
church consultant emphasizes the importance of eye contact between preacher
and audience.

Spurgeon, Charles Haddon
"Preaching—in a Natural Style." *Banner of Truth* (Jan 1972): 33. Addresses 1338
the need for preachers to pay attention to delivery. The truth they speak from
the Word of God should be delivered, insists the author, in a natural manner
that is an extension of their personalities.

Stromer, Walter F.
"Your Voice Is Your Fortune?" *Christian Ministry* 4 (July 1973): 19–21. A 1339

speech professor offers several insights into and practical methods for improving sermon delivery.

History—Individual Preachers

Abbott, Don
"Ian Paisley: Evangelism and Confrontation in Northern Ireland." *Today's*   1340
Speech 21 (Fall 1973): 49-55. Examines the role of Paisley, fundamentalist preacher, in the inception of civil unrest in Northern Ireland. His preaching tactics and political maneuvers, writes the author, reveal the style of the Reformation preachers.

Ackworth, John
"Sermon Topics." *Bibliotheca Sacra* 101 (1944): 102-4. Catalogs the sermon   1341
topics of Charles Haddon Spurgeon, telling how many came from each book of the Bible.

Anderson, Floyd Douglas
"*Dispositio* in the Preaching of Hugh Latimer." *Speech Monographs* 35   1342
(1968): 451-61. Examines the delivery, structure, and content of Latimer's sermons, which moved his sixteenth-century audiences. The author demonstrates that Latimer was no slave to preaching form.

Anonymous
"Harry Emerson Fosdick." *Christianity Today*, 24 October 1969, p. 31. A   1343
brief account of Fosdick's career, focusing on his role in the fundamentalist-modernist controversy.

"The Thundering Scot." *Christianity Today*, 27 October 1972, pp. 26-27. A   1344
comment on John Knox's key role in the Scottish Reformation and on his contribution to education and the church.

Aquila, Dominic A.
"Apostle in Virginia." *Presbyterian Journal*, 26 January 1977, pp. 7-8, 19.   1345
Samuel Davies, an eighteenth-century preacher, enjoyed a balanced ministry of church planting and Bible preaching for thirty-eight years, according to this biographical study.

Auksi, Peter
"Wyclif's Sermons and the Plain Style." *Archive for Reformation History*   1346
66 (1975): 5-23. Attributes the plain style of John Wyclif's sermons to the example of Christ, statements from Scripture, and the pattern of the primitive church. The author also discusses Wyclif's use of a conventional premise of classical rhetorical theory.

Barlow, Richard B.
"Thomas Bradbury (1677-1759): Pulpit Firebrand and Defender of the   1347
Protestant Succession." *Andover Newton Quarterly* 18 (1978): 172-77. A brief
overview of the fiery Protestant dissenter and fearless crusader during Queen
Anne's stormy reign.

Barnds, William Joseph
"Jonathan Swift, Preacher." *Anglican Theological Review* 40 (1958): 42-47.   1348
A summary of Swift's ideas about preaching, including his approach to
sermon preparation and delivery.

Barnes, T. D.
"The Emperor Constantine's Good Friday Sermon." *Journal of Theologi-*   1349
cal Studies 27 (1976): 414-23. Examines the setting, date, and message of
Constantine's Good Friday Sermon, delivered in A.D. 317 on the occasion of
Constantine's audience having been released from the oppression of another's
rule.

Barnhouse, Donald Grey
"Giant Among Bible Teachers." *Eternity* 9 (Jan 1958): 7-9, 48. Traces the   1350
life of A. C. Gaebelein, outstanding teacher and preacher and the founder of
Our Hope.

Barrois, Georges A.
"Calvin and the Genevans." *Theology Today* 21 (1965): 458-65. Sixty-six   1351
sermons by John Calvin on Isaiah 13-29 are shown to contain the principal
themes of his theology, and then several of these themes are surveyed.

Batson, E. Beatrice
"The Artistry of John Bunyan's Sermons." *Westminster Theological Jour-*   1352
nal 38 (1976): 166-81. Examines specific sermons for structure, rhetoric, and
applications. The author notes Bunyan's use of character-sermons and
question-answer sessions following his sermons.

Bennett, Hiram R.
"Jonathan Swift, Priest." *Anglican Theological Review* 39 (1957): 131-38.   1353
Focuses on many facets of Swift, one of whose many talents was preaching.

Bishop, John
"P. T. Forsyth: Preaching and the Modern Mind." *Religion in Life* 48   1354
(1979): 303-8. Reviews Forsyth's theology of preaching in *Positive Preaching
and the Modern Mind* (see RHT[1], entry 159).

Brentnall, John
"John Hieron of Breadsall." *Banner of Truth* (Nov 1969): 34-40. Portrays   1355

the life, ministry, and character of Hieron, a seventeenth-century preacher known for his reverence for God and his patient ministry to his people.

"William Bagshawe: The Apostle of the Peak." *Banner of Truth* (Nov **1356**
1967): 3–8. Probes the ministry of Bagshawe in seventeenth-century England. His faithful proclamation of God's Word for more than half a century is acknowledged.

Burleigh, John H. S.
"St. Augustine: Pastor and Preacher." *Union Seminary Quarterly Review* **1357**
20 (May 1965): 343–54. Examines Augustine's episcopal duties, preaching, ethical emphasis, and doctrinal controversies. His preaching, says the author, was a sentence-by-sentence, often word-by-word exposition, and he sometimes used the allegorizing method of interpretation.

Carter, C. Sydney
"John Williams: A Statesman Bishop." *Evangelical Quarterly* 20 (1948): **1358**
147–56. A biographical sketch of Williams (1583–1651).

Carter, Joseph C.
"Russell Conwell's *Lectures on Oratory*." *Foundations* 12 (1969): 47–65. A **1359**
transcription of Conwell's class lectures, some remarks by William Saurman, and an introduction and conclusion by the author. The lectures reflect Conwell's philosophy of oratory and his stimulating methods of teaching.

Chandler, Daniel R.
"Preston Bradley on Preaching." *Religious Communication Today* (Sep **1360**
1978): 11–14. Traces Bradley's thoughts on selected rhetorical topics.

Chazan, Robert
"Confrontation in the Synagogue of Narbonne: A Christian Sermon and a **1361**
Jewish Reply." *Harvard Theological Review* 67 (1974): 437–57. Reviews the preaching of Friar Paul Christian in the thirteenth century, the purpose of which was to evangelize the Jews.

Coleman, William L.
"Billy Sunday: A Style Meant for His Time and Place." *Christianity Today*, **1362**
17 December 1976, pp. 14–17. A look at Sunday and his evangelistic campaign in New York in 1917.

Costas, Orlando
"Influential Factors in the Rhetoric of Augustine." *Foundations* 16 (1973): **1363**
208–21. A study of the intellectual and theological forces that shaped Augustine's rhetorical theory.

Dabney, Robert L.
    "Dabney on Preaching." Edited by Paul Helm. *Banner of Truth* (Mar   **1364**
1976): 17-23. Discusses gospel sermons, historical sermons, and the interpretation of the Word for the congregation.

Davis, R. E.
    "Billy Sunday: Preacher-Showman." *Southern Speech Journal* 32 (1966):   **1365**
83-97. Examines Sunday's appeals, techniques, content, and effectiveness,
concluding that he was "a brilliant success" as a showman but "tended to fall
short" as an evangelist.

Donovan, Daniel D.
    "Saint John Chrysostom: Spokesman for Christ." *Homiletic and Pastoral*   **1366**
Review 75 (Oct 1974): 62-66. Explains why Chrysostom was such an out-
standing speaker. The author mentions in part the great amount of time
Chrysostom devoted to the preparation of sermons.

Doyle, G. Wright
    "Augustine's Sermonic Method." *Westminster Theological Journal* 39   **1367**
(1977): 213-38. An excursion into the milieu that helped to shape Augustine's
sermons. The author also explains Augustine's sermon preparation.

Ellis, William E.
    "Edgar Young Mullins and the Crisis of Moderate Southern Baptist Lead-   **1368**
ership." *Foundations* 19 (1976): 171-85. Rehearses the crisis atmosphere faced
by this president of Southern Baptist Theological Seminary (1899-1928), an
atmosphere created by the evolution controversy and prohibition.

Epp, Theodore H.
    "God Used a Man." *Good News Broadcaster* 23 (Apr 1965): 6-7. Describes   **1369**
the effect of T. Myron Webb's radio preaching on many people, including the
author.

Eubank, Wayne C.
    "Palmer's Century Sermon, New Orleans, January 1, 1901." *Southern*   **1370**
Speech Journal 35 (1969): 28-39. Examines the final sermon that Benjamin
Morgan Palmer preached by popular demand, analyzing its setting, outline,
organization, proofs, style, and delivery, and the reaction it produced.

Evans, W. Glyn
    "Tell It Like It Is." *Moody Monthly* 69 (Jan 1969): 28-29, 45-46, 51. De-   **1371**
scribes the way D. L. Moody preached, speaking to people persuasively
through a familiarity with the Bible and spiritual power.

Francis, Alan F.
"William Griffiths: The Apostle of Gower." *Banner of Truth* (May 1970): **1372**
21–30. A short biography of Griffiths, an English preacher in the late 1700s.

Franklin, Benjamin
"I Remember George Whitefield." *Eternity* 21 (July 1970): 30–31. Franklin **1373**
recounts in his memoirs the magnetism of Whitefield's preaching, his oratorical gift, and Franklin's personal response to Whitefield's preaching.

Franklin, J. D. R.
"Prerequisites for Preaching." *Christianity Today*, 31 January 1969, p. 15. **1374**
Singles out certain gems in John Newton's writings on qualifications for, and
spiritual tone in, preaching.

Freeman, William
"Cotton Mather and Homiletics." *Central States Speech Journal* 27 (1976): **1375**
218–24. Investigates Mather's view on the covenant of grace, credibility and
reason, and their relationship to his homiletical theory.

Gordon, Alasdair B.
"James Kidd of Aberdeen." *Banner of Truth* (Nov 1973): 29–32. The life of **1376**
Kidd, a nineteenth-century preacher and scholar in Scotland whose strong
personality and good study habits gave power to his preaching.

"Some Sidelights on Ralph Erskine." *Banner of Truth* (Sep 1969): 20–22. **1377**
Highlights of the life of Erskine (1685–1752), a Scottish preacher.

Graham, Billy
"Biblical Authority in Evangelism." *Christianity Today*, 22 October 1976, **1378**
pp. 14–16. Recounts the author's decision to follow the Bible as God's authoritative Word, and enjoins others to "preach the Scriptures with authority."

"Billy Graham: Spanning the Decades." *Christianity Today*, 7 November **1379**
1969, p. 34. An interview with Graham on the twentieth anniversary of his
first evangelistic campaign. He recounts the beginning of his ministry and
especially the publicity given his first campaign.

Green, Lowell C.
"Justification in Luther's Preaching on Luke 18:9–14." *Concordia Theo-* **1380**
logical Monthly 43 (1972): 732–47. Lists five suggestions for preaching doctrinal sermons, all of which emerged from a study of Martin Luther's pulpit
work.

Gundry, Stanley N.
"Grand Themes of D. L. Moody." *Christianity Today*, 20 December 1974, **1381**
pp. 4–6. Cites quotations of Moody, and demonstrates several themes emphasized and exemplified by him.

Hagan, Michael R.
"J. N. Darby, the Brethren Movement, and Lay Ministry." *Religion in Life*   1382
44 (1975): 347-62. A professor of communication examines the life and
ministry of Darby, emphasizing Darby's concern that laymen be free to preach.

Hamilton, James E.
"Finney: An Appreciation." *Christianity Today*, 8 August 1975, pp. 13-16.   1383
Thoughts on the influence of Charles G. Finney, presented through an histori-
cal survey of his life.

Hasler, Richard A.
"John Witherspoon, Pastor in Politics." *Christianity Today*, 29 September   1384
1972, pp. 11-12, 14. An examination of Witherspoon's career in light of the
current tension between the minister's prophetic and pastoral functions.

Herget, Winfried
"Preaching and Publication: Chronology and the Style of Thomas   1385
Hooker's Sermons." *Harvard Theological Review* 65 (1972): 231-39. Traces
Hooker's sermons through the process of publication, noting, among other
things, the variations in published sermons.

Herzog, Frederick L.
"Theologian of the Word of God." *Theology Today* 13 (1956): 315-31.   1386
Discusses Karl Barth as a theologian, but devotes one section to his expe-
riences as a young preacher.

Hickin, Leonard
"Charles Kingsley (1819-1875)." *Expository Times* 86 (1975): 146-50. A   1387
sketch of a great preacher whose sermons attracted those who seldom attended
church, and who was one of few Church of England clergymen regarded by
the queen as a favorite preacher.

Hobbs, Herschel H.
"Reflections on My Ministry." *Southwestern Journal of Theology* 15   1388
(Spring 1973): 71-77. Reflects on a forty-year ministry, providing insights that
would profit young preachers.

Hodges, Graham R.
"Fosdick at 90." *Christian Century*, 22 May 1968, p. 684. An overview of   1389
Harry Emerson Fosdick's multifaceted contribution to Protestantism by way
of writing, preaching, and church involvement.

Hope, Norman V.
"A Reminder from John Knox." *Christianity Today*, 27 October 1972,   1390
pp. 5-6. Finds in Knox an example of the power of prophetic preaching, and

locates his contribution as a Reformer and pulpiteer in his ability to apply the Bible to his own day.

Hopkins, Paul A.

"What Made the Man?" *Eternity* 12 (Mar 1961): 14–18, 35–40, 42. Gives an 1391
interesting look at the things that surrounded the life of Donald Grey Barnhouse and how they affected his preaching.

Horne, Charles M.

"The Power of Paul's Preaching." *Bulletin of the Evangelical Theological* 1392
Society 8 (1965): 111–16. An exegetical study of I Corinthians 2:1–5, concluding
that Paul reached sinful men only by presenting God's message with His
methods and in His power.

Hornsby, J. T.

"James Allen of Gayle." *Evangelical Quarterly* 15 (1943): 40–55. A 1393
biographical account of Allen (1734–1804), including a discussion of his
preaching.

Houghton, S. M.

"George Whitefield and Welsh Methodism." *Evangelical Quarterly* 22 1394
(1950): 276–89. Reviews Whitefield's field preaching in Wales and his friend-
ship with Howel Harris.

"Spurgeon and His Sermons." *Banner of Truth* (Oct 1973): 17–26. Describes 1395
the manner of and movement in Charles Haddon Spurgeon's sermons. The
author has read Spurgeon's sermons for forty years and views them as excellent
examples of biblical preaching.

Humphreys, David

"Thomas Hooker." *Banner of Truth* (Feb 1968): 30–36; (Mar 1968): 32–40; 1396
(Apr 1968): 25–36. The life and preaching ministry of Hooker, a seventeenth-
century English clergyman.

Johnson, George

"Calvinism and Preaching." *Evangelical Quarterly* 4 (1932): 244–56. 1397
Analyzes the style and goal of John Calvin's preaching.

Jones, Bob

"Moody and Sankey." *Faith for the Family* (Nov 1973): 6–9. Looks at the 1398
effect on the world of D. L. Moody's preaching, and at the relationship between
Moody and Ira D. Sankey in this ministry of faith.

"Sam Jones: Great Evangelist." *Faith for the Family* (Sep 1973): 9–10. 1399

Killian, Charles
"John Wesley: A Speech Critic." *Asbury Seminarian* 24 (Apr 1970): 7-14. A   **1400**
compilation of Wesley's advice on delivery—hand gestures, facial expression,
voice level, and speech clarity.

Kimnach, Wilson H.
"Jonathan Edwards' Early Sermons: New York, 1722-1723." *Journal of*   **1401**
Presbyterian History 55 (1977): 255-66. A study of twenty-four unpublished
sermons revealing Edwards's early naiveté and orthodoxy.

Lampton, William E.
"Worldliness: Helmut Thielicke's Quest for Relevant Preaching." *Southern*   **1402**
Speech Journal 34 (1969): 245-55. Focuses on Thielicke's rhetoric and his
attraction of the masses during World War II, when he defied Hitler's tirades
against religion, and in the present.

Larkin, William J.
"A. W. Blackwood: Teacher of Preachers." *Moody Monthly* 74 (Nov 1973):   **1403**
87-88, 90-91. Outlines the life, ministry, and books of Andrew W. Blackwood,
who had a passion for biblical preaching and people, who was pastor of
several Presbyterian churches, and who became professor of homiletics at
Princeton Theological Seminary.

"C. E. Macartney: Champion of the Faith." *Moody Monthly* 73 (Jan 1973):   **1404**
47-52. Reflects on Clarence Edward Macartney's character and preaching style.

"Donald Grey Barnhouse." *Moody Monthly* 76 (Feb 1976): 123-25. A pastor   **1405**
recounts the expository preaching ministry of Barnhouse, revealing his convictions of the truthfulness of God's Word and the clarity of his preaching.

Lazenby, Walter
"Exhortation as Exorcism: Cotton Mather's Sermons to Murderers." *Quar-*   **1406**
terly Journal of Speech 57 (1971): 50-56. A professor of English illustrates how
Mather took advantage of every conceivable current event in his sermons.

Leavenworth, J. Lynn
"John Mason Peck's Ministry and the Flow of History." *Foundations* 17   **1407**
(1974): 259-67. A summary, analysis, and application for today of the principles
of Peck, a pioneer evangelist, educator, and organizer in the Mississippi valley.

Lee, Philip
"Karl Barth as Preacher and Pastor." *Union Seminary Quarterly Review* 28   **1408**
(Fall 1972): 87-92. Uses Barth to show the need for sermons to contain the
Word of God, for the pastor to shepherd the flock of Christ, and for reforma-
tion in the parish to meet people's individual needs.

Lindsell, Harold
"Reflections on a Crusader." *Christianity Today,* 2 July 1971, p. 23. Makes   **1409**
observations on Billy Graham, reviewing the strongpoints of his ministry.

McAlister, Virginia Clemens, and Roberts, Mary M.
"Peter Marshall's Sermon Approach: Innovative or Traditional?" *Southern*   **1410**
Speech Journal 35 (1970): 315-23. Analyzes Marshall's preaching, concluding
that he followed the best of rhetorical traditions. The authors quote from
Marshall's wife to give insight into the man and his sermon preparation.

McCord, James I.
"The Faith of John Knox." *Princeton Seminary Bulletin* 65 (Dec 1972):   **1411**
16-21. A narrative of Knox's life, focusing especially on the faith that sustained
him as a preacher and Reformer.

McGuire, Michael D., and Patton, John H.
"Preaching in the Mystic Mode: The Rhetorical Art of Meister Eckhart."   **1412**
Communication Monographs 44 (1977): 263-72. Examines Johannes Eckhart's
adaptation of homiletical principles extant in his time.

Mackerness, E. D.
"F. W. Robertson (1816-1853): A Thinker in the Pulpit." *Evangelical Quar-*   **1413**
terly 29 (1957): 218-29. Analyzes Robertson's sermons, and discusses his
theology.

McKirachan, J. Frederick
"The Preaching of Paul Tillich." *Princeton Seminary Bulletin* 53 (Jan   **1414**
1960): 33-42. A detailed analysis.

Macleod, John
"Charles Simeon (1759-1836)." *Evangelical Quarterly* 9 (1937): 46-63. A   **1415**
sketch of Simeon's preaching and life.

McLoughlin, William G., Jr.
"Billy Sunday Was His Real Name." *Pulpit Digest* 36 (Oct 1955): 93-113. A   **1416**
condensation of the book by the same title (see RHT[1], entry 386).

More, Robert, Jr.
"Asahel Nettleton and Evangelistic Methods." *Banner of Truth* (Oct 1970):   **1417**
29-37. Discusses Nettleton's methods, compares them to Charles G. Finney's,
and evaluates their results.

Morris, Calvin
"Martin Luther King, Jr.: Exemplary Preacher." *Journal of the Inter-*   **1418**
denominational Theological Center 4 (Spring 1977): 61-66.

Morris, Lee
"Projecting Pastoral Care in Revival Preaching: Billy Graham." *Pastoral*   1419
Psychology 19 (June 1968): 33-41. Explores how Graham projects pastoral
care in his preaching, analyzing examples in his sermons.

Murray, Iain H.
"Charles Hodge (1797-1878)." *Banner of Truth* (Feb 1958): 12-18. A brief   1420
biography with one of Hodge's sermon outlines appended to it.

"Dabney." *Banner of Truth* (Mar 1967): 1-4, 20; (May 1967): 12-15. A   1421
historical account of the life and ministry of Robert L. Dabney, a Presbyterian
preacher-theologian of Virginia in the nineteenth century.

"The Forgotten Spurgeon." *Banner of Truth* (Mar 1962): 16-32; (Feb 1963):   1422
1-72. Discusses Charles Haddon Spurgeon's method of preaching, the content
of his messages, his theology, and his reprinted sermons.

"George Whitefield: A Spur to Ministers." *Banner of Truth* (Apr 1970):   1423
32-40. Examines Whitefield's contributions to preaching. Prominent in them,
says the author, are Whitefield's love, humility, and fellowship with God.

"A Hundred Years Ago: I, C. H. Spurgeon and the 1859 Revival." *Banner*   1424
of Truth (Feb 1959): 4-11. An analysis of Charles Haddon Spurgeon's influence
in the English revival of 1859.

"An Introduction to Jonathan Edwards (1703-1758)." *Banner of Truth* (Feb   1425
1958): 2-11. A brief treatment of Edwards's life and ministry.

"John Brown, D.D. (1787-1858)." *Banner of Truth* (Sep 1961): 16-21. A   1426
biographical sketch that discusses Brown's view of exegesis, according to
which the sermon must be derived from and fully related to the text.

"John Elias, 1774-1841." *Banner of Truth* (Apr 1957): 5-14. An account and   1427
analysis of Elias's life and ministry.

"John Flavel." *Banner of Truth* (Sep 1968): 1-10. A discussion of Flavel's   1428
life, the popularity of his works, his impact on his congregation, and his
spiritual preparation for preaching.

"Jonathan Edwards." *Banner of Truth* (Dec 1974): 23-32; (Apr 1975): 7-18.   1429
Describes the early life of Edwards, an American theologian-preacher, including his schooling, conversion, and character.

"Joseph Irons and 150 Years Ago." *Banner of Truth* (Nov 1968): 1-6. A   1430
historical account of Irons (emphasizing his prayer life and diligent study)
and of Grove Chapel, where he ministered.

"Robert Murray McCheyne." *Banner of Truth* (Feb 1957): 14-23. A brief   1431
biography of McCheyne, and a summary of his teachings.

"Thomas Jolly of Wymondhouses." *Banner of Truth* (July 1967): 13-17.   1432
Records the ministry of Jolly, a seventeenth-century itinerant preacher in

England. The author treats the persecution Jolly experienced and his stead-
fastness in preaching the gospel.

"Whitefield and the Evangelical Revival in Scotland." *Banner of Truth*   1433
(Apr 1970): 8-24. Discusses the revival of the 1700s in Scotland, revealing the
preparations made for George Whitefield's first visit, the commencement of
the revival, and its effects.

"Whitefield in 'the Jerusalem of England.'" *Banner of Truth* (Jan 1971):   1434
17-28. An address given on the anniversary of George Whitefield's death, in
which the author provides a historical account of Whitefield's ministry in and
around London.

"William Jay: The Preacher." *Banner of Truth* (Apr 1971): 15-30. Reviews   1435
Jay's life and ministry, emphasizing the importance of his preaching during
his day.

Oke, C. Clare
"Paul's Method Not a Demonstration but an Exhibition of the Spirit."   1436
Expository Times 67 (1955): 35-36. Explains the meaning of *apodeixis* in
I Corinthians 2:4, relating it to Paul's method of proclaiming the gospel.

Osborn, Ronald E.
"In the Fight to Set Men Free: Harry Emerson Fosdick (1878-1969)."   1437
Encounter 31 (1970): 177-81. A memorial address recognizing the breadth of
Fosdick's influence, the preeminence of his preaching, and the characteristics
of his pulpit ministry.

Owens, James H., Sr.
"Billy Graham—A Contemporary Micaiah." *Christianity Today*, 30 July   1438
1965, p. 24. Compares Graham to a prophet of old with "a message of peace,
love, and reconciliation."

Panosian, Edward M.
"America's Theologian-Preacher." *Faith for the Family* (Nov 1976): 12-13,   1439
42-43. Argues that Jonathan Edwards played a strategic role in bridging the
gap between the colonial and revolutionary periods.

"The Awakener." *Faith for the Family* (Jan 1976): 16-18. Depicts George   1440
Whitefield as a co-worker with Jonathan Edwards and John Wesley, and as a
well-balanced man of faith.

Parkander, Dorothy J.
"Puritan Eloquence: The Sermons of Samuel Ward of Ipswich." *Anglican*   1441
Theological Review 41 (1959): 13-22. Examines Ward, a Puritan preacher, and
his ideas about preaching.

Patton, John H.
"Wisdom and Eloquence: The Alliance of Exegesis and Rhetoric in   1442
Augustine." *Central States Speech Journal* 28 (1977): 96-105. Discusses Augustine's closely connected exegetical and rhetorical precepts.

Peerlinck, Francis
"Rudolf Bultmann: Preaching and Liturgy." *Worship* 47 (1973): 450-62.   1443
Analyzes the liturgical elements in Bultmann's sermons along with his suggestions about preaching and the liturgical service.

Peterson, Raymond A.
"Jeremy Taylor's Theology of Worship." *Anglican Theological Review* 46   1444
(1964): 204-16. Indicates the scope of Taylor's liturgical, homiletical, and ascetical writings, as well as his theological presuppositions.

Phillips, Robert A., Jr.
"Fosdick and the People's Concerns." *Foundations* 13 (1970): 262-76. Dis-   1445
cusses Harry Emerson Fosdick's sermons decade by decade, showing the problems of each decade and Fosdick's response to those problems.

Pitts, John
"The Genius of Charles Haddon Spurgeon." *Christianity Today*, 27   1446
February 1970, pp. 6-8. Explores various features of Spurgeon's pulpit genius that account for his success.

Pollock, John C.
"The Human Side of Billy Graham." *Eternity* 17 (May 1966): 8-10, 38.   1447
Looks at Graham's private life, daily routine, devotional life, and manner with people.

"One Man's Furrow." *Christianity Today*, 13 September 1974, pp. 14, 17-18,   1448
21. An historical assessment of Billy Graham's impact.

Purcell, Malcolm
"Preacher for the Ages." *Moody Monthly* 71 (Apr 1971): 26-27, 47-49. A   1449
biographical sketch of George Whitefield, analyzing his great orations and message.

Quillian, Joseph D., Jr.
"Albert Outler as Pastor." *Perkins School of Theology Journal* 27 (Spring   1450
1974): 29-35. A biographical summary that offers insights into the methods of Outler, an influential churchman, including Outler's methods of preaching and teaching.

Reeves, Dudley
"Charles Simeon in Scotland." *Banner of Truth* (Jan 1973): 15-21. Relates   1451
the preaching ministry of Simeon, an eighteenth-century preacher.

"David Bogue and Scotland." *Banner of Truth* (Nov 1974): 26–32. Tells of   **1452**
the life and ministry of Bogue, a nineteenth-century preacher who showed
much love for the people and ability to train preachers.

"James Haldane." *Banner of Truth* (July 1971): 18–24; (Apr 1972): 24–30.   **1453**
An account of the conversion and spiritual development of Haldane, an
eighteenth-century Scottish naval officer, showing how God carefully shaped
him into a preacher.

"Rowland Hill in Scotland." *Banner of Truth* (July 1973): 43–48. Describes   **1454**
the lively and direct preaching of Hill, an English aristocrat turned preacher.

"Whitefield in Scotland." *Banner of Truth* (Mar 1977): 23–32. Delineates   **1455**
the motivation and character of George Whitefield's preaching in Scotland, as
well as principles governing his itinerant preaching.

Rongione, Louis A.
"Augustine the Preacher." *Homiletic and Pastoral Review* 77 (July 1977):   **1456**
50–56. Examines factors that made Augustine a great preacher.

Rowe, David L.
"Elon Galusha and the Millerite Movement." *Foundations* 18 (1975):   **1457**
252–60. Reviews the life and leadership of a leading Baptist preacher of the
1800s.

Rudolph, Erwin R.
"Richard Baxter: A Fugitive Life." *Eternity* 23 (Apr 1972): 37–39. An   **1458**
account of Baxter's life, a list of his literary contributions, and a discussion of
the qualities of his preaching.

Rupp, George
"The 'Idealism' of Jonathan Edwards." *Harvard Theological Review* 62   **1459**
(1969): 209–26. Examines Edwards's works and his "idealism," faith in the
immediacy of God's presence and at the same time an embracing of the order
of natural law.

Russell, C. Allyn
"J. C. Massee: Unique Fundamentalist." *Foundations* 12 (1969): 330–56.   **1460**
Discusses the life and ministry of Massee.

"John Roach Straton: Accusative Case." *Foundations* 13 (1970): 44–72. Tests   **1461**
the claim that Straton, a Baptist pastor, was a social prophet of the early 1900s.

"William Bell Riley: Architect of Fundamentalism." *Foundations* 18 (1975):   **1462**
26–52. Reviews the life and thought of Riley, a gifted fundamentalist preacher.

Sayre, Francis B., Jr.
"An Interview with Francis B. Sayre, Jr." Interviewed by Robert Graham   **1463**

Kemper. *Christian Ministry* 3 (Jan 1972): 37-42. Sayre, the chief administration officer and preacher at Washington National Cathedral, speaks out for preaching the Word of God, even while he values other forms of communication.

Schafer, Thomas A.
"The Role of Jonathan Edwards in American Religious History." *Encounter* 30 (1969): 212-22. Surveys Edwards's role in early New England Protestantism as preacher, theologian, and promoter of the Great Awakening. 1464

Scofield, C. I.
"Jesus Christ as a Preacher." *Bibliotheca Sacra* 100 (1943): 546-53. Analyzes the preaching method of Jesus Christ. 1465

Scott, Manuel L.
"The Lord Came Preaching." *Christianity Today,* 26 April 1968, pp. 6-7. Contends that the Gospels provide an authentic portrait of Jesus Christ as a preacher, and that our distinctives should be the same as His. 1466

Secrett, A. G.
"Philip Doddridge and the Evangelical Revival of the Eighteenth Century." *Evangelical Quarterly* 23 (1951): 242-59. A biography of Doddridge (1702-1751), and an account of his influence on the eighteenth-century revival. 1467

Shaw, Ian
"Auguste Francke: Man of Active Faith." *Banner of Truth* (July 1975): 23-28. Portrays the preaching and orphanage ministries of Auguste H. Francke in eighteenth-century Germany, noting his compassion for the poor and service to the Lord. 1468

Shelley, Bruce
"Charles E. Fuller: Taking Risks on Radio." *Eternity* 27 (May 1976): 25-26, 35-37. A survey of the life of Fuller, a fundamentalist preacher, and an estimate of the impact of his radio program, "Old Fashioned Revival Hour." 1469

"James McGready: Hellfire on the Frontier." *Eternity* 27 (Jan 1976): 29-30, 32. A glimpse of the violent preaching style of revivalist McGready and his influence on camp meetings. 1470

Shindler, Robert
"Dr. Nettleton: The New England Evangelist." *Banner of Truth* (Oct 1975): 19-25. Presents the internal struggle preceding Asahel Nettleton's conversion as a key factor in his becoming an evangelist. 1471

Simpson, Edmund K.
"Spurgeon's Intellectual Qualities." *Evangelical Quarterly* 6 (1934): 381-97. Discusses Charles Haddon Spurgeon's word choice and preaching style. 1472

Sleeth, Ronald E.

"Bultmann and the Proclamation of the Word." *Princeton Seminary* 1473
Bulletin, new series, 2 (1979): 153–62. Examines Rudolf Bultmann's contribution to preaching theory.

"What Is the Matter with Preaching? A Fosdick Retrospective." *Perkins* 1474
School of Theology Journal 32 (Sum 1979): 28–30. Restates some of Harry Emerson Fosdick's principles on topical preaching and the use of the Bible in sermon preparation.

Smellie, Alexander

"A Field Preacher." *Banner of Truth* (July 1960): 11–19. A biography of 1475
John Blackader, reprinted from the author's book *Men of the Covenant: The Story of the Scottish Church in the Years of Persecution* (1903).

Snyder, Howard A.

"John Wesley: A Man for Our Times." *Christianity Today*, 23 June 1972, 1476
pp. 8–11. Discusses six elements of Wesley's success, three regarding his message, three his method.

Sobosan, Jeffrey G.

"Newman's Preaching: Theory and Practice." *Homiletic and Pastoral* 1477
Review 74 (Dec 1973): 66–71.

Spurgeon, Charles Haddon

"John Wesley." *Banner of Truth* (May 1969): 15–20; (June 1969): 43–48; 1478
(July 1969): 54–58. Comments on Wesley's character and preaching style.

Stanwood, Paul Grant

"John Cosin as Homilist, 1595–1671/72." *Anglican Theological Review* 47 1479
(1965): 276–89. Looks at Cosin's interests and sermons.

Stefun, Bonaventure

"St. Augustine, Preacher." *Homiletic and Pastoral Review* 64 (1964): 591–96. 1480
Considers the success of Augustine's preaching in light of his use of Scripture in sermons.

Stegmaier, Norma K.

"Mark Hopkins and His Baccalaureate Sermons." *Southern Speech Com-* 1481
munication Journal 37 (1972): 259–68. Analyzes Hopkins's twenty baccalaureate sermons, considered his most successful speeches, for their content, purposes, ideas and arguments, and proofs.

Stonier, Geoffrey

"Isaac Watts and Preaching." *Banner of Truth* (Dec 1974): 3–8. Identifies 1482
Watts as the connecting link between the Puritan preachers and the Evangelical Awakening. The author describes Watts as a preacher and hymn writer.

Straton, Hillyer H.
"Melito of Sardis, Preacher Extraordinary." *Anglican Theological Review*   **1483**
29 (1947): 167-70. Reviews the reasons for Melito's excellence as a preacher.
The author bases observations on a recently discovered sermon by Melito on
Christ's passion.

Sugden, Howard F., and Wiersbe, Warren W.
"Rediscovering a Preacher's Preacher." *Moody Monthly* 71 (Jan 1971): 50,   **1484**
52-56. A sketch of George H. Morrison's life and ministry in Scotland,
emphasizing his biblical preaching and devotion to people.

Tade, George T.
"Rhetorical Aspects of the *Spiritual Exercises* in the Medieval Tradition of   **1485**
Preaching." *Quarterly Journal of Speech* 51 (1965): 409-18. Examines the
persuasive power of *Spiritual Exercises*, written by Ignatius of Loyola, and its
vivid language and word pictures.

Thomas, Geoffrey
"Alexander Comrie." *Banner of Truth* (Feb 1969): 4-8; (Mar 1969): 29-35. A   **1486**
description of the public and private life of Comrie, a faithful Dutch preacher
in the 1700s.

"Jonathan Scott." *Banner of Truth* (Mar 1970): 30-35. Sketches the character   **1487**
and life of Scott, an eighteenth-century English army captain who became
first a Christian and then a preacher.

Thomas, Gordon L.
"Hugh Latimer: Preacher *ad populum*." *Quarterly Journal of Speech* 51   **1488**
(1965): 28-34. Highlights the life of Latimer and his messages, relationships,
social and economic concerns, aggressiveness, style, and general pulpit skill.

Turnbull, Ralph G.
"Jonathan Edwards and Great Britain." *Evangelical Quarterly* 30 (1958):   **1489**
68-74. Discusses Edwards's style of preaching and some of the literature that
helped to shape it.

Ulback, Edward
"John Chrysostom, Preacher." *Bibliotheca Sacra* 95 (1938): 328-42. A biog-   **1490**
raphy of Chrysostom, with an analysis of his preaching and style of ministry.

Van Groningen, Gerard
"That Balanced Young Preacher." *Outlook* 21 (Aug 1971): 10-11. Examines   **1491**
Zechariah's preaching and its impact on the people. The author points out
that Zechariah preached the "full counsel of God."

Wakeley, J. B.
"Whitefield's Last Days." *Banner of Truth* (Apr 1970): 4-7. Depicts George   **1492**
Whitefield's last sermon and his death.

Walk, Donald A.
"The Foolishness of Preaching." *Homiletic and Pastoral Review* 76 (May   **1493**
1976): 30-32. Discusses Paul's style when preaching to the Corinthians
(I Corinthians 1:17-2:15) and the reasons for that style.

Walker, Charles
"Thomas Chalmers: A Christian Strategist." *Banner of Truth* (May 1969):   **1494**
29-36. Presents Chalmer's influence on the restoration of biblical preaching
in nineteenth-century Scotland.

Walls, Andrew F.
"James Lee of Shadoxhurst: A Study in Evangelical Religion in the Bleak   **1495**
Age." *Evangelical Quarterly* 32 (1960): 34-44. A biography of Lee (1792-1865)
that comments on the nature of his preaching.

Wardin, Albert W., Jr.
"J. Whitcomb Brougher, Sr.: The Portland Years." *Foundations* 13 (1970):   **1496**
73-78. Describes Brougher, a Baptist pastor who exerted great influence for
moral and social change in Oregon from 1904 to 1910.

Warlick, Harold C., Jr.
"Fosdick's Preaching Method." *Religion in Life* 41 (1972): 509-23. Ex-   **1497**
amines the preaching style of Harry Emerson Fosdick, describing it as pastoral
counseling from the pulpit.

Webber, F. R.
"Walther in the Pulpit." *Concordia Theological Monthly* 32 (1961): 621-26.   **1498**
Details contributions of C. F. W. Walther to the pulpit.

White, Richard C.
"Dwight E. Stevenson: Teacher of Preachers." *Lexington Theological*   **1499**
Quarterly 10 (Apr 1975): 1-6. A biography of Stevenson, a respected homiletics
professor, in which the author sets forth insights for the pastor who takes
preaching seriously.

"Melito of Sardis: Earliest Christian Orator?" *Lexington Theological*   **1500**
Quarterly 2 (1967): 82-91. Introduces the recently discovered paschal homily
of Melito of Sardis. This second-century homily may be, writes the author, the
earliest known Christian use of rhetoric in preaching.

Wiersbe, Warren W.
"Baxter: Frail, but Effective." *Moody Monthly* 76 (Jan 1976): 112-16. Reveals   **1501**

the heart of Richard Baxter, a seventeenth-century English preacher who preached the truth of God's Word with compassion.

"F. W. Robertson: The Sad, Lonely Pastor." *Moody Monthly* 73 (Feb 1973): 1502
52–57. A biographical sketch that focuses on the trials of Robertson's life as well as his contributions to preaching.

"The Fighting Mystic." *Moody Monthly* 77 (Dec 1976): 107–9; (Jan 1977): 1503
123–25. Looks at the life of F. B. Meyer, a nineteenth-century English preacher, who stood against tremendous obstacles and preached in what was then an unconventional manner.

"A Formula That Works." *Moody Monthly* 77 (Apr 1977): 117–21. Com- 1504
ments on the formula used by Joseph Kemp to do the work of God: Kemp prayed, taught the Bible, and evangelized.

"Frank W. Boreham: The Man and His Writings." *Moody Monthly* 75 (Oct 1505
1974): 83–87. Recounts the life of Boreham, an industrious preacher and prolific writer who pastored in New Zealand and Australia in the early twentieth century.

"G. Campbell Morgan: Prince of Expositors." *Moody Monthly* 75 (Dec 1506
1974): 67–71. Credits Morgan's fine sermons to his long hours of studying the Word of God, and describes them as doctrinally sound and devotionally appealing.

"Ironside: Preaching Without Gimmicks." *Moody Monthly* 77 (Oct 1976): 1507
143–47. Characterizes Harry A. Ironside's ministry as one of preaching God's Word in simplicity and love and without gimmicks.

"Joseph Parker: Ecclesiastical Eagle." *Moody Monthly* 74 (Dec 1973): 59–62. 1508
An overview of the life and ministry of Parker, a nineteenth-century English preacher who lived for his preaching alone.

"The Little Fair Preacher of Anwoth." *Moody Monthly* 73 (June 1973): 1509
69–72. A biographical sketch of Samuel Rutherford, the seventeenth-century Scottish preacher.

"Maclaren: Devoted and Disciplined." *Moody Monthly* 75 (June 1975): 1510
99–101. Presents Alexander Maclaren as a man of disciplined study, hard work, and concentration on the preaching of God's Word.

"Mr. Moody's Friend." *Moody Monthly* 73 (Dec 1972): 51–56. Examines the 1511
life and ministry of Henry Drummond, a Scottish preacher of the nineteenth century.

"Pastor as Shepherd, Prophet, Builder." *Moody Monthly* 74 (May 1974): 1512
77–80. Reviews the life and books of Charles E. Jefferson, who maintained a fine balance between pastoring and preaching.

"Phillips Brooks on Preaching." *Moody Monthly* 72 (Feb 1972): 61–65. A **1513**
biographical sketch of Brooks, a Christian humanist and the preacher of
timeless themes.

"Sangster of Westminster: A Big Man." *Moody Monthly* 74 (Mar 1974): **1514**
73–75. Reveals the compassion of William Edwin Sangster, a twentieth-century
English pastor who in his preaching combined scholarship with a love for
his congregation.

"A Scholar but Not a Recluse." *Moody Monthly* 77 (Mar 1977): 155–59. **1515**
Reviews the ministry of W. H. Griffith Thomas, showing his prayer life,
disciplined study, and clarity of presentation.

"Sidelights on Charles H. Spurgeon." *Moody Monthly* 73 (Mar 1973): **1516**
55–56, 58–61. Identifies notable characteristics of Charles Haddon Spurgeon.

"Varley: Gospel Wholesaler." *Moody Monthly* 76 (June 1976): 97–101. **1517**
Sketches the life of Henry Varley, the itinerant preacher who greatly challenged
D. L. Moody for God's service.

"W. R. Nicoll: Minister, Editor, Knight." *Moody Monthly* 73 (Nov 1972): **1518**
73–76. Describes the life and ministry of Nicoll, best known for editing *The
Expositor's Bible*.

"Whyte: 'A Deevil of a Laddie.'" *Moody Monthly* 75 (Apr 1975): 105–9. A **1519**
biographical sketch of Alexander Whyte, revealing a lifetime of study and
forty-seven years of preaching in Edinburgh.

Wilson, J. Christy
"The Significance of Samuel Zwemer." *Princeton Seminary Bulletin* 61 **1520**
(Autumn 1967): 51–60. Examines the impact of Zwemer, a preacher and mis-
sionary to Muslims.

Wirt, Sherwood E.
"George Whitefield: The Awakener." *Moody Monthly* 79 (Sep 1978): 55, **1521**
60, 62, 64. Describes the life, person, and ministry of George Whitefield.

Wood, A. Skevington
"Luther as a Preacher." *Evangelical Quarterly* 21 (1949): 109–21. Analyzes **1522**
six aspects of Martin Luther's preaching, including his simplicity, his connection with the biblical text, and his freedom of form.

Woods, Rich
"Billy Sunday: The Baseball Evangelist." *Faith for the Family* (Sep 1976): **1523**
12–13, 44–45. The story of how God moved Billy Sunday from the baseball
field to the pulpit.

History—Groups

Agonito, Joseph A.
"The Significance of Good Preaching: The Episcopacy of John Carroll."   1524
American Ecclesiastical Review 167 (1973): 697-704. Discusses ways in which
Carroll, a native American and the first Roman Catholic bishop in the United
States, helped to cultivate good preachers.

Andrews, J. H. B.
"The Rise of the Bible Christians." *Preacher's Quarterly* 11 (1965): 51-58. A   1525
discussion of the Bible Christians, who broke off from the Methodist Church
in East Cornwall and North Devon, England. The author devotes much space
to the preachers in this movement.

Bailey, Ivor
"The Challenge of Change: A Study of Relevance Versus Authority in the   1526
Victorian Pulpit." *Expository Times* 86 (1974): 18-22. Compares the preaching
ministries of Charles Haddon Spurgeon and F. W. Robertson, assessing the
tension between orthodoxy, with its risk of irrelevance, and liberalism, with
its risk of obscuring revelation.

Ban, Joseph D.
"Two Views of One Age: Fosdick and Straton." *Foundations* 14 (1971):   1527
153-71. A review of the public and written records of John Roach Straton, a
spokesman for fundamentalism, and Harry Emerson Fosdick, a spokesman
for moderate progressives.

Basney, Lionel
"The Heyday of the Sermon." *Christian Herald* 99 (Feb 1976): 4, 6, 10, 12. A   1528
historical survey of great preachers and their influence, beginning with Paul
and Peter and concluding with D. L. Moody and Phillips Brooks.

Cox, James W.
"'Eloquent . . . , Mighty in the Scriptures': Biblical Preachers from Chry-   1529
sostom to Thielicke." *Review and Expositor* 72 (1975): 189-201. A sketch of the
lives and analysis of the preaching of such men as John Chrysostom, Martin
Luther, Charles Haddon Spurgeon, Karl Barth, and Helmut Thielicke.

"The Southern Baptist Pulpit, 1845-1970." *Review and Expositor* 67 (1970):   1530
195-202. Traces major themes in Southern Baptist preaching, identifying
men who were typical of their periods.

Cragg, Gerald R.
"Training the Ministry—the Older Tradition." *Andover Newton Quarterly*   1531
8 (1968): 223-34.

Davies, Horton

"Elizabethan Puritan Preaching." *Worship* 44 (1970): 93-108, 154-70. **1532**
Examines the Elizabethan Puritans and their emphasis on preaching, the
simple structure of their sermons, the distinguishing characteristics of their
hermeneutics, their sermonic styles, and their favorite topics.

Dayton, Donald W., and Sider, Lucille Dayton

"Women as Preachers: Evangelical Precedents." *Christianity Today,* 23 **1533**
May 1975, pp. 4-7.

De Jong, Peter Y.

"Preaching and the Synod of Dort." *Banner of Truth* (Dec 1968): 21-36. **1534**
Reminds the reader that the Synod of Dort showed great interest in preaching
by defining it and by showing its urgency, character, content, and aim.

Eppinger, Paul D.

"Four Great Baptist Preachers and the Theology of Preaching." *Founda-* **1535**
tions 11 (1968): 110-26. A study and critique of the preaching of Harry Emerson
Fosdick, Robert J. McCracken, Gene E. Bartlett, and Stephen F. Olford.

Haselden, Kyle

"Priests and Preachers." *Christian Century,* 30 June 1965, p. 830. An **1536**
analysis of the rise of preaching in Roman Catholicism and its overall decline
in Protestantism.

Hayden, Eric W.

"Eighteenth-Century Pulpit Preparation." *Banner of Truth* (Mar 1972): **1537**
36-40; (May 1972): 16-18. Excerpts from letters between Joshua Thomas and
Benjamin Francis on, among other things, sermon preparation.

"Spurgeon and Moody: Parallel Lives." *Moody Monthly* 73 (Apr 1973): **1538**
61-66. Shows the similarities between Charles Haddon Spurgeon and D. L.
Moody in character, appearance, and dependence on the Holy Spirit.

MacInnes, George

"African Parish: Formation or Inspiration?" *Worship* 44 (1970): 588-97. A **1539**
look at the preaching of the Catholic church in Africa, uncovering problems
and making suggestions that Protestant preachers can read with profit.

Macleod, Donald

"Fosdick-Sockman-Scherer." *Princeton Seminary Bulletin* 63 (Dec 1970): **1540**
6-8. A remembrance of three preachers shortly after their deaths: Harry
Emerson Fosdick, Ralph W. Sockman, and Paul Scherer.

Reist, Irwin W.

"John Wesley and George Whitefield: A Study in the Integrity of Two **1541**

Theologies of Grace." *Evangelical Quarterly* 47 (1975): 26-40. Compares Wesley and Whitefield, using quotations from their works.

Seaton, Jack
"Philip and Matthew Henry." *Banner of Truth* (Feb 1975): 1-8. Sketches   1542
the lives, character, and ministries of this father and son.

Semple, James H.
"Passing the Torch of Evangelism." *Christianity Today*, 27 October 1967,   1543
p. 15. Traces the historical links between the conversion experiences of great
evangelists from D. L. Moody through Billy Graham.

Smylie, James H.
"Protestant Clergymen and American Destiny: I, Promise and Judgment,   1544
1781-1800." *Princeton Seminary Bulletin* 55 (Apr 1962): 62-73. Analyzes the
preachments of various clergymen between 1781 and 1800, discovering two
dominant themes: promise and judgment.

Smylie, John E.
"Protestant Clergy and American Destiny: II, Prelude to Imperialism,   1545
1865-1900." *Princeton Seminary Bulletin* 55 (Apr 1962): 74-84. Analyzes the
way Protestant clergymen viewed history and so shaped the future American
destiny from 1865 to 1900.

Southard, Samuel
"The Pulpit Heritage of Louisville and Nashville." *Pulpit* 36 (Jan 1965):   1546
8-10. A professor of the psychology of religion analyzes four types of preachers
that have contributed to the present preaching tradition in that region:
exhorter, narrator, administrator, and inquirer.

Starkloff, Carl F.
"Barth and Loyola on Communication of the Word of God." *Scottish*   1547
Journal of Theology 27 (1974): 147-61. Compares the views of Karl Barth and
Ignatius of Loyola on the preacher's attitudes, functions, and preaching.

Vander Hart, Mark
"The Place of Preaching and the CRC." *Outlook* 22 (Nov 1972): 22-24.   1548
Traces the place of preaching in the Christian Reformed Church, finding it to
occupy a very important position.

Van Gorp, Sheryl
"The CRC and the Place of Preaching." *Outlook* 23 (Jan 1973): 12-14.   1549
Traces the history of preaching in the Christian Reformed Church and
analyzes its purpose—to "bring Christ to others."

History—Periods

Barclay, William
"The Life and Message of the Early Church." *Preacher's Quarterly* 11 **1550**
(1965): 187-90, 246-61; 12 (1966): 4-10, 81-88, 155-63, 248-56. Contains many
helpful and interesting insights into the first-century church and the message
its spokesmen preached.

Bell, L. Nelson
"Then and Now." *Christianity Today,* 26 May 1967, pp. 28-29. A look at **1551**
the focal points of preaching in the early church: the sin problem and
redemption. The author contends that preaching has deteriorated since that
era.

De Jong, Peter Y.
"The Throbbing Heart of Reformatory Preaching." *Torch and Trumpet* **1552**
12 (Dec 1962): 10. Explores some of the causes of the Reformation.

Heald, John C.
"Apocalyptic Rhetoric: Agents of Anti-Christ from the French to the **1553**
British." *Today's Speech* 23 (Spring 1975): 33-37. Argues that sermons on the
Book of Revelation were the basis of military and economic allegiance of New
England citizens between 1774 and 1776. The author supplies examples of
how the Apocalypse was used to interpret current events.

Huntley, Frank L.
"Heads for an Essay on the Seventeenth Century Funeral Sermon in **1554**
England." *Anglican Theological Review* 38 (1956): 226-34. Examines the
purposes and structure of the seventeenth-century funeral sermon.

Jasper, F. N.
"Preaching in the Old Testament." *Expository Times* 80 (1969): 356-61. **1555**
Argues that preaching played a very important part in the worship of preexilic
Israel and that therefore to eliminate preaching from our worship is to forsake
our Old Testament heritage.

Muirhead, Ian A.
"Preaching and Theology in the Thirteenth Century and To-day." *Exposi-* **1556**
tory Times 59 (1948): 312-14. Views distinctives of Dominican and Franciscan
preachers against the historical background of the thirteenth century, and
analyzes their transition to more academic pursuits.

Murray, Iain H.
"Ministerial Training: A Sketch of Theological Education in the 16th and **1557**
17th Centuries." *Banner of Truth* (Apr 1959): 12-21. Sketches theological
instruction, particularly in England.

"The Presentation of the Gospel and the Doctrines of Grace." *Banner of* 1558
Truth (Feb 1957): 23-28. Traces the relationship between preaching such doctrines as election and sovereignty and the occurrence of revivals in the church.

"The Puritan View of the Ministry and Its Relation to Church Govern- 1559
ment." *Banner of Truth* (Aug 1957): 24-34. A study of the Puritan movement,
with comments on the Puritans' view of preaching.

Robertson, J. D.
"Focus in Preaching." *Asbury Seminarian* 10 (Spring 1956): 3-6. Discusses 1560
the role of contemporary preaching.

Smith, Edward O., Jr.
"The Doctrine of the Prince and the Elizabethan Episcopal Sermon: 1561
1559-1603." *Anglican Theological Review* 45 (1963): 83-92. Considers sermons
prepared to cultivate a royal mystique.

Stamm, Frederick Keller
"Preaching: Challenge at Mid-Century." *Pulpit Digest* 31 (Dec 1950): 11-20. 1562
Looks at the stature of Christian preaching during the first half of this
century.

History—Theory

Casteel, John L.
"Conceptions of Preaching in the Yale Lectures." *Anglican Theological* 1563
Review 26 (1944): 65-74. The central idea emerging from the Yale lectures is
that preaching is divinely inspired utterance.

Dieter, Otto A.
"*Arbor picta:* The Medieval Tree of Preaching." *Quarterly Journal of* 1564
Speech 51 (1965): 124-44. Discusses the origin of the *arbor picta,* a homiletical
model for preaching from before the sixteenth century. Included are remarks
about aspects of the tree that are valid today.

Dod, Albert B.
"The Origin of the Call for Decisions." *Banner of Truth* (Dec 1963): 9-15. 1565
Discusses the history of the invitation, which originated with Charles G.
Finney.

McGee, Michael C.
"Thematic Reduplication in Christian Rhetoric." *Quarterly Journal of* 1566
Speech 56 (1970): 198-204. Analyzes the sermon's argumentative structure and
the development of rhetorical theory in the early Christian period. The author
also notes changes that have occurred in sermon delivery.

More, Robert, Jr.
"The Historical Origins of 'the Altar Call.'" *Banner of Truth* (Dec 1969): 1567
25-31. Defines the phrase "altar call," and analyzes it biblically and historically.

Osborn, Ronald E.
"A Functional Definition of Preaching: A Tool for Historical Investigation
and Homiletical Criticism." *Encounter* 37 (1976): 53-72. A historian proposes
a definition of preaching.

1568

Teaching

Adams, Jay E.
"A Method for Discovering Good Models: Study of Taped Sermons."
Journal of Pastoral Practice 3, 2 (1979): 143-46. Advocates the use of video
tapes in the study of the content and form of preaching and of the preacher's
vocal characteristics.

1569

Bass, George M.
"Videotape: A Prescription for Preaching." *Lutheran Quarterly* 20 (1968):
381-88. Surveys some problems of preaching and suggests video tape as a
good vehicle for correcting them.

1570

Burke, John
"Preaching: The Synthetic Act of the Believer." *Homiletic and Pastoral
Review* 77 (Oct 1976): 20-26. Argues that seminary curricula must renew their
emphasis on preaching because of preaching's proven capability of giving
believers insight and meaning to their faith.

1571

Davis, H. Grady
"The Teaching of Homiletics: The Present Situation in American Seminaries." *Encounter* 22 (1961): 197-207. Summarizes the consensus in homiletics
about a theology of preaching and about procedures for teaching preaching.

1572

Heetland, David
"Can Homiletics Be an Academic Discipline?" *Church Management* 51
(Mar 1975): 17-18. Discusses the qualifications of a preacher who has preached
for many years for teaching homiletics, and the direction homiletics should
take in the future.

1573

Hiltner, Seward
"The Teaching of Practical Theology in the United States During the
Twentieth Century." *Princeton Seminary Bulletin* 61 (Autumn 1967): 61-75.
Surveys advances made in teaching practical theology (including preaching)
in the United States.

1574

Lotz, David W.
"Preparation for Proclamation: Reflections on Undergraduate Theological
Education for Ministry." *Currents in Theology and Mission* 4 (1977): 76-86.

1575

Shows how theological education, including undergraduate ministerial education, prepares one for present proclamation of the gospel.

Macleod, Donald
"The American Academy of Homiletics." *Princeton Seminary Bulletin* 61   **1576**
(Win 1968): 6-8. Discusses the recently formed academy.

"Preaching and Recycling." *Princeton Seminary Bulletin* 65 (July 1972):   **1577**
3-6. After recognizing H. Grady Davis's contribution to homiletics, the author
gives his opinions on how to improve homiletic pedagogy.

Murray, Iain H.
"C. H. Spurgeon's Views on Training for the Ministry." *Banner of Truth*   **1578**
(July 1960): 25-32. Examines Charles Haddon Spurgeon's method for training
preachers, and contrasts it with modern methods.

Nes, William Hamilton
"Homiletics as a Theological Discipline." *Anglican Theological Review*   **1579**
43 (1961): 61-70. Defines preaching as a faithful, lucid, and comprehensible
articulation of Christian faith and practice; and argues that preaching is not
merely the acquisition of skills, but one theological discipline related to others.

Nichols, J. Randall
"What Should We Teach the Preacher?" *Military Chaplain's Review* [3]   **1580**
(Spring 1974): 23-31. Demonstrates the importance of grounding preachers in
the dynamics of law, religious language, the theology of communication, and
the function of conflict in communication.

Skudlarek, William
"Homiletics in the Roman Catholic Seminary." *Worship* 46 (1972): 77-85.   **1581**
Contends that because of preaching's centrality in the ministry, the purpose of
studying Bible, theology, and church history in seminary is to become a better
preacher. The author also includes suggestions about teaching homiletics.

Sleeth, Ronald E.
"The Teaching of Preaching." *Pulpit* 24 (Oct 1953): 20-21. Calls for several   **1582**
important emphases in teaching homiletics.

Townsend, Howard William
"Speech Course for Theological Students." *Western Speech* (May 1952):   **1583**
185-92.

Ward, Ronald A.
"Teaching the New Testament." *Christianity Today*, 13 May 1966, pp. 6-8.   **1584**
Gives a rationale for teaching the New Testament in an academic setting with
more relevance, and discusses the relationship between "secondary" and scientific exegesis.

Ziegler, Jesse H.
"Selection and Training of Candidates for the Ministry: Education in 1585
Pastoral Theology: Some American Approaches." *Expository Times* 74 (1962):
69–72. Surveys approaches to pastoral education in North American schools.

Bibliography

Barber, Cyril J.
"How to Find Those Elusive Illustrations." *Christianity Today*, 30 January 1586
1976, pp. 24–25. Identifies several publications rich with illustrations, and
mentions topics for which they are particularly helpful.

Cleath, Robert L.
"Communication and Christian Witness: Ten Top Books of the Decade." 1587
Christianity Today, 14 October 1966, pp. 40–42. Lists and annotates the ten
most significant books on communication and witness published during the
past decade. Thirty members of the Speech Association of America selected the
list.

Custer, Stewart
"Tools for Bible Exposition." *Biblical Viewpoint* 3 (1969): 139–41; 4 (1970): 1588
59–61, 147–48. An annotated bibliography of recommended books on biblical
geography, archaeology, and poetry.

Edwards, O. C., Jr.
"Synoptic Exegesis for Preaching." *Homiletic* 4 (1979): 1–5. Lists significant 1589
exegetical helps for preachers on the synoptic Gospels.

Ford, D. W. Cleverley
"I Recommend You to Read: IX, Books on Preaching, 1952–1967." *Exposi-* 1590
tory Times 79 (1967): 68–71. Reviews six books that represent the thought on
preaching during this period.

Homrighausen, Elmer G.
"Preaching in the Sixties." *Pulpit Digest* 52 (Jan 1972): 7–10. A partial report 1591
on books about preaching published in the 1960s, accompanied by a brief
historical introduction to that decade.

Litfin, A. Duane
"The Five Most-Used Homiletics Texts." *Christianity Today*, 10 August 1592
1973, p. 14. Describes the five most popular homiletics texts, based on a survey
of 177 seminaries.

MacLennan, David A.
"Resources for Preaching." *Review and Expositor* 51 (1954): 48-61. Suggests   1593
resources for sermon ideas and illustrations, such as Bible versions, literature,
current events, slogans, and observation of people.

Macleod, Donald
"Preaching: A Bibliography for Christians." *Christianity Today*, 10 August   1594
1973, pp. 12-14, 16-19. Lists books in the categories of history, theology, the
office, theory, interpretation, biography, dialogue, worship, the Christian year,
communication, and anthologies.

"Published Sermons." *New Pulpit Digest* 55 (Sep 1975): 34-35. Discusses   1595
the decline of sermon publishing, and offers a bibliography of resources that do
exist.

Mitchell, Henry H.
"The 'New' Phenomenon of Black Preaching." *Homiletic* 4 (1979): 6-10. An   1596
overview of significant books and trends in black preaching today.

Nichols, J. Randall
"The Pedagogy of Preaching." *Homiletic* 2 (1977): xi-xv. Reviews books   1597
and articles in the field of homiletic pedagogy.

Osborne, Sumner, Jr.
"A List of Expository Books." *Bibliotheca Sacra* 109 (1952): 63-72. A bibliog-   1598
raphy of expositions on each book of the Bible. Books included are for the
student of the English Bible and are predominantly premillennial.

Scherer, Paul
"Bibliography for Ministers: Homiletics." *Union Seminary Quarterly*   1599
Review 15 (Nov 1959): 39-44. Classifies works on the preaching office, the
communication of the gospel, sermons, and reference books.

Steichen, Alan J.
"A Bibliographic Review of Preaching." *Worship* 45 (1971): 334-51. Lists   1600
books published in America between 1965 and 1971, dealing mostly with
preaching as communication and as theology. The last section includes books
discussing unique types of preaching in the Catholic church.

TeSelle, Sallie McFague
"Parable, Metaphor, and Narrative." *Homiletic* 2 (1977): iii-vi. An overview   1601
and brief analysis of writings on parables, metaphors, and narratives, and on
their relationship to preaching.

Wiersbe, Warren W.
"Books About the Ministry." *Moody Monthly* 72 (Oct 1971): 48, 50, 52-53.   1602

Identifies eight books that encourage and enlighten preachers concerning their character and function.

"Dargan: Historian of Preaching." *Moody Monthly* 75 (Feb 1975): 81-83. **1603** Lists a number of books that deal with the history of preaching, and explains their value to the preacher. The main work mentioned is Edwin C. Dargan's *A History of Preaching* (see RHT[1], entry 421).

"The Later Yale Lectures." *Moody Monthly* 72 (Mar 1972): 67-71. A list of **1604** several men and their published Yale lectures that have assisted the author in his ministry. He outlines their theories on preaching and the ministry.

"On Reading Other Men's Sermons." *Moody Monthly* 75 (Jan 1975): 83-87. **1605** Advises preachers to read other preachers' sermons to strengthen their own, then lists collections available. The author also warns against imitation and plagiarism.

"Those Yale Lectures on Preaching." *Moody Monthly* 72 (Jan 1972): 61-63. **1606** Discusses the Yale lectures and most notably Henry Ward Beecher's, which the author describes as wordy and tedious but full of "gems."

"Walking with the Giants." *Moody Monthly* 71 (July 1971): 60-63. Lists **1607** biographies of preachers that will help the pastor in his ministry and sermon preparation.

"When You Preach on the Apostles." *Moody Monthly* 73 (May 1973): 61-65. **1608** Mentions books available as resources to preaching on the apostles, and offers suggestions on how to preach on the apostles.

"Where to Meet Those Preachers of the Past." *Moody Monthly* 73 (Oct **1609** 1972): 63-64, 66. A list of biographical material on great preachers of the past, and an explanation of why this material is important for today's preacher.

Theses and Dissertations

Abstracts for many of these dissertations appear in *Dissertation Abstracts International*, a reference work available at most university and college libraries. Dissertations in that work are followed by the abbreviation DA, which in turn is followed by volume and page numbers. Because in recent years each volume of *Dissertation Abstracts* is divided into two sections, A and B, the section letter concludes the entry. The first dissertation listed below, then, is included in *Dissertation Abstracts* and is located in volume 35 on page 2376 of section A.

General Works

Adams, Douglas G.
"Humor in the American Pulpit from George Whitefield Through Henry **1610** Ward Beecher." Th.D., Graduate Theological Union, 1974. DA 35:2376-A.

Allen, Ronald James
"Feeling and Form in Exegesis and Preaching: An Essay in Hermeneutics **1611** and Homiletics Based on the Philosophy of Art of Susanne K. Langer." Ph.D., Drew University, 1977. DA 38:2858-A.

Andrus, Paul Frederick
"A Study in Augmented Preaching." S.T.D., Emory University, 1973. **1612**

Barrie, Marilyn Horton
"The Effect of Cognitive Complexity and Audience Attitude on Persuasive **1613** Strategies." Ph.D., University of Kansas, 1977. DA 38:7018-A.

Baumann, J. Daniel
"Preaching Within the Evangelical Free Church of America." Th.D., Boston **1614** University School of Theology, 1967. DA 28:1885-A.

Benton, Donald R.
"Preaching in the Pastoral Context." D.Min., Southern Methodist University, **1615**
1974.

Brockhaus, Herman Henry
"Suggestion as a Means of Persuasion, with Special Application to the **1616**
Religious Revival." M.A., University of Wisconsin, 1937.

Brubaker, Robert C.
"An Adventure in Preaching." Ph.D., United Theological Seminary, 1976. **1617**

Buck, Edwin Francis, Jr.
"A Study of the H. M. S. Richards Lectureship with Emphasis upon Some **1618**
of the Basic Elements of Persuasive Preaching." Ph.D., Michigan State University, 1968. DA 29:1973-A.

Button, Carl Lloyd
"The Rhetoric of Immediacy: Baptist and Methodist Preaching on the **1619**
Trans-Appalachian Frontier." Ph.D., University of California, Los Angeles,
1972. DA 33:435-A.

Carlson, Bruce Lyman
"A Process for Growth in Preaching Competency." D.Min., Drew University, **1620**
1977. DA 38:7388-A.

Carmack, William Ross, Jr.
"Invention in the Lyman Beecher Lectures on Preaching: The Lecturers' **1621**
Advice on Gathering and Selecting Sermon Material." Ph.D., University of
Illinois, 1958. DA 19:2683.

Coburn, Kimball Boyd, Sr.
"Prophetic Preaching from a Pastoral Base." D.Min., School of Theology at **1622**
Claremont, 1975. DA 36:3792-A.

Crist, John David
"Teaching the Parables in the Local Church Using Cognitive Field Theory." **1623**
Rel.D., School of Theology at Claremont, 1975. DA 36:3779-A.

Dickens, George Dean
"Implications for Preaching in Selected Communications Research and **1624**
Experiments, 1963-1973." Th.D., Southwestern Baptist Theological Seminary,
1974.

Dickinson, Buford Allen
"The Hearing of the Word." Ph.D., School of Theology at Claremont, 1976. **1625**
DA 37:1630-A.

Eason, Henry Fincher
"Semantic Models Supporting the Sermon Themes of Five Contemporary   1626
Preachers." Ph.D., University of Denver, 1961.

Egertson, Paul Wennes
"Sacramental Rhetoric: The Relation of Preaching to Persuasion in   1627
American Lutheran Homiletics." Ph.D., School of Theology at Claremont,
1976. DA 37:1639-A.

Elder, Marjorie Jeanne
"Present-Day American Pulpit Humor." M.A., University of Wisconsin,   1628
1950.

Fukada, Robert Mikio
"Language and Culture in Christian Preaching: A Case Study in Japanese   1629
Protestantism." D.Min., School of Theology at Claremont, 1979. DA 40:1539-A.

Hackett, Charles Dudleigh
"Hermeneutical and Homiletical Implications of Merleau-Ponty's Theory   1630
of Linguisticality." Ph.D., Emory University, 1976. DA 37:2245-A.

Hall, Glenn Edward
"An Experimental Field Investigation of the Effects of Source Credibility   1631
and Dogmatism on the Evaluation of a Belief-Discrepant Message by Religious
Fundamentalists." Ph.D., University of Southern California, 1975. DA 37:6837-A.

Hall, Robert Gordon
"Praxis and Preaching: The Development of Righteousness as Solidarity   1632
Within the Biblical Tradition and Its Value to a Christian Community."
D.Min., School of Theology at Claremont, 1977. DA 38:1467-A.

Harrell, Douglas Arthur
"The Relationship of Life-Situation Preaching to Pastoral Counseling."   1633
D.Min., School of Theology at Claremont, 1976. DA 37:1631-A.

Hatch, Leonard J.
"Lay Contributions to Sermon Preparations." D.Min., Eastern Baptist   1634
Theological Seminary, 1976. DA 37:1622-A.

Heetland, David
"Toward an Interpersonal Theory of Preaching." Th.D., Iliff School of   1635
Theology, 1975.

Heflin, James Larohn
"An Evaluation of the Use of Humor in the Sermon." Th.D., Southwestern   1636
Baptist Theological Seminary, 1974.

Hilton, Robert Morton

"A Comparative Analysis of the Meaning and Function of Guilt in Current   **1637**
Psychological Theory and Contemporary Formulations of Preaching." Th.D.,
School of Theology at Claremont, 1965. DA 27:526-A.

Hubbard, Lorenzo

"Christian Preaching: A Healer of Black Racial Hostilities." D.Min., School   **1638**
of Theology at Claremont, 1978. DA 39:1649-A.

Hunter, Edward Gordon

"Humor in the Pulpit." D.Min., School of Theology at Claremont, 1978.   **1639**
DA 39:1650-A.

Jabusch, Willard Francis

"An Exploration of the Crisis and New Approaches in Contemporary   **1640**
Catholic Preaching." Ph.D., Northwestern University, 1968. DA 29:2382-A.

Johnson, Clair Emery

"*Verbum vocale:* Biblical Preaching Today." Th.D., Union Theological   **1641**
Seminary in the City of New York, 1965. DA 26:2352.

Johnson, Dudley Vincent, Jr.

"The Intersection of Persuasion Theory and Preaching." Rel.D., School of   **1642**
Theology at Claremont, 1975. DA 36:3794-A.

Jones, Jerry L.

"A Survey of the Audience Expectation Factors with an Analysis of Preaching   **1643**
in the Churches of Christ in the South in 1972." Th.D., New Orleans Baptist
Theological Seminary, 1974.

Kelley, Duane D.

"A Pastor-Led Bible Teaching Program for a Small Church." D.Min.,   **1644**
Southwestern Baptist Theological Seminary, 1974.

Kendall, Robert Dean

"A Rhetorical Study of Religious Drama as a Form of Preaching: An   **1645**
Exploration of Drama as a Complement to Monolog Preaching." Ph.D.,
University of Minnesota, 1973. DA 34:2800-A.

Kerley, William Clarence

"Dominant Emphases in Preaching: An Investigation into the Warrack   **1646**
Lectures." Th.D., Southwestern Baptist Theological Seminary, 1969.

Kilsby, Mary Ellen

"The New Hermeneutic and the Sermon as an Art Form: A Discussion of   **1647** the Sermon Enlightened by the New Hermeneutic Theologians and a Philosophy of Artistic Communication." D.Min., School of Theology at Claremont, 1978. DA 39:939-A.

Lambert, Kenneth Maurice
"Preaching with Purpose." D.Min., Southern Methodist University, 1975. 1648

Lojek, Helen Heusner
"Ministers and Their Sermons in American Literature." Ph.D., University 1649
of Denver, 1977. DA 38:787-A.

Ludlow, Dorothy Paula
"'Arise and Be Doing': English 'Preaching' Women, 1640-1660." Ph.D., 1650
Indiana University, 1978. DA 39:5664-A.

McCollister, John Charles
"A Study of the Theories of Homiletics of the American Lutheran Church." 1651
Ph.D., Michigan State University, 1969. DA 30:5518-A.

McCormick, James Ray
"Preaching as Experience." Ph.D., School of Theology at Claremont, 1971. 1652

McFadden, Roy Patton
"A Planned Program of Preaching and Teaching for a Mission Church." 1653
D.Min., Southwestern Baptist Theological Seminary, 1976.

McKinney, James Ronald
"Creating and Conducting a Diversified Program of Preaching at the 1654
Wateree Baptist Church, Camden, South Carolina." D.Min., Southern Baptist
Theological Seminary, 1977.

McReynolds, James E.
"A Study of the Relationship of Sensitivity Group Insights to the Preaching 1655
Ministry of the Church." D.Min., Vanderbilt University Divinity School, 1972.
DA 33:1822-A.

Madden, Thomas Joseph
"Kingdom and Community: The Eschatological Preaching as Interpreted 1656
by Père Marie-Joseph Lagrange." Ph.D., University of Notre Dame, 1978. DA
39:2993-A.

Martin, John Lee
"Homiletical Implications of Ian Ramsey's Philosophy of Religious Lan- 1657
guage." Louisville Presbyterian Theological Seminary, 1976.

Mathis, Don R.
"The Development of a Program of Preaching to Meet Selected Needs of   **1658**
Members of the Southside Baptist Church of Princeton, Kentucky." D.Min.,
Southern Baptist Theological Seminary, 1976.

Mayfield, James Leonard
"An Analysis of Expectations for the Responsibility Concerning Topic   **1659**
Selection of Protestant Ministers as Preachers." Ph.D., Michigan State University, 1964. DA 26:545.

Miller, Harold Allen
"A Comparison of the Forms of Support Used in Contemporary American   **1660**
Protestant Pulpit Address with the Forms of Support Used in Other Contemporary American Public Address: A Content Analysis." Ph.D., University of
Minnesota, 1962. DA 24:2665.

Morgan, Bruce M.
"Preaching to Middlescents of the First Baptist Church of Griffin, Georgia,   **1661**
with Emphasis upon Lay Participation and Perception." D.Min., Southern
Baptist Theological Seminary, 1976.

Olbricht, Thomas Henry
"Methods of Sermon Preparation and Delivery Employed by Clergymen in   **1662**
Iowa City and Cedar Rapids." M.A., State University of Iowa, 1953.

Parrott, Bob Winson
"Biblical Preaching and the Use of Humor." D.Min., Southern Methodist   **1663**
University, 1977.

Patton, John H.
"The Contemporary American Pulpit as Rhetorical Situation." Ph.D.,   **1664**
Indiana University, 1974. DA 35:2427-A.

Primrose, Robert A.
"An Analysis of Preaching on Social Issues in the Quad Cities." Ph.D.,   **1665**
University of Iowa, 1972. DA 32:7117-A.

Randolph, John Thomas
"Future Oriented Preaching." S.T.D., Emory University, 1972.   **1666**

Richardson, Donald Porter
"The Pulpit Discourse of the Baptist General Conference in the Greater   **1667**
Minneapolis–St. Paul Area: A Study of Role [with] Appendix." Ph.D., University of Minnesota, 1968. DA 29:1977-A.

Richmond, Kent Douglas
"The Figure of Jesus in the Lyman Beecher Lectures in Preaching." Ph.D.,   **1668**
Garrett Theological Seminary, 1971.

Riegert, Eduard Richard
"A Kerygmatic Interpretation of the Gospel Lessons Appointed in the   **1669**
Lutheran Church for the Season of Trinity." Th.D., Princeton Theological
Seminary, 1967. DA 28:3759-A.

Sands, Leo Richard
"Contemporary Roman Catholic Preaching: Its Inventional Characteris-   **1670**
tics." Ph.D., Pennsylvania State University, 1975. DA 37:695-A.

Schleifer, Herman William, Jr.
"The Place of Preaching in the Evangelical Lutheran Church." S.T.D.,   **1671**
Temple University, 1960. DA 27:2191-A.

Scott, Harold Edgar
"The Renewal of Preaching in the Roman Catholic Church in America."   **1672**
Th.D., Princeton Theological Seminary, 1966. DA 27:1920-A.

Seyler, Robert Lewis
"A Christian Understanding of Anger: New Testament Preaching as Coun-   **1673**
seling from the Sermon on the Mount, Matthew 5:21-26, 38-42." D.Min.,
School of Theology at Claremont, 1977. DA 38:1464-A.

Simonian, Vahe Harold
"The Quest for Biblical Preaching." Th.D., School of Theology at Clare-   **1674**
mont, 1970. DA 31:2488-A.

Strawser, Ray A.
"Authority, Authenticity and Authentication in Contemporary Preaching."   **1675**
Ph.D., Wesley Theological Seminary, 1975

Sunukjian, Donald Robert
"The Homiletical Theory of Expository Preaching." Ph.D., University of   **1676**
California, Los Angeles, 1974. DA 35:1275-A.

Taylor, Rodney Glen
"The Relationship of Preaching to Mental Health with Jesus as the Model   **1677**
in Selected Lukan Passages." Th.D., New Orleans Baptist Theological Seminary, 1973.

Terry, Thomas Roy
"A Program for Improving Life-Situation Preaching at Sardis Baptist   **1678**
Church, Timmonsville, South Carolina." D.Min., Southern Baptist Theologi-
cal Seminary, 1976.

Trotter, Frank Edward, Jr.
"Preaching and Modern Literature: A Theological/Cultural Investigation." **1679**
Ph.D., Wesley Theological Seminary, 1975.

Trower, Katherine Bache
"The Plowman as Preacher: The Allegorical and Structural Significance of **1680**
Piers the Plowman in *Piers Plowman*." Ph.D., University of Illinois, 1968.
DA 30:712-A.

Venden, Louis
"A Critical Analysis of Contemporary Seventh-Day Adventist Preaching **1681**
and a Constructive Proposal of Guiding Principles for Homiletical Pedagogy."
Ph.D., Princeton Theological Seminary, 1979. DA 40:1537-A.

Waltner, James H.
"The Authentication Preaching in the Anabaptist-Mennonite Tradition." **1682**
Ph.D., School of Theology at Claremont, 1971.

Widmer, Reinhold Rubin
"Roman Catholic Ecumenism and Its Implications for Evangelical Preach- **1683**
ing." Ph.D., Fuller Theological Seminary, 1970.

Woodell, Charles Harold
"The Preacher in Nineteenth-Century Southern Fiction." Ph.D., University **1684**
of North Carolina at Chapel Hill, 1974. DA 35:3707-A.

Worley, Robert C.
"Teaching-Preaching in the Early Church and Today." Ed.D., Columbia **1685**
University, 1967. DA 28:5141-A.

Preaching and Theology

Bell, Robert L.
"An Evaluation of the Practical Potential of Rudolf Bultmann's Theological **1686**
Insights for Contemporary Preaching." Ph.D., San Francisco Theological
Seminary, 1971.

Ireland, Robert Roy
"Preaching with the Theology of Schubert Ogden." D.Min., School of **1687**
Theology at Claremont, 1977. DA 38:1475-A.

Johnson, W. Walter
"Preaching as Ethical Action: A Response to the Concentration on Preach- **1688**
ing in Barth and Bultmann from the Viewpoint of Practical Theology." Th.D.,
Princeton Theological Seminary, 1969. DA 30:3086-A.

Leavey, Thomas Edward
"Christ's Presence in Word and Eucharist: Illustrated by Karl Barth's   **1689**
Doctrine of the Word of God and Contemporary Sacramental Theologians'
Doctrine of Christ's Activity in the Eucharist." Ph.D., Princeton University,
1968. DA 29:4548-A.

Litfin, A. Duane
"Theological Presuppositions and Preaching: An Evangelical Perspective."   **1690**
Ph.D., Purdue University, 1973. DA 34:6154-A.

Stuempfle, Herman G., Jr.
"Law and Gospel in Contemporary Lutheran Preaching, with Special   **1691**
Reference to Oswald C. J. Hoffmann and Edmund A. Steimle." Th.D., School
of Theology at Claremont, 1971. DA 32:1617-A.

Turner, Walter Glenn
"Towards an Apologetic Foundation for Christian Proclamation in a   **1692**
Pluralistic Age." Ph.D., Southern Baptist Theological Seminary, 1977. DA
38:6785-A.

Topics of Preaching

Gold, Aaron Sholom
"Can the Sermon Be an Effective Learning Technique for Forming Judg-   **1693**
ments of Marriage and Family-Life Problems?" Ed.D., Columbia University,
1967. DA 28:1295-A.

Jones, Hugh Geraint Martin
"A Survey of Protestant Preaching in the Area of Ecology." D.Min., Vander-   **1694**
bilt University Divinity School, 1972. DA 33:1819-A.

Masters, Earl Wayne
"Preaching the Resurrection." D.Div., Vanderbilt University Divinity   **1695**
School, 1972. DA 33:1821-A.

Murray, Stuart Eldon
"From Text to Sermon in Colossians." D.Min., Eastern Baptist Theological   **1696**
Seminary, 1975. DA 36:3786-A.

Stanton, James M.
"Preaching on Death: Its Procedures and Possibilities." D.Min., School of   **1697**
Theology at Claremont, 1975. DA 36:3810-A.

Thrasher, Charles Audrey
"A Planned Program of Preaching on Marriage and Family Enrichment." **1698**
D.Min., Southwestern Baptist Theological Seminary, 1974.

Whitehead, Brady B., Jr.
"Preaching Response to the Death of Martin Luther King, Jr." Th.D., **1699**
Boston University School of Theology, 1972. DA 33:2489-A.

Williamson, Edgar Roland
"Preaching Paul's Doctrine of Justification by Faith to Modern Man." **1700**
D.Min., Southern Methodist University, 1975.

The Congregation

Good, Menno Eckman
"A Study of Kinesthetic Involvement of a Congregation in the Preaching **1701**
Event." D.Min., Eastern Baptist Theological Seminary, 1975. DA 36:3781-A.

Kutter, Joseph Ray
"Discovering the Felt Needs of the Members of the First Baptist Church of **1702**
Arlington as a Source for Preaching." D.Min., Drew University, 1978.

Odom, Wayne C.
"The Preaching Ministry Serves an Educational Role Through an Effective **1703**
Small Group Process." D.Min., Southern Methodist University, 1977.

Watson, Larry M.
"The New Person in the Church Pew." Ph.D., Eden Theological Seminary, **1704**
1973.

Wentworth, Thomas Richard
"A Trained Laity: A Key to the Renewal of Preaching." D.Min., Eastern **1705**
Baptist Theological Seminary, 1977. DA 38:2191-A.

Wildman, Robert Bryant
"Congregational Involvement in the Preaching Process." D.Min., Louisville **1706**
Presbyterian Theological Seminary, 1977.

The Setting—Liturgical

Burke, William John
"The Development of the Theology of the Liturgical Sermon in the Forma- **1707**
tion of the Constitution on the Sacred Liturgy of the Second Vatican Council."
S.T.D., Catholic University of America, 1968. DA 30:792-A.

Empereur, James Lester
"A Critical Evaluation of Rudolf Otto's Liturgical Theology and Practice." **1708**
Ph.D., Graduate Theological Union, 1972. DA 33:3757-A.

The Setting—Special Occasions

Sprague, Richard Lewis
"The Funeral Sermon: An Homiletic Vehicle of Celebration and Affirma-   **1709**
tion." D.Min., Vanderbilt University Divinity School, 1974. DA 35:2389-A.

The Sermon

Bailey, Robert Wilson
"The Revitalization of the Preaching Event, with Emphasis upon Lay   **1710**
Participation and Perception." S.T.D., Southern Baptist Theological Seminary,
1970. DA 31:4250-A.

Barber, Harvey Dwaine
"The Utilization of Drama, Dialogue and Audio-Visual Aids in Preaching."   **1711**
D.Min., Southwestern Baptist Theological Seminary, 1973.

Bartholomew, Gilbert Leinbach
"An Early Christian Sermon-Drama: John 8:31-59." Ph.D., Union Theo-   **1712**
logical Seminary in the City of New York, 1974. DA 35:1738-A.

Bogdanovich, John V.
"An Inquiry into Selected Elements of Interest and Attention Embodied in   **1713**
the Sermon on the Mount." M.A., Washington Theological Seminary, 1950.

Bontrager, John Kenneth
"The Story Sermon as a Ministry to Children and Adults in the Light of   **1714**
Psychological Insight and New Testament Understanding of Parable." D.Min.,
School of Theology at Claremont, 1977. DA 38:1471-A.

Calcagno, J. S.
"The Nature of the Oratorical Illustration and Its Use in the Sermon." M.A.,   **1715**
Catholic University of America, 1956.

Cameron, Maxwell Ian
"Heaven Beleagured: A Literary Study of the Long Parliament Sermons."   **1716**
Ph.D., University of Toronto, 1974. DA 36:1518-A.

Dunkle, William F.
"Preaching Values in the Church Year for Evangelical Protestantism." 1717
Th.M., Union Theological Seminary in Virginia, 1950.

Erb, John David
"Is There a Positive Correlation Between Successful Preaching and the Use 1718
of Vivid Imagery Word-Concepts?" M.A., Ohio State University, 1938.

Ewbank, Henry Lee
"Objective Studies in Speech Style with Special Reference to One Hundred 1719
English Sermons." Ph.D., University of Wisconsin, 1932.

Fenner, Allan H.
"The Preacher as a Composer." S.T.M., Lutheran Theological Seminary 1720
(Gettysburg), 1949.

Klose, Paul Charles
"The Use of Imagination in Preaching." Th.M., Northern Baptist Theo- 1721
logical Seminary, 1950.

Kotchkiss, Robert V.
"Metaphor in the Communication of Spiritual Truth." Th.M., Pittsburgh 1722
Theological Seminary, 1959.

Lacy, Donald Charles
"Preaching as a Lay/Clergy Event." D.Min., Christian Theological Semi- 1723
nary, 1976.

Liddle, Noël Ivan
"Fundamental Principles of Homiletics Inherent in Literary Expression." 1724
Th.D., Northern Baptist Theological Seminary, 1959.

McGettrick, Garvin
"Incorporating the Dialogical Principle into Preaching." D.Min., South- 1725
western Baptist Theological Seminary, 1973.

Manes, Everett E.
"The Use of Illustration in Contemporary Preaching." A.M., University of 1726
Chicago, 1935.

Parsons, Ronald John
"Lay Perception and Participation in the Communication of the Sermon." 1727
Ph.D., Boston University Graduate School, 1966. DA 27:1439-A.

Rife, Carl B.
"The Understanding and Utilization of Feedback in the Preaching Situation." D.Min., Wesley Theological Seminary, 1973. 1728

Rogne, David George
"First Person Preaching." D.Min., School of Theology at Claremont, 1977. 1729
DA 38:1088–A.

Saylor, Donald Ray
"Literary Devices of Attention in Contemporary Preaching." Th.M., 1730
Southern Baptist Theological Seminary, 1956.

Simms, Stewart Broadus, Jr.
"A Nine Months Planned Program of Preaching Utilizing Creative Presen- 1731
tations and Evaluative Techniques." D.Min., Southwestern Baptist Theological
Seminary, 1974.

Stinespring, James Monroe
"The Use of Hermeneutic by Selected Modern Preachers." Ph.D., Southern 1732
Baptist Theological Seminary, 1978.

Thorpe, Archer H., Jr.
"Testing Innovative Forms of Preaching." D.Min., Southwestern Baptist 1733
Theological Seminary, 1975.

Delivery

Chadwick, Thomas Wilford
"A Study to Determine What a Pastor Is Communicating Nonverbally from 1734
the Pulpit." D.Min., Eastern Baptist Theological Seminary, 1976. DA 37:1622–A.

Hovee, Gene Herbert
"The Concept of Effective Delivery in the Yale Lectures on Preaching." 1735
Ph.D., University of Illinois, 1966. DA 27:4374–A.

Szawara, Mary Jill
"Temporal Aspects of Variable Spontaneity in Homilies." Ph.D., Saint 1736
Louis University, 1975.

History—Individual Preachers

Aho, Gerhard
"The Preaching of F. G. Hedberg." Ph.D., University of Illinois at Urbana- 1737
Champaign, 1972. DA 33:5860–A.

Alpert, Helle M.
"Robert Keayne: Notes of Sermons by John Cotton and Proceedings of the   **1738**
First Church of Boston from 23 November 1639 to 1 June 1640." Ph.D., Tufts
University, 1974. DA 35:3667-A.

Anderson, Floyd Douglas
"The King's Preacher: A Rhetorical Analysis of the Sermons of Hugh   **1739**
Latimer Preached Between January, 1548, and Lent, 1550." Ph.D., University of
Illinois, 1967. DA 28:3283-A.

Anderson, James Lee
"An Evaluation of the Communicative Factors in the Radio Preaching of   **1740**
Walter A. Maier of the Tenth Lutheran Hour Series in 1942-1943." Th.D.,
Southwestern Baptist Theological Seminary, 1976.

Anderson, James William
"The Grace of God and the Non-Elect in Calvin's Commentaries and   **1741**
Sermons." Th.D., New Orleans Baptist Theological Seminary, 1976.

Apel, William Dale
"The Understanding of Salvation in the Evangelistic Message of Billy   **1742**
Graham: A Historical-Theological Evaluation." Ph.D., Northwestern University, 1975. DA 37:4435-A.

Arlington, Larry David
"Moses A. Williams: A Rhetoric of Preaching and Praying." Ph.D., University of Oregon, 1973. DA 34:1393-A.   **1743**

Ashby, Jerry Paxton
"John Albert Broadus: The Theory and the Practice of His Preaching."   **1744**
Th.D., New Orleans Baptist Theological Seminary, 1968.

Baker, James Donald
"An Examination of the 'Baptist Hour' Preaching of Herschel H. Hobbs   **1745**
from 1958-1968." Th.D., New Orleans Baptist Theological Seminary, 1970.

Banks, Edward C.
"A Study of the Rhetorical and Homiletical Theory and Practice of Doctor   **1746**
Gerald Hamilton Kennedy, Bishop of the Methodist Church." Ph.D., Michigan
State University, 1966. DA 27:1135-A.

Barnard, Lawrence Reginald
"Christology and Soteriology in the Preaching of John Chrysostom." Th.D.,   **1747**
Southwestern Baptist Theological Seminary, 1974.

Bastian, Dwight R.
"A Homiletical Analysis of Ernest Fremont Tittle's Sermons on War and   **1748**
Peace from 1918 to 1949." S.T.D., Garrett-Evangelical Theological Seminary,
1975.

Batson, Trenton Wayne
"Arminianism in New England: A Reading of the Published Sermons of   **1749**
Benjamin Colman, 1673–1747." Ph.D., George Washington University, 1974.
DA 35:2377-A.

Benefield, LeRoy
"Lee Rutland Scarborough and His Preaching." Th.D., Southwestern   **1750**
Baptist Theological Seminary, 1970.

Bennett, Harold Repton
"A Rhetorical Analysis of the Preaching of Evangelist Hiram S. Walters,   **1751**
President of the West Indies Union Conference of Seventh-Day Adventists."
Ph.D., Michigan State University, 1971. DA 32:3470-A.

Bennett, Homer Douglas
"A Rhetorical Study of the Preaching Characteristics of Clovis Gillham   **1752**
Chappell." Ph.D., Bowling Green State University, 1972. DA 33:3824-A.

Best, Larry Grant
"Classical *partitiones orationis* in the Homilies of Aelfric: An Overview."   **1753**
Ph.D., University of Connecticut, 1977. DA 38:4838-A.

Bryson, Harold Thomas
"A Critique of the Expository Preaching of Thomas Alan Ogle Redpath."   **1754**
Th.D., New Orleans Baptist Theological Seminary, 1971.

"The Expository Preaching of W. A. Criswell in His Sermons on the   **1755**
Revelation." Th.M., New Orleans Baptist Theological Seminary, 1967.

Burke, Ronald Kevin
"Samuel Ringgold Ward: Christian Abolitionist." Ph.D., Syracuse Univer-   **1756**
sity, 1975. DA 37:1869-A.

Burns, Robert Elwood
"A Development of Criteria for Effective Preaching from an Analysis of the   **1757**
Preaching of Henry Ward Beecher." S.T.D., Garrett-Evangelical Theological
Seminary, 1975. DA 36:6158-A.

Butler, Arthur F.
"Hugh Latimer: The Religious Thought of a Reformation Preacher."   **1758**
Ph.D., Kent State University, 1976. DA 37:5193-A.

Butler, Francis Joseph
"John Henry Newman's *Parochial and Plain Sermons* Viewed as a Critique   **1759**
of Religious Evangelicalism." S.T.D., Catholic University of America, 1972. DA
33:1217-A.

Butler, Jennifer Bailey
"An Analysis of the Oral Rhetoric of Mordecai Wyatt Johnson: A Study of   **1760**
the Concept of Presence." Ph.D., Ohio State University, 1977. DA 38:6394-A.

Butts, John R.
"A Rhetorical Study of the Preaching and Speaking of Batsell Barrett   **1761**
Baxter." Ph.D., Michigan State University, 1970. DA 31:4308-A.

Carl, William Joseph, III
"Old Testament Prophecy and the Question of Prophetic Preaching: A   **1762**
Perspective on Ecclesiastical Protest to the Vietnam War and the Participation
of William Sloane Coffin, Jr." Ph.D., University of Pittsburgh, 1977. DA
38:5121-A.

Cherry, Harold Ross
"A Rhetorical Analysis of the Preaching of Clovis Gillham Chappell."   **1763**
Ph.D., Michigan State University, 1970. DA 31:6194-A.

Chester, Vera
"The Rhetorician as Theologian: A Study of the Sermons of John Henry   **1764**
Newman." Ph.D., Marquette University, 1971. DA 33:387-A.

Collins, Thomas Francis
"The Image of America in the Writings of Newell Dwight Hillis." Ph.D.,   **1765**
University of Iowa, 1974. DA 35:2166-A.

Conklin, Royal Forrest
"The Public Speaking Career of William Gannaway (Parson) Brownlow."   **1766**
Ph.D., Ohio University, 1967. DA 28:3289-A.

Conrad, F. Leslie, Jr.
"The Preaching of George Whitefield, with Special Reference to the   **1767**
American Colonies: A Study of His Published Sermons." S.T.D., Temple University, 1959. DA 27:3106-A.

Corvin, William Rayford
"The Rhetorical Practice of Paul Tillich." Ph.D., University of Oklahoma,   **1768**
1968. DA 29:1309-A.

Daniel, Charles Edgar, Jr.
"The Significance of the Sermons of Wenzeslaus Linck." Ph.D., Ohio State   **1769**
University, 1968. DA 30:650-A.

Darrow, Diane Marilyn
"Thomas Hooker and the Puritan Art of Preaching." Ph.D., University of   1770
California, San Diego, 1968. DA 29:1535-A.

Davis, Douglas Walter, Jr.
"A Rhetorical Study of the Early Preaching of Edward Eggleston." Ph.D.,   1771
Indiana University, 1971. DA 32:4745-A.

Dayka, Ernest
"A Rhetorical Criticism of the Preaching of Harold Cooke Phillips." Ph.D.,   1772
Case Western Reserve University, 1969. DA 31:3073-A.

DeBrand, Roy Everett
"An Analysis of the Preaching of Wallace Bassett Using the Homiletical   1773
Method of H. C. Brown, Jr." Th.D., Southwestern Baptist Theological
Seminary, 1975.

Dirks, Marvin J.
"Lay Expectation Factors in Relation to the Preaching of Helmut Thie-   1774
licke." Th.D., Boston University School of Theology, 1968. DA 29:1945-A.

Dorr, Luther Maxwell, Sr.
"A Critique of the Preaching of William Edwin Robert Sangster." Th.D.,   1775
New Orleans Baptist Theological Seminary, 1968.

Dowdle, Thad Robert
"A Study of the Homiletical Theory of Andrew Watterson Blackwood."   1776
Th.D., New Orleans Baptist Theological Seminary, 1971.

Earnest, James David
"A Study of John Henry Newman's *Oxford University Sermons*." Ph.D.,   1777
Yale University, 1978. DA 40:266-A.

Fain, William Maurice
"A Study of the Preaching of Timothy Dwight." Th.D., New Orleans   1778
Baptist Theological Seminary, 1970.

Felt, Shirley Ann Rader
"John Donne's Sermons and the *ars moriendi*." Ph.D., University of Cali-   1779
fornia, Riverside, 1975. DA 37:5846-A.

Gardner, David M.
"The Evangelistic Preaching of George A. Buttrick as a Model for Preach-   1780
ing in the First Baptist Church, Greenville, Kentucky." D.Min., Southern
Baptist Theological Seminary, 1976.

Gericke, Paul W.
"A Critical Study of the Preaching of Robert Greene Lee." Th.D., New 1781
Orleans Baptist Theological Seminary, 1964.

Gertner, Willis Stanley
"Paul E. Scherer: Preacher and Homiletician." Ph.D., Wayne State Univer- 1782
sity, 1967. DA 28:3284-A.

Grimes, Gordon Wayne
"An Analysis of the Preaching of Frederick William Robertson as Evidenced 1783
in His Sermons and Bible Studies." Th.D., Southwestern Baptist Theological
Seminary, 1976.

Gundry, Stanley N.
"Ruin, Redemption, Regeneration: The Proclamation Theology of Dwight 1784
L. Moody, Evangelist." S.T.D., Lutheran School of Theology at Chicago,
1975. DA 36:7483-A.

Haba, James Charles
"A Study of Abraham Wright's *Five Sermons, in Five Several Styles; or,* 1785
Ways of Preaching." Ph.D., Cornell University, 1967. DA 28:1396-A.

Hagan, Michael R.
"The Concept of Christian Ministry Revealed in the Writings of John 1786
Nelson Darby (1800-1882)." Ph.D., University of Washington, 1967. DA
28:1926-A.

Herin, Thomas James
"Luke 12:13-14:35 as an Introduction to Luke as Preacher." Ph.D., Union 1787
Theological Seminary in the City of New York, 1974. DA 35:1213-A.

Horton, O. Charles
"An Analysis of Selected Published Sermons of Billy Graham." Th.M., 1788
New Orleans Baptist Theological Seminary, 1967.

Humbertson, Robert Donald
"The Rhetorical Theory of Joseph Fort Newton." Ph.D., Ohio State Uni- 1789
versity, 1976. DA 37:4700-A.

Hunt, Paul Robert
"John Everard: A Study of His Life, Thought, and Preaching." Ph.D., 1790
University of California, Los Angeles, 1977. DA 38:4845-A.

Jenkins, Ronald Bradford
"The Life and Sermons of Henry Smith." Ph.D., University of North 1791
Carolina at Chapel Hill, 1976. DA 37:5142-A.

Kennedy, Larry Wells
"The Fighting Preacher of the Army of Tennessee: General Mark Perrin   1792
Lowrey." Ph.D., Mississippi State University, 1976. DA 37:7920-A.

King, George William
"Robert Bunger Theime, Jr.'s Theory and Practice of Preaching." Ph.D.,   1793
University of Illinois at Urbana-Champaign, 1974. DA 35:8055-A.

Kleinhans, Robert G.
"Erasmus' Doctrine of Preaching: A Study of *Ecclesiastes, sive de ratione*   1794
concionandi." Th.D., Princeton Theological Seminary, 1968. DA 29:2790-A.

Kruppa, Patricia Stallings
"Charles Haddon Spurgeon: A Preacher's Progress." Ph.D., Columbia   1795
University, 1968. DA 32:360-A.

Kurtz, Arnold A.
"A Rhetorical Analysis of the Preaching of Dr. Clarence Edward Macartney,   1796
Twentieth Century Exponent of the Traditional Orthodoxy." Ph.D., Michigan
State University, 1966. DA 27:3160-A.

Landry, Fabaus
"The Preaching of Harry Emerson Fosdick: An Analysis of Its Intent,   1797
Style, and Language." D.Div., Vanderbilt University Divinity School, 1972.
DA 33:1820-A.

Larson, Barbara Ann
"A Rhetorical Study of the Preaching of the Reverend Samuel Davies in   1798
the Colony of Virginia from 1747 to 1759." Ph.D., University of Minnesota,
1969. DA 30:3126-A.

Lawler, Thomas Matthew Coogan
"The English Works of St. John Fisher: A Study of Homiletic and Devo-   1799
tional Method in the Age of Erasmus." Ph.D., Yale University, 1967. DA
29:902-A.

Linn, Edmund Holt
"The Rhetorical Theory and Practice of Harry Emerson Fosdick." Ph.D.,   1800
State University of Iowa, 1952. DA 28:5170-A.

Litchfield, Landis Hugh
"An Analysis of the Homiletical Method of Dr. J. Wallace Hamilton."   1801
Th.D., Southwestern Baptist Theological Seminary, 1971.

Lloyd, Mark Brooks
"A Rhetorical Analysis of the Preaching of Bishop Francis Asbury." Ph.D.,   1802
Michigan State University, 1967. DA 28:3801-A.

Loring, Eduard Nuessnee
"Charles C. Jones: Missionary to Plantation Slaves, 1831-1847." Ph.D.,   1803
Vanderbilt University, 1976. DA 37:2254-A.

McCauley, Morris L.
"The Preaching of the Reverend Rowland Hill (1744-1833), Surrey Chapel,   1804
London." Ph.D., Louisiana State University, 1974. DA 35:4728-A.

McDow, Malcolm Ray
"A Study of the Preaching of James Stuart Stewart." Th.D., New Orleans   1805
Baptist Theological Seminary, 1968.

"A Study of the Preaching of Peter Marshall." Th.M., New Orleans Baptist   1806
Theological Seminary, 1965.

McGilly-McCoy, Catherine Anne
"A Rhetorical Analysis of the Speeches of Paul Perigord During World   1807
War I." Ph.D., Florida State University, 1977. DA 38:1737-A.

McKenzie, Gordon Moore
"Doctor John Sutherland Bonnell's Theory and Practice of Preaching."   1808
Ph.D., Michigan State University, 1970. DA 31:4313-A.

Maguire, Robert Clark
"The Analysis and Criticism of the Persuasive Discourse of the Rev. Peter   1809
C. Yorke, 1894-1898." Ph.D., University of California, Los Angeles, 1967. DA
28:3802-A.

Mercer, Jerry Lee
"A Study of the Concept of Man in the Sermons of John Wesley." Th.D.,   1810
School of Theology at Claremont, 1970. DA 31:2486-A.

Meyer, Edward Cecil
"The First Protestant Handbook on Preaching: An Analysis of the *De*   1811
formandis concionibus sacris seu de interpretatione scriptuarum populari
libri II of Andreas Hyperius in Relation to Medieval Homiletical Manuals."
Ph.D., Boston University Graduate School, 1967. DA 28:1891-A.

Miesner, Donald Robert
"Chiasm and the Composition and Message of Paul's Missionary Ser-   1812
mons." S.T.D., Christ Seminary in Exile, 1974. DA 36:2926-A.

Mitchell, James Nathaniel
"Nat Turner: Slave, Preacher, Prophet, and Messiah, 1800-1831." D.Min., 1813
Vanderbilt University Divinity School, 1975. DA 37:5197-A.

Morris, Aubrey Leon
"A Study of Psychological Factors in the Evangelistic Preaching of Billy 1814
Graham." Th.D., Southern Baptist Theological Seminary, 1966. DA 27:1438-A.

Nowell, Arris Patterson
"A Study of the Preaching of Thomas Dewitt Talmage." Th.D., New 1815
Orleans Baptist Theological Seminary, 1974.

Oswalt, Jerry Eugene
"A Critical Analysis of the Published Sermons and Lectures of Clovis 1816
Gillham Chappell." Th.D., New Orleans Baptist Theological Seminary, 1969.

Prichard, Samuel Van Orden
"Theodore Ledyard Cuyler's Theory and Practice of Preaching." Ph.D., 1817
Pennsylvania State University, 1972. DA 34:1400-A.

Regehr, John
"The Preaching of Christoph Blumhardt (1842-1919) [with] Supplement." 1818
2 vols. Th.D., Southern Baptist Theological Seminary, 1970. DA 31:1367-A.

Renaker, David Wilson
"The Biographical Sermon as a Biblical Method in the Preaching of 1819
F. B. Meyer." Th.D., Southwestern Baptist Theological Seminary, 1967.

Rhoads, Forrest Neil
"A Study of the Sources of Marshall Keeble's Effectiveness as a Preacher." 1820
Ph.D., Southern Illinois University, 1970. DA 31:3687-A.

Ritthamel, Franklin Carl Walter
"Luther's Principles of Teaching as Reflected in His Preached Sermons, 1821
1528-1532." Th.D., Concordia Seminary, 1965.

Rogers, Ernest Eugene
"A Study of the Evangelistic Methodology and Preaching of Edward Earl 1822
Cleveland." Ph.D., Michigan State University, 1967. DA 28:5182-A.

Savage, Nancy
"The Preaching Career of Rabbi Morris Adler, with Special Attention to 1823
Selected Sermons, 1958-1966." Ph.D., Wayne State University, 1971. DA
32:6589-A.

Schaper, Robert Newell
"The Preaching of John Donne, with an Investigation of Its Mystic and   1824
Poetic Elements and Their Place in the Task of Preaching." Th.D., School of
Theology at Claremont, 1973. DA 34:3534-A.

Schuda, Robert Bernard
"A Study of Laurence Sterne's Sermons: Yorkshire Background, Ethics, and   1825
Index." Ph.D., University of Wisconsin-Madison, 1975. DA 36:8081-A.

Seltman, Kent Daniels
"Henry Fielding, the Preacher: A Study of the Layman's Sermons in His-   1826
torical and Rhetorical Context." Ph.D., University of Nebraska, 1974. DA
35:5425-A.

Shaw, Wayne Eugene
"God's Herald: A Rhetorical Analysis of the Preaching of James S. Stewart."   1827
Ph.D., Indiana University, 1969. DA 30:5099-A.

Shelly, Harold Patton
"Richard Sibbes: Early Stuart Preacher of Piety." Ph.D., Temple University,   1828
1972. DA 33:6443-A.

Shelton, Robert M.
"The Relationship Between Reason and Revelation in the Preaching of   1829
Harry Emerson Fosdick." Th.D., Princeton Theological Seminary, 1965. DA
26:3514.

Simons, Robert George
"The Personal Realization of the Religious System: Revelation in New-   1830
man's Anglican Sermons, 1839-1843." S.T.D., Catholic University of America,
1977. DA 38:860-A.

Smith, Glenn Don
"A Rhetorical Biography: An Analysis of Selected Sermons Preached by   1831
Martin Luther." Ph.D., University of Nebraska, 1971. DA 32:4155-A.

Spangler, Russell Melvin
"A Rhetorical Study of the Preaching of Pastor David Wilkerson." Ph.D.,   1832
Michigan State University, 1969. DA 31:851-A.

Stevens, George Sheldon
"A Study of the Homiletical Theory of Roy Allan Anderson." Ph.D.,   1833
Michigan State University, 1968. DA 29:3710-A.

Stevens, Paul Wateson
"A Critical Examination of the Preaching of George Arthur Buttrick." 1834
Th.D., New Orleans Baptist Theological Seminary, 1972.

Stookey, Laurence Hull
"The Biblical Theology of Memory in the Sermons of John Donne." 1835
Th.D., Princeton Theological Seminary, 1971. DA 32:2793-A.

Storer, Clement Allyn Alden
"Elijah Kellogg: 19th Century New England Orthodox Preacher." Ph.D., 1836
Michigan State University, 1969. DA 31:1212-A.

Sullivan, John Harold
"Theodore Parker Ferris: The Man, His Method and Message." D.Min., 1837
School of Theology at Claremont, 1976. DA 37:1631-A.

Sumrall, Philip Ernest
"A Study of the Preaching of James David Grey." Th.D., New Orleans 1838
Baptist Theological Seminary, 1979.

Sunukjian, Donald Robert
"Patterns for Preaching: A Rhetorical Analysis of the Sermons of Paul in 1839
Acts 13, 17 and 20." Th.D., Dallas Theological Seminary, 1972.

Trimble, John Clifton
"The Rhetorical Theory and Practice of John W. McGarvey." Ph.D., 1840
Northwestern University, 1966. DA 27:2219-A.

Trout, John Moore, III
"Alan of Lille and the Art of Preaching in the Twelfth Century." Ph.D., 1841
Rutgers University, 1972. DA 33:4292-A.

Tucker, Austin Boyett
"Monroe Elmon Dodd and His Preaching." Th.D., Southwestern Baptist 1842
Theological Seminary, 1971.

Turner, R. Edward
"A Critical Analysis of the Concept of Preaching in the Thought of Ellen 1843
G. White." Ph.D., School of Theology at Claremont, 1979. DA 40:1150-A.

Vaughn, Vernon Damon
"A Critical Study of the Preaching of Samuel Porter Jones." Th.D., New 1844
Orleans Baptist Theological Seminary, 1962.

Wallenstein, Martin Albert
"The Rhetoric of Isaac Watts's Hymns, Psalms, and Sermons." Ph.D.,   **1845**
Indiana University, 1979. DA 40:543-A.

Walton, Arthur B.
"Stephen's Speech." Th.D., Grace Theological Seminary, 1972.   **1846**

White, Larry A.
"Rhetoric of James A. Pike: A Humanistic Criticism." Ph.D., Southern   **1847**
Illinois University, 1975. DA 36:7052-A.

White, W. D.
"John Henry Newman, Anglican Preacher: A Study in Theory and Style."   **1848**
Ph.D., Princeton University, 1968. DA 29:3213-A.

Wietfeldt, Willard James
"The Emblem Literature of Johann Michael Dilherr (1604-1669): An   **1849**
Important Preacher, Educator and Poet in the Seventeenth Century in Nürn-
berg." Ph.D., University of Illinois at Urbana-Champaign, 1974. DA 35:7884-A.

Wilson, Donald W.
"A Rhetorical Study of the Preaching of Pastor George Vandeman." Ph.D.,   **1850**
Michigan State University, 1966. DA 27:3151-A.

Wilson, Henry Steward
"The Speaking God: Luther's Theology of Preaching." Ph.D., Drew Uni-   **1851**
versity, 1977. DA 38:7392-A.

Womack, Morris Maloney
"A Study of the Life and Preaching of John Chrysostom." Ph.D., Wayne   **1852**
State University, 1967. DA 28:3288-A.

History—Groups

Anderson, James Russell
"Pentecost Preaching of Acts 2: An Aspect of Hutterite Theology." 2 vols.   **1853**
Ph.D., Southern Baptist Theological Seminary, 1971. DA 32:7075-A.

Barton, John Marion
"The Preaching on 'Herald of Truth' Radio, 1952-1969." Ph.D., Pennsyl-   **1854**
vania State University, 1975. DA 36:4090-A.

Bever, Ronald Doyle
"An Analysis of Speaking in the American Restoration Movement, 1820-   **1855**
1849." Ph.D., Northwestern University, 1968. DA 29:3699-A.

Carter, Lawrence Edward
"Motivation and Preaching: Content Analysis of Sermons by Two Preachers **1856** in the Light of Abraham H. Maslow's Theory of Need-Values." Ph.D., Boston University Graduate School, 1979. DA 40:315-A. The two preachers are William A. Jones, Jr., and Otis A. Maxfield.

Chaney, Charles Leonard
"God's Glorious Work: The Theological Foundations of the Early Mis- **1857** sionary Societies in America, 1787-1817." Ph.D., University of Chicago, 1973.

Creasy, William Charles
"A Study of the Development of the Popular Motives of *Health*, *Wealth*, **1858** *Power*, and *Success* in Practical Theology of the Early Disciples of Christ, as It Appeared in Their Periodicals Through 1850, with Some Consideration of Their Meaning for Today's Preacher." D.Div., Vanderbilt University Divinity School, 1971. DA 32:2175-A.

Fribley, Peter Craven
"The Pulpit Ministry to Alienation: A Dialectical Study of Alienation and **1859** the Preaching Ministries of Gerald Kennedy and George Arthur Buttrick, Using Sociological Criteria from Robert A. Nisbet and Theological Criteria from Paul Tillich and H. Richard Niebuhr, with Particular Emphasis upon 'Redemptive Alienation' as a Positive Heuristic for the Understanding of Sermonic Discourse." Ph.D., Princeton Theological Seminary, 1974. DA 35:3103-A.

Goodell, John
"The Triumph of Moralism in New England Piety: A Study of Lyman **1860** Beecher, Harriet Beecher Stowe, and Henry Ward Beecher." Ph.D., Pennsylvania State University, 1976. DA 37:4431-A.

Hickey, Timothy Roy
"Methodist Preaching at the Time of the Formation and Development of **1861** the Detroit Annual Conference of the Methodist Church: 1856-1869." Ph.D., University of Michigan, 1969. DA 30:4045-A.

Ivy, Quinton Sherwood
"The Homiletical Methods and Theories of Three Contemporary Preachers **1862** in the American Baptist Convention." Th.D., Boston University, 1965. DA 26:6196. The three preachers are Clarence Cranford, Carlyle Marney, and Robert McCracken.

Keith, James Melvin
"The Concept of Expository Preaching as Represented by Alexander **1863** Maclaren, G. Campbell Morgan, and David Martyn Lloyd-Jones." Th.D., Southwestern Baptist Theological Seminary, 1975.

Kolb, Erwin
"A Study of the Applications Used in the Sermons of the Concordia Pulpit   **1864**
of the Years 1955-1964." Th.D., Concordia Seminary, 1967.

Loucks, Clarence Melvin
"Mass Evangelistic Methodology: Charles Grandison Finney and William   **1865**
Franklin Graham." Th.M., Fuller Theological Seminary, 1973.

Miller, Philip V.
"Fosdick and Scherer: Their Sermons Judged by Their Theories; and the   **1866**
Speeches in the Acts of the Apostles." D.Min., Southern Methodist University,
1974.

Niedenthal, Morris J.
"Preaching the Presence of God: Based on a Critical Study of the Sermons   **1867**
of Paul Tillich, Karl Barth and Herbert H. Farmer." Th.D., Union Theological
Seminary in the City of New York, 1969. DA 30:2137-A.

Owens, Raymond Eugene
"Preaching in a Revivalist Tradition: The Influence of Revivalism on   **1868**
Southern Baptist Preaching, 1845-1877." Th.D., Union Theological Seminary
in the City of New York, 1967. DA 28:1515-A.

Riga, Peter John
"Penance in Ambrose, Leo and in the Sermons of Reconciliation of   **1869**
the Roman Archdeacon." Th.D., Graduate Theological Union, 1974. DA
35:3112-A.

Schmidt, Martin John
"The Proclamation of the Risen Jesus Christ in Lutheran Preaching: A   **1870**
Content Analysis of Selected Sermons, Representing Ninety-Seven Years of
Preaching Within the Lutheran Church-Missouri Synod, as Found in *Magazin
fuer ev. luth. Homiletik und pastoral Theologie* (1877-1929) and *The Con-
cordia Pulpit* (1930-1973)." Ed.D., Columbia University, 1974. DA 35:2429-A.

Scruggs, Julius Richard
"A Comparative Study of the Social Consciousness of Harry Emerson   **1871**
Fosdick and Martin Luther King, Jr." D.Min., Vanderbilt University Divinity
School, 1975. DA 37:398-A.

Streight, Charlotte Culver
"The Rhetoric of the Apostle Paul and the Prophets: A Comparative   **1872**
Study." Ph.D., University of Southern California, 1977. DA 38:4449-A.

Vitrano, Steven P.
"The Chicago Sunday Evening Club: A Study in Contemporary Preach-   1873
ing." Ph.D., Michigan State University, 1966. DA 27:1952-A.

Winter, Terry Walter Royne
"Effective Mass Evangelism: A Study of Jonathan Edwards, George White-   1874
field, Charles Finney, Dwight L. Moody and Billy Graham." Th.D., Fuller
Theological Seminary, 1968.

Young, Robert Charles
"The Authority for Preaching Among the Disciples of Christ, 1868-1969."   1875
Ph.D., Ohio University, 1978. DA 39:2992-A.

Zeitler, Lester E.
"Preaching Christ to the Glory of God for the Salvation of the Hearer: An   1876
Analysis of the Preaching Proposed in the *Magazin für ev.-luth. Homiletik
und pastoraltheologie*, 1877-1929." Ph.D., Concordia Seminary, 1968.

History—Periods

Benton, Robert Milton
"The American Puritan Sermon Before 1700." Ph.D., University of   1877
Colorado, 1967. DA 29:559-A.

Briscoe, Marianne Grier
"The Relation of Medieval Preaching Manuals to the Medieval English   1878
Morality Plays." Ph.D., Catholic University of America, 1975. DA 36:1490-A.

Collins, Naomi Feldman
"Oliver Cromwell's Protectorate Church Settlement: The Commission for   1879
the Approbation of Publique Preachers: The Triers and the Commission for
the Ejecting of Scandalous, Ignorant and Insufficient Ministers and School-
masters: The Ejectors." Ph.D., Indiana University, 1970. DA 31:5978-A.

Creighton, Linn James
"Reconciliation in American Protestant Preaching, 1910-1960." Th.D.,   1880
Princeton Theological Seminary, 1972. DA 33:1218-A.

Crew, Phyllis Mack
"A Question of Authority: Reformed Preaching and Iconoclasm in the   1881
Netherlands, 1543-1570." Ph.D., Cornell University, 1974. DA 35:2893-A.

Ellis, William Preston, Jr.
"A Study of the Nature of the Expository Sermon in the United States from   1882
1940-1968." Th.D., New Orleans Baptist Theological Seminary, 1971.

Gane, Erwin Roy
"The Historical Significance of the Scriptural Exegesis Employed in Some   **1883**
Sixteenth-Century English Sermons." Ph.D., University of Nebraska-Lincoln,
1976. DA 38:410-A.

Grosjean, Paul Eugene
"The Concept of American Nationhood: Theological Interpretation as   **1884**
Reflected by the Northern Mainline Protestant Preachers in the Late Civil
War Period." Ph.D., Drew University, 1977. DA 38:7390-A.

Hendricks, Dan Lee
"The Bern Reformation of 1528: The Preachers' Vision, the People's Work,   **1885**
an Occasion of State." Ph.D., Duke University, 1977. DA 38:7391-A.

Holton, Oscar Dile, Jr.
"The Victorian Sermon as Literature." Ph.D., Texas Technological College,   **1886**
1967. DA 28:3144-A.

Kennel, LeRoy E.
"Communication Constructs in Contemporary American Protestant   **1887**
Preaching, 1940-1965." Ph.D., Michigan State University, 1966. DA 27:3158-A.

Lesser, Marvin Xavier
"'All for Profit': The Plain Style and the Massachusetts Election Sermons   **1888**
in the Seventeenth Century." Ph.D., Columbia University, 1967. DA 28:2253-A.

Liefeld, Walter Lewis
"The Wandering Preacher as a Social Figure in the Roman Empire."   **1889**
Ph.D., Columbia University, 1967. DA 28:4254-A.

Loefflath-Ehly, Victor Paul
"Religion as the Principal Component of World-Maintenance in the   **1890**
American South from the 1830's to 1900 with Special Emphasis on the Clergy
and Their Sermons." Ph.D., Florida State University, 1978. DA 39:3640-A.

Mason, Paul Henry
"The Value of Preaching for Contemporary Protestant Worship: An Evalu-   **1891**
ation of the Controversy Since 1928." Th.D., Southwestern Baptist Theological
Seminary, 1974.

Mastriani, Ralph Louis
"*Wisdom, Who Is Christ* and Its Relationship to the Medieval Sermon."   **1892**
Ph.D., St. Louis University, 1977. DA 38:5444-A.

Miller, Joseph Morgan
"Foundations of Evangelism: A Study of the Revival of Pastoral Preaching   **1893**
During the Twelfth Century." Ph.D., Indiana University, 1970. DA 31:3685-A.

Skudlarek, William F.
"Assertation Without Knowledge? The Lay Preaching Controversy of the   **1894**
High Middle Ages." Ph.D., Princeton Theological Seminary, 1976. DA
37:2964-A.

History—Theory

Reimer, Dalton Wayne
"Approaches to Preaching: An Analysis of Twentieth-Century Concepts   **1895**
and Theories of Preaching." Ph.D., Northwestern University, 1971. DA
32:3467-A.

Teaching

Bartow, Charles Louis
"An Evaluation of Student Preaching in the Basic Homiletics Courses at   **1896**
Princeton Theological Seminary: A Farmerian Approach to Homiletical
Criticism." Ph.D., New York University, 1971. DA 32:1668-A.

Bresee, W. Floyd
"An Analysis of Homiletics Teaching Methods Advocated by Contemporary   **1897**
Homiletic Authorities in the United States." Ph.D., Northwestern University,
1971. DA 32:3461-A.

Chamberlain, Charles Dow
"A Project in Training Lay Speakers to Assist Pastors in the Preaching   **1898**
Ministry in Multi-Station Charges." Ph.D., Garrett-Evangelical Theological
Seminary, 1974.

Appendix
List of Periodicals

Addresses of all periodicals appearing in the bibliography are given to assist one in soliciting, directly from the publishers, information about obtaining copies of back issues, and in ordering new subscriptions. As much as possible these addresses are current as of 1982.

For periodicals with more than one address, only that of the subscription office is supplied. For periodicals that are published outside North America and that maintain an American office for subscribers on this continent, only the American address is given.

Included in the addresses are the names of the schools, societies, or companies, if any, that publish the periodicals.

America
  106 W. 56th St.
  New York, NY 10019

American Baptist Quarterly
  1106 S. Goodman St.
  Rochester, NY 14620

The American Ecclesiastical Review
  (no longer published)

Andover Newton Quarterly
  Andover Newton Theological School
  210 Herrick Rd.
  Newton Centre, MA 02159

Anglican Theological Review
  600 Haven St.
  Evanston, IL 60201

Archive for Reformation History
  Gütersloher Verlagshaus
  4830 Gütersloh I
  Königstrasse 23
  Postfach 2368
  West Germany

The Asbury Seminarian
  Asbury Theological Seminary
  204 N. Lexington Ave.
  Wilmore, KY 40390

Augustinian Studies
  The Augustinian Institute
  Villanova University
  Villanova, PA 19085

Austin Seminary Bulletin
Austin Presbyterian Theological
Seminary
100 E. 27th St.
Austin, TX 78705

The Banner
2850 Kalamazoo Ave., S.E.
Grand Rapids, MI 49508

The Banner of Truth
Box 621
Carlisle, PA 17013

The Baptist Program
Southern Baptist Convention
460 James Robertson Pkwy.
Nashville, TN 37219

Biblical Viewpoint
Bob Jones University
Greenville, SC 29614

Bibliotheca Sacra
Dallas Theological Seminary
3909 Swiss Ave.
Dallas, TX 75204

*Bulletin of the Evangelical Theological
Society*
(see *Journal of the Evangelical
Theological Society*)

Calvin Theological Journal
Calvin Theological Seminary
3233 Burton St., S.E.
Grand Rapids, MI 49506

Central States Speech Journal
Central States Speech Association
Department of Speech
Iowa State University
Ames, IA 50011

The Chaplain (no longer published)

The Christian Century
407 S. Dearborn St.
Chicago, IL 60605

Christian Graduate
Universities and Colleges Christian
Fellowship Associates
38 De Montfort St.
Leicester LE1 7GP
United Kingdom

Christian Herald
Chappaqua, NY 10514

Christianity Today
Box 1915
Marion, OH 43305

Christian Life
396 E. Saint Charles Rd.
Wheaton, IL 60187

Christian Minister
Estella House
47A Main Road
Claremont, Cape Town
South Africa

The Christian Ministry
Christian Century Foundation
407 S. Dearborn St.
Chicago, IL 60605

Church Administration
The Sunday School Board
Southern Baptist Convention
127 Ninth Ave., N.
Nashville, TN 37234

*Church Management: The Clergy
Journal*
Box 1625
Austin, TX 78767

The Clergy Review
Tablet Publishing Co.
48 Great Peter St.
London SW1P 2HB
United Kingdom

Communication Monographs
The Speech Communication
Association
5105 Backlick Rd.
Annandale, VA 22003

Communication Quarterly
Caroline Drummond, Executive
Secretary
Eastern Communication Association
Department of Speech—265-65
Temple University
Philadelphia, PA 19122

Concordia Theological Monthly
(no longer published)

Covenant Quarterly
The Evangelical Covenant Church of
America
5101 N. Francisco Ave.
Chicago, IL 60625

Currents in Theology and Mission
Christ Seminary-Seminex
539 N. Grand Blvd.
St. Louis, MO 63103

Dialog
2375 Como Ave., W.
St. Paul, MN 55108

Dimension
St. Charles Seminary
Overbrook
Philadelphia, PA 19151

The Drew Gateway
Drew Theological School
Madison, NJ 07940

The Duke Divinity School Review
Divinity School of Duke University
Durham, NC 27706

Encounter
Christian Theological Seminary
Box 88267
Indianapolis, IN 46208

Eternity
Evangelical Ministries
1716 Spruce St.
Philadelphia, PA 19103

The Evangelical Quarterly
The Paternoster Press
Paternoster House
3 Mount Radford Crescent
Exeter EX2 4JW
United Kingdom

Evangelical Recorder
25 Ballyconnor Ct.
Willowdale, Ontario M2M 4B3
Canada

The Expository Times
T. & T. Clark
36 George St.
Edinburgh EH2 2LQ
United Kingdom

Faith at Work
Box 1138
Columbia, MD 21044

Faith for the Family
Bob Jones University
Greenville, SC 29614

Foundations
(see *American Baptist Quarterly*)

The Good News Broadcaster
Back to the Bible Broadcast
Box 82808
Lincoln, NE 68501

Harvard Theological Review
Scholars Press
101 Salem St.
Box 2268
Chico, CA 95927

Homiletic
3510 Woodley Rd., N.W.
Washington, DC 20016

Homiletic and Pastoral Review
Catholic Polls, Inc.
86 Riverside Dr.
New York, NY 10024

International Review of Mission
World Council of Churches
Room 1062
475 Riverside Dr.
New York, NY 10115

Interpretation
Union Theological Seminary
in Virginia
3401 Brook Rd.
Richmond, VA 23227

The Journal of Christian Reconstruction
Chalcedon
Box 158
Vallecito, CA 95251

Journal of Communication
The Annenberg School Press
Box 13358
Philadelphia, PA 19101

The Journal of Pastoral Care
Association for Clinical Pastoral
Education
475 Riverside Dr., Suite 450
New York, NY 10115

Journal of Pastoral Practice
Presbyterian and Reformed
Publishing Co.
Box 817
Phillipsburg, NJ 08865

Journal of Presbyterian History
Presbyterian Historical Society
425 Lombard St.
Philadelphia, PA 19147

Journal of Psychology and Theology
Rosemead School of Psychology
Biola University
13800 Biola Ave.
LaMirada, CA 90639

Journal of the Academy of Parish Clergy
(current information unavailable)

The Journal of the Evangelical Theological Society
Simon J. Kistemaker
Reformed Theological Seminary
5422 Clinton Blvd.
Jackson, MS 39209

The Journal of the Interdenominational Theological Center
671 Beckwith St., S.W.
Atlanta, GA 30314

The Journal of Theological Studies
Journals Department
Oxford University Press
Walton St.
Oxford OX2 6DP
United Kingdom

The King's Business
Biola University
13800 Biola Ave.
LaMirada, CA 90639

Lexington Theological Quarterly
Lexington Theological Seminary
631 S. Limestone St.
Lexington, KY 40508

Liguorian
Liguori Dr.
Liguori, MO 63057

Lumen Vitae
184 rue Washington
1050 Brussels
Belgium

The Lutheran Quarterly
(no longer published)

Luther Theological Seminary Review
(current information unavailable)

Military Chaplains' Review
U.S. Army Chaplain Board
Myer Hall, Building 1207
Fort Monmouth, NJ 07703

The Minister's Quarterly
297 Park Ave., S.
New York, NY 10010

Missionary Monthly
Reformed Bible College
Box 6181
Grand Rapids, MI 49506

Moody Monthly
2101 W. Howard St.
Chicago, IL 60645

The New Pulpit Digest
(see *Pulpit Digest*)

The Other Side
Jubilee, Inc.
300 W. Apsley St.
Philadelphia, PA 19144

The Outlook
4855 Starr St., S.E.
Grand Rapids, MI 49506

Pastoral Life
Society of St. Paul (Canfield)
Canfield, OH 44406

Pastoral Psychology
Human Sciences Press
72 Fifth Ave.
New York, NY 10011

*The Perkins School of Theology
Journal*
The Perkins School of Theology
Southern Methodist University
Dallas, TX 75275

The Preacher's Quarterly
(see *Worship and Preaching*)

Preaching Today
(no longer published)

The Presbyterian Journal
Box 3075
Asheville, NC 28802

Present Truth
(no longer published)
c/o *Verdict*
Box 1311
Fallbrook, CA 92028

The Priest
Our Sunday Visitor, Inc.
Noll Plaza
Huntington, IN 46750

The Princeton Seminary Bulletin
Princeton Theological Seminary
Princeton, NJ 08540

*Proceedings of the Catholic Homiletic
Society Charter Convention*
(current information unavailable)

Proclaim
The Sunday School Board
Southern Baptist Convention
127 9th Ave., N.
Nashville, TN 37234

Psychology for Living
Narramore Christian Foundation
1409 N. Walnut Grove Ave.
Rosemead, CA 91770

The Pulpit (no longer published)
c/o *The Christian Ministry*
407 S. Dearborn St.
Chicago, IL 60605

Pulpit Digest
Box 5199
Jackson, MS 39216

The Quarterly Journal of Speech
William Work, Executive Secretary
Speech Communications Association
5105 Backlick Rd.
Annandale, VA 22003

The Reformation Review
International Council of Christian
   Churches
756 Haddon Ave.
Collingswood, NJ 08108

The Reformed Journal
William B. Eerdmans Publishing Co.
255 Jefferson, S.E.
Grand Rapids, MI 49503

Reformed Review
Western Theological Seminary
Holland, MI 49423

Religion in Life
Abingdon
201 Eighth Ave., S.
Nashville, TN 37202

Religious Communication Today
(current information unavailable)

Review and Expositor
Southern Baptist Theological
   Seminary
2815 Lexington Rd.
Louisville, KY 40280

The Saint Luke's Journal of Theology
The School of Theology
The University of the South
Sewanee, TN 37375

Scottish Journal of Theology
Scottish Academic Press Ltd.
33 Montgomery St.
Edinburgh, Scotland EH7 5JX
United Kingdom

Search
The Sunday School Board
Southern Baptist Convention
127 Ninth Ave., N.
Nashville, TN 37234

The Seminary Review
Cincinnati Christian Seminary
2700 Glenway Ave.
Cincinnati, OH 45204

*The Southern Speech Communication
   Journal*
Southern Speech Communication
   Association
Department of Communication
University of South Florida
Tampa, FL 33620

The Southern Speech Journal
(see *The Southern Speech
   Communication Journal*)

Southwestern Journal of Theology
School of Theology
Southwestern Theological Seminary
Fort Worth, TX 76122

Spectrum: Christian Communications
(no longer published)

*Spectrum: International Journal of
   Religious Education*
(no longer published)

Speech Monographs
(see *Communication Monographs*)

*The Sunday School Times and
   Gospel Herald*
Union Gospel Press
2000 Brookpark Rd.
Cleveland, OH 44109

Tenth
Tenth Presbyterian Church
1700 Spruce St.
Philadelphia, PA 19103

Theological Markings
United Theological Seminary of the
   Twin Cities
3000 5th St., N.W.
New Brighton, MN 55112

Theological Studies
Georgetown University
37th and O St., N.W.
Washington, DC 20057

Theology Digest
Box 6036
Duluth, MN 55806

Theology Today
Box 29
Princeton, NJ 08540

Today's Speech
(see *Communication Quarterly*)

Torch and Trumpet
(see *The Outlook*)

TSF News and Reviews
c/o *TSF Bulletin*
Theological Students Fellowship
233 Langdon
Madison, WI 53703

Union Seminary Quarterly Review
3041 Broadway at Reinhold Niebuhr
    Place
New York, NY 10027

*Western Journal of Speech
    Communication*
Gary D. Keele
Executive Secretary, Western Speech
    Communication Association
Department of Communication Arts
California State Polytechnic
    University
Pomona, CA 91768

Western Speech
(see *Western Journal of Speech
    Communication*)

The Westminster Theological Journal
Westminster Theological Seminary
Chestnut Hill
Philadelphia, PA 19118

Wisconsin Lutheran Quarterly
(current information unavailable)

World Vision
World Vision International
919 W. Huntington Dr.
Monrovia, CA 91016

Worship
St. John's Abbey
Collegeville, MN 56321

Worship and Preaching
Methodist Publishing House
Wellington Rd., Wimbledon
London SW19 8EU
United Kingdom

Index of Authors

I

J

K

Index of Personal Subjects